divine
STRONGHOLDS

divine
STRONGHOLDS

RESOLVING CONTROL ISSUES
WITH PATTERNS OF HIS PRESENCE

TERRY TEYKL WITH LYNN PONDER

PRAYER POINT PRESS

Divine Strongholds
Resolving Control Issues with Patterns of His Presence
Copyright © 2008 Dr. Terry Teykl
Published by Prayer Point Press
Edited by Lynn Ponder

First Printing, March 2008

Unless otherwise indicated, all Scripture quotations are from the Holy Bible, New International Version © 1973, 1978, 1984 by the International Bible Society. Used by permission of Zondervan Publishing House.

ISBN: 1-57892-115-5
Printed in the United States of America

Prayer Point Press
2100 N. Carrolton Dr.
Muncie, Indiana 47304
To order: www.prayerpointpress.com
To order, call toll-free: (888) 656-6067

To Allen, Jan and Jini, my partners in ministry, who have all given of themselves in countless, immeasurable ways to serve the call of Jesus on their lives:

*for hundreds of hours on the road
and "Old Blue"
for Chautauqua, NY; Kearney, NE; Melvin, IL
for Jini's garage and Jan's loft
and laying cards in the Indiana winter
for building shelves
and hauling boxes
for laughing
and crying
and believing*

Thank you.

CONTENTS

Introduction   9

Chapter One - What is a Stronghold?   19

Chapter Two - Religion vs Passion   49

Chapter Three - Pride vs Humility   69

Chapter Four - Sedition vs Honor   95

Chapter Five - Parochialism vs Unity   123

Chapter Six - Judgment vs Grace   151

Chapter Seven - Fear vs Faith   179

Chapter Eight - Get a (Worship) Life   209

Chapter Nine - Crafted Prayer   247

Chapter Ten - A Tale of Two Cities   273

Notes   289

Introduction

Several years ago, at a small, rural church in Indiana, I taught a seminar session on some common issues I felt were plaguing many of today's churches. I called the issues "strongholds," not because I had done a lot of research about that concept in advance, but because it just seemed instinctively to be the right term. My audience on that late winter afternoon was a comfortable group of primarily pastors, about 50 if I recall correctly, in a quaint little sanctuary that wouldn't have held many more. As I spoke, I scribbled out notes on a small blackboard that stood on an easel in front of the piano. Low-tech and low-key, that seminar didn't create a tidal wave of church reform; maybe not even a ripple in the bathtub. Nevertheless it was significant to me because it was a revelatory moment. And I always remember revelatory moments.

Anyone who has ever done a good bit of public speaking knows what it's like to really connect with an audience. Their eyes light up and their heads nod. They smile or laugh or cry, and then nudge their friend or spouse with an elbow in a gesture of silent affirmation. On this day there was a lot of nodding, poking and laughing as I talked somewhat informally about these ideas that I had jotted down on a piece of paper only days before.

I knew immediately that these strongholds were a very real part of church life. I knew because of the response I was getting from those pastors, and I knew because of the familiar feel of the Holy Spirit's presence as I spoke. I knew because I had been seeing and feeling them in churches for many years. At the end of the day, when I and my staff looked at what had formed on the chalkboard, we all agreed it was the embryo of a book.

Sometimes knowing that something is true is the easy part; explaining why it is true is the more difficult task. And more difficult still is understanding how to put that knowledge to work. Just about everyone knows that the law of gravity is true. Some scientists or physicists can even explain in detailed calculations why it is true. What is most helpful, though, is that someone figured out how to harness the power of gravity in a waterfall to produce electricity.

Several years ago when I did that seminar, I knew that the strongholds existed. So did everyone else in the room. But it has taken me a long time and, in fact, the writing of another book, to ponder why and how they exist corporately, and even more importantly for those of us who love the local church and would like to see it rescued from itself, how we might harness the power to produce something good.

The book I'm referring to is called *The Presence Based Church*, and it is definitely a prequel to this one. If you haven't read it, I would recommend that you do. Although it's not necessary to the understanding of this book, the content in each sheds light on the other.

In *The Presence Based Church*, I described two opposing church models, one called the consumer based church (or the Martha church) and the other called the Presence based church (or the Mary church). The names were derived from the scene in

Luke 10:38-42 in which Jesus is dining at the home of his good friends, sisters Mary and Martha. In short, Mary is sitting at Jesus' feet soaking up everything he is saying, while Martha is frantically busy in the kitchen making preparations for the meal. When Martha finally gets angry and rebukes her sister for being so lazy, Jesus lovingly confronts her:

> Martha, Martha, the Lord answered, you are worried and upset about many things, but only one thing is needed. Mary has chosen what is better, and it will not be taken away from her (Luke 10:41-42).

We depicted the Martha church as an institution that caters to the needs and desires of people, who in essence become the coveted consumers in the competitive church market. In our economy, the whims and trends of consumers drive merchants to offer better goods and services at a lower price. Likewise, consumer based churches are driven to give church shoppers more of what they want and less of what they don't want in an effort to fill the seats on Sunday morning and lay claim to their market share of members. The consumer based church model is primarily about the sheep—getting them, keeping them and counting them.

Let me very briefly summarize the characteristics we used to illustrate this model:

Religious Activities—Church life teems with activities available for every age and social group.

Crisis Motivated Prayer—The prayer life of the church focuses on asking God to meet specific needs by intervening in the lives of those who are struggling, grieving, ill or distressed.

Competition—The consumer based church model turns local congregations into competitors who evaluate their success by comparing themselves to each other.

Sheep Shifting—Unfortunately, true evangelism suffers

when churches are vying for people's attention. Instead of bringing new converts into the kingdom, they are content to "shift the sheep" from one building to another, creating the illusion of church growth.

Jesus as Mascot—Jesus is often relegated to a supporting role as the mascot (who cheers on the real team) rather than being revered and worshiped as master.

Pastor Fetch—The pastor of this church spends most of his time trying to keep the people happy, and in the process can lose his vision for ministry or become vulnerable to fatigue and frustration.

Image Consciousness—The "image" of the church—everything from the style of worship on Sunday to the paint colors and landscaping—must keep up with market trends.

Personality Driven Leadership—The church's reputation rests on the skills, education, personality and even physical appearance of the pastor (and to some degree his family also).

Controlites—When a church caters to people, it empowers them and will eventually relinquish aspects of ownership to them. When people are striving for control, the Holy Spirit backs away.

In contrast to the consumer based church, the Presence based church is all about inviting and welcoming the Presence of God. It places Jesus, the new Ark of the Covenant, in the very center of life just as the Israelites did in the Old Testament, and it desires to be known and distinguished by his name and glory. In short, it is more about him than them. This church, like Mary, is always at the master's feet, listening, seeking and worshiping.

The Presence Based Church book portrays the Mary church model with these attributes:

Levitical Worship—Worship is a high priority in this church and doesn't just happen on Sunday morning. It is more of a lifestyle than an activity and permeates all aspects of church life.

First Love Prayer—Prayer goes way beyond getting needs met to praying just to know and be known by God. This church seeks God's face, not just his hand.

Compassion—Because of their fascination with Jesus, they mirror his compassion for the lost and have a distinctive burden for the Great Commission.

Presence Evangelism—When the Presence of God is real, it is unmistakable. It draws people in and changes lives, with or without a polished Power Point presentation.

Revelation of Jesus—Pressing deeper and deeper into the heart of God, the Presence based church is fueled by the incremental revelation of the savior's glory.

Pastor Betterdish—This pastor chooses what is better. Because his people release him to do so, he is free to be with God, seeking his approval and not man's.

Humility—Since worship and prayer are outward signs of an inner dependence on God, the Mary church has a healthy desperation for God's Presence and is not given to self promotion or arrogance.

Presence Drawn Leadership—Because the leadership is released to seek the Lord's heart and guidance in all matters, conflict is kept to a minimum. Decisions are made by praying through to consensus rather than by taking sides and voting.

Divine Habitation—Where God's Presence is invited and welcomed consistently for a period of time, he does more than just visit; he will take up residence and "inhabit."

WHO'S IN CHARGE?

At the heart of the struggle between these opposing church

models is the issue of control. Are people groups within the church jockeying back and forth, pulling strings and applying pressure in order to see that their will be done? Or is God being allowed free rein to lead, work and move so that his kingdom is being established in and through the church? The question of control goes all the way back to Adam and Eve in the Garden of Eden, and man has been bumping and tumbling down that slippery slope ever since.

As Christians we have a post-fall mentality, and I've always thought as a pastor and writer that we should preach and teach more on the pre-fall world that God created. It is an amazing picture of what God intended for his creation. His desire was that man should live in perfect harmony and union with him, interacting together in the Garden and enjoying the abundance and beauty of the unspoiled earth. It was his wish that he and his man-likeness would be co-regents, ruling this new dominion in complete and single-minded agreement. Of course man didn't last long in the pre-fall arrangement; in fact, just a day or so. The whole scene occupies only one page in my Bible out of nearly 1,000, so I guess it is little wonder that there aren't many books written about it or sermons preached on it. We don't have much material there to draw from; just enough to give us a compelling glimpse at what might have been.

As sons of Adam and daughters of Eve, the way we are inclined to think is just mixed up in a wholesale manner.

Nevertheless, when Adam and Eve fell, the seamless unison between our minds and God's went out the window. Stinking thinking entered the picture, and the crusade for control was on. The moment the first husband and wife bit off more than they could chew, the curse of carnal thinking was etched into the DNA of humankind and then passed down to every generation starting with the first two babies ever conceived, Cain and Abel, and continuing all the way through ancient and modern history to the present. No person, culture, race or civilization has been immune. As sons of Adam and daughters of Eve, the way we are inclined to think is just mixed up in a wholesale manner.

Notice that the serpent didn't tempt the man and woman with lust or greed or power. It was the promise of knowledge, of wisdom equivalent to that of God himself, which he used to bring utopia to a quick and screeching halt. He needed nothing more than the enticing fruit from the tree of the knowledge of good and evil. Adam and Eve couldn't resist. Satan went after their minds, not by accident or because it was simply convenient, but because that was his battlefield of choice, and his tactics haven't changed much in two thousand years.

Satan's target is still our minds. He wants to feed the curse of carnal thinking because he knows that as long as we are in agreement with the serpent, we are out of sync with our heavenly Father. If we are in control, God is not. Francis Frangipane wrote:

> You will remember that the location where Jesus was crucified was called "Golgotha," which meant "place of the skull." If we will be effective in spiritual warfare, the first field of conflict where we must learn warfare is the battleground of the mind; i.e., the "place of the skull." For the territory of the uncrucified thought-life is the beachhead of satanic assault in our lives. To defeat the devil, we must be crucified in the place of the skull. We must be renewed in the spirit of our minds!

The evil one knows that where he can win the minds of men, he gains the will and destiny of that generation. "For as he thinks in his heart, so is he" (Proverbs 23:7, *New King James Version*). One only needs to look at the terror groups and brutal regimes of the Middle East to see examples of entire generations of men and women in bondage to carnal systems of thinking that refuse to acknowledge God. On a grand scale, such mindsets have enormous destructive power. The carnal mind that is controlled by Satan, void of any understanding of God's nature and kingdom, can commit such atrocities that it is hard for most of us to comprehend.

That's the extreme end of the spectrum. On an individual level, carnal thinking can almost appear harmless, even admirably dedicated. "Marthas" are hard workers who toil tirelessly in the kitchen (or the nursery, or the choir, or the men's ministry) and seem to be content until something doesn't go their way or someone moves their table without permission. And suddenly Martha is on a rampage and the battle is on.

In any setting where people build relationships and interact together, carnal thinking inevitably leads to turf wars and control conflicts that cripple the institution.

Carnal thinking says, "This is my kitchen (project, ministry, building, etc) and I'm in charge. I know what's best, so don't get in my way." In any setting where people build relationships and interact together, this kind of thinking inevitably leads to turf wars and control conflicts that cripple the institution. What starts with one or two people grows to include 10 or 12. As the numbers get bigger, the conflict escalates, and more people take sides. Anger, manipulation, distrust, and fear are just a few of the poisonous fruits.

I see evidence of such tribal control issues that affect the body of Christ everywhere I travel. Whether it is a Hindu law banning Christians from baptizing in Mumbai, or two ladies in Beaumont, Texas who won't let their pastor get the mail, the source of the problem is the same—stinking thinking. For Christ's church, the price is high. Ruling our own world requires a huge investment of time and resources, and the casualty rate is tragic.

The consumer based church and the Presence based church models represent two opposing sides of the control battle being waged for our minds, and that is pretty much where *The Presence Based Church* left off. Either a church is afflicted with carnal thinking and therefore spending much of its energy in mediation and damage control, or it is unified by a single mind to wait on, worship and welcome the Presence of God. In this book, I want to take this same line of thinking into a new dimension—the formation of corporate strongholds.

Father, teach us to worship you; not stuff, personalities, traditions or power. If there is any idolatry in our community, expose it and expel it. Like Daniel may we never bow to any other. Amen.

(1 Chronicles 16:29; Daniel 3:28)

1

WHAT IS A STRONGHOLD?

On a recent trip to England, I visited the Tower of London. At first glance, it is easy to see why it is one of the country's most acclaimed historical treasures and tourist attractions. Nestled in the heart of one of the world's key metropolitan, cultural, financial and political cities, it stands as an almost surreal reminder of an age that to me seems more like fable than history. Little snippets of every fairy tale I have read to my grandchildren, and every movie I have ever seen set in a medieval castle with warriors and women, kings and traitors, all danced around in my head at once. It was like seeing something completely make-believe suddenly spring to life.

Dating back to the year 1078, when William the Conqueror ordered the first phase of the walled castle built, the Tower of London isn't tall compared to the other modern buildings that surround it. But it is nevertheless still an impressive, foreboding structure that feels larger than it really is. When you walk through the dark inner chambers and secluded courtyard, the city seems far away. The sense of imprisonment is quite imaginable. Over the centuries that kings and queens lived in the Tower, it became a place well-known for the captivity, torture and deaths of hundreds of enemies and "traitors," including several queens and royal family members. You can still see etchings carved in the stone by prisoners held in chains inside the various dungeons. Ironically, you can also view the collection of Crown Jewels still used by the royal family today as part of the tour. If ever I've seen a real-life representation of a stronghold, the Tower of London was it.

In the *New International Version* of the Bible that I generally use for personal study, the word stronghold(s) appears 50 times, 49 times in the Old Testament and once in the New Testament. Of the 50 references, 40 of them use the term to refer to a physical place of refuge such as a fortress, a walled city, or hiding place that was heavily defended where a man would go to find protection from his enemies.

In many of these references it is David whom we find seeking sanctuary in the stronghold, such as in 1 Samuel 23:14 which says, "David stayed in the desert strongholds and in the hills of the Desert of Ziph. Day after day Saul searched for him, but God did not give David into his hands." As a military commander and one who spent a good part of his life running from people who wanted to kill him, David was very familiar with strongholds and had a deep appreciation for the safety they offered.

So it isn't too surprising then that when David wrote the Psalms, he used the term metaphorically several times in describing how he felt about God, such as in this passage: "The Lord is my light and my salvation— whom shall I fear? The Lord is the stronghold of my life— of whom shall I be afraid?" (Psalm 27:1). For David, the Lord was his ultimate source of shelter and retreat, his refuge and salvation from the enemies of doubt and fear that assailed him.

After considering the consistent usage of the term "stronghold" in the Old Testament, it is interesting that in the one and only reference in the New Testament, the meaning of the word seems to have been turned inside out. It does not refer to a place of safety, but rather a force that clearly opposes God and can hold us captive. In this letter to the Corinthian Christians, Paul is encouraging them to come against the strongholds and tear them down:

> For though we live in the world, we do not wage war as the world does. The weapons we fight with are not the weapons of the world. On the contrary, they have divine power to demolish strongholds. We demolish arguments and every pretension that sets itself up against the knowledge of God, and we take captive every thought to make it obedient to Christ (2 Corinthians 10:3-5).

So is a stronghold a good thing or a bad thing? Do we flee to it, or fight it? I think the answer can be either. A fortress is just a fortress. Whether it is a place of protection or imprisonment depends entirely on who lives there.

The strongholds we erect today are not castles or fortresses made of brick and mortar. That concept is about as relevant for the contemporary local church body as the Tower of London is to the city that surrounds it. To understand how strongholds form and affect churches today, we need to define them in a new context with new terms.

The kind of stronghold that Paul alluded to in 2 Corinthians is not a physical place, but a mental structure that we erect thought by thought, and then lock together with the opinions of others and our own validating experiences. He talks about a stronghold as an argument or pretension that "sets itself up against the knowledge of God." From this example, I want to define a stronghold as **a belief system—a pattern of thinking, attitudes and expectations—that influences behavior and invites spiritual domination.**

Notice that in this definition, a stronghold is neither good nor bad in and of itself. This is important because much of the literature that has been written about strongholds in recent years has alluded to them pretty much exclusively as conditions of evil influence and even demonic oppression. And much of this same material deals with individual, personal strongholds rather than strongholds as they appear in a group. For example, popular teacher and author Beth Moore, in her book *Praying God's Word*, talks about strongholds this way:

A stronghold is anything that exalts itself in our minds, "pretending" to be bigger or more powerful than our God. It steals much of our focus and causes us to feel overpowered. Controlled. Mastered. Whether the stronghold is an addiction, unforgiveness toward a person who has hurt us, or despair over a loss, it is something that consumes so much of our emotional and mental energy that abundant life is strangled....[1]

I think Moore is right on in her assessment of how a stronghold overpowers our thinking, and she goes on to offer good practical help to those individuals struggling with personal strongholds of this nature. But I think there are other forms of strongholds that books like this don't address.

I'm not going to deal with individual strongholds since others have done that; I'm interested in how they function corporately in churches. And I am going to insist that strongholds can be either positive or negative, depending on the content of the mental structure that is built.

This definition of a stronghold has been carefully crafted to convey a lot of information in very few words. It also may be a different approach to the topic of strongholds than you have seen or heard before. Since it is foundational to your understanding of the rest of this book that you get a clear picture of this concept in your mind, I'd like to expound just a little bit on each part of the definition.

A belief system is the term I use to describe the basic

framework of the stronghold, and it is made up of three components: a pattern of thinking, attitudes and expectations. While these terms seem pretty self-explanatory, they each offer a distinctive building block to the overall definition.

The word "pattern" is significant because patterns form habits. Strongholds are not formed just from random ideas or thoughts, but from patterns that we put together over time. Thought one leads to thought two which leads to thought three and so on. Patterns have a certain logic to them, and they can be repeated.

Attitudes, on the other hand, involve our emotions. Attitudes aren't always logical or well-reasoned, they just are. But attitudes can involve very powerful feelings that define who we are and how we relate to those around us.

The important thing to note about expectations is that expecting something to happen is very different from wanting it to happen, or even hoping it will happen. It is the difference between confident belief and wishful thinking. Whether we expect a certain outcome or just hope for it powerfully affects how we walk through the process of trying to achieve it.

A stronghold is a pattern of thinking, attitudes and expectations—that influences behavior and invites spiritual domination.

The next part of the definition, that a stronghold "influences behavior," is also very important and is a key concept to understand when trying to evaluate whether or not a stronghold is present in your church. You may be able to identify several thought processes or beliefs that you think are at work. However, if they are not affecting the way people behave, then they are not really strongholds. They may be commonly held ideas or perceptions, and they may even be widely accepted and embraced by most everyone in the congregation. But until that system of ideas starts producing corresponding actions, it's just rhetoric. You will want to keep this in mind later on as we talk about divine strongholds, because there is a lot of rhetoric in the church today that sounds good but is not producing action. Strongholds will always be connected to behavior.

Finally, I have said that a stronghold invites spiritual domination, which means that it creates favorable conditions in the spiritual realm for supernatural activity. I will talk more about this part of the definition later in this chapter when I address carnal strongholds and divine strongholds separately.

FORMATION OF A STRONGHOLD

Before we look at specific kinds of strongholds, I want to consider how the belief system of any stronghold might form. The following "steps" do not necessarily represent a rigid sequence, but rather a general pattern for stronghold formation. All of these take place as a stronghold forms, but they may be intertwined or happening simultaneously, and the cycle may repeat itself over and over. At some point, the stronghold takes control, but the process continues, which just further reinforces the belief system.

Seed thought—Strongholds start with a seed thought, an idea that has the potential to germinate in our minds and grow, eventually altering the way we think and behave. Seed thoughts are energy producing ideas that often appear to be validated by real life experiences. Of the thousands of ideas that pass through our minds every day, a few have innate power to capture our attention.

Meditation—When a seed thought takes hold, we brood or meditate on it—replaying it over and over and over. We give it priority above other thoughts in our minds until it becomes a mental "high place." It may even become an obsession. The longer we meditate, the more energy we draw from the seed thought, and the more we commit to it.

Expectations and attitudes—As our meditation becomes

a familiar pattern of thinking, attitudes (strong feelings) form. We develop expectations about how the new ideas might influence ourselves and those around us.

Behavior—We test the thought pattern by acting on it. As we do, we may adjust our thought patterns, attitudes and expectations with each trial until we see the same results consistently.

Belief system—Attitudes and expectations solidify into a belief system which defines how we respond to people and situations. We create a statement of faith or a script, which is an explanation and defense of what we believe. The statement of faith enables us to clearly communicate the belief system to others.

Confession—With the belief system firmly in place, we continue to act the stronghold out in our daily lives, forming habits that repeat themselves based on our ideological fortress. As we act, we talk through the script (or statement of faith), reassuring ourselves and others that the patterns of thinking, attitudes and expectations are well founded and trustworthy.

Since strongholds live in our minds, a "corporate stronghold," could be defined as **a situation in which a significant percentage of a definable group of people all share and act on the same belief system.** In other words, enough people within a particular group must be living in the stronghold so that the group as a whole begins to take on the behavioral characteristics. Either directly or indirectly it becomes a part of the group's identity.

Within a church setting for example, strongholds spread much like a virus, from direct exposure to a carrier. Relationships and social networks within the congregation are breeding grounds where seed thoughts, attitudes and expectations get passed back and forth, tested and adjusted. With only one or two active carriers, spread of the stronghold is very slow. But as more and more catch it, the numbers begin to increase exponentially. The process of stronghold formation, both in an individual and in a church, is measured in months and years, not days and weeks. Of the strongholds I see operating in churches, some could probably be traced back decades, while others seem to have a more recent origin. In some cases the formation was triggered by a specific event, in others, the development runs parallel to social or political changes in the surrounding community. Regardless of the cause, churches often don't recognize the stronghold until it's well established for the same reason that you don't always realize you're gaining weight until you wake up one day and can't zip your pants. The change is almost always gradual and subtle.

A corporate stronghold is a situation in which a significant percentage of a definable group of people all share and act on the same belief system.

Let me give you an image that might help you visualize the formation process. A man moves to a farm with a fishing pond about a half mile from the house. Every day, he gets in his truck and drives out to the pond to fish. At first, the drive is slow and bumpy as the farmer guides his truck through tall weeds and maneuvers around obstacles in the path. He wonders if he might be charting a new course every day. But before long, he begins to see two identical tracks emerge where his truck tires have worn down the grass. Eventually, after weeks and weeks of driving back and forth to the pond, the tracks become such deep, well-worn ruts, that the farmer doesn't even have to hold the steering wheel. He simply points the truck in the right direction, and it coasts along the familiar grooves.

I call this the "groove principle," and it illustrates how thought processes that we repeat frequently can cut such deep grooves in our minds that it becomes easier and easier for us to reach the same destination. As we form these mental ruts, the thought process eventually becomes effortless, and in fact so natural that any other outcome is impossible. These grooves are the subway lines through which strongholds are fed. This is an important concept to keep in mind throughout this book, and especially as we talk about dismantling one stronghold and establishing another in its place.

CARNAL STRONGHOLDS

To say that the church today is conflicted is an understatement. I was riding in a car with a pastoral leader who oversees a group of churches in his denomination, and with little prodding he began telling me story after story of tensions, disputes and all out wars going on in the congregations he served. Most of his time, he told me, was spent sorting through piles of letters from disgruntled laity and clergy and putting out fires. He felt like a referee instead of a spiritual leader. Despite all his efforts to bring resolution and minister healing, the list of casualties grew longer every week. He was so discouraged that he had all but given up.

When the corporate thought patterns of the consumer based church persist over time, they create grooves that eventually lead to the formation of carnal strongholds. (These strongholds are carnal in the sense that they are "of the flesh" or "relating to physical appetites," not carnal because they are sexual or sensual.) These strongholds are like hidden mines; you don't necessarily know they are there until you step on one.

I came face to face with one such mine very early in my ministry in a small central Texas church I had been assigned to pastor. Before I had preached my first sermon, I was approached by a community leader (and church member) who "warned" me of the impending danger. In an almost fatherly manner, he put his hand on my shoulder, looked me straight in the eyes and said, "Don't you preach to us about loving black people. If you do, you'll be gone." And he had a short list of names to prove his point.

That's a carnal stronghold.

As I mentioned before, one thing that makes carnal strongholds so difficult to address is that often, by the time the belief system has really taken hold, it is so deeply ingrained into the corporate mindset that it seems normal. Strongholds become part of a church's identity, and are generally widely accepted and embraced by all. In fact, the deception is so complete that damaging behavior is routinely carried out in the name of God, or at least the party line. It feels comfortable and, as long as nothing happens to bring that stronghold out into the light where it can be seen for what it is, it is never dealt with.

To attack a stronghold head on is hazardous and frequently creates a situation in which everyone loses.

When a stronghold is confronted head on, however, it is almost always explosive. That's what the church leader that I rode with was experiencing first hand. To attack one head on is hazardous and frequently creates a situation in which everyone loses.

As a result of my contact with hundreds of churches, I have identified six distinctive carnal strongholds that I see plaguing churches of all sizes and flavors: religion, pride, sedition, parochialism, judgment and fear. We are going to examine each one separately, but first I want to focus on three threads that are common to all of them: idolatry, cognitive closure and the susceptibility to demonic activity.

Idolatry

Reading the story of the Israelites in the Old Testament gives one the impression that they suffered from some kind of spiritual amnesia. Despite being God's chosen people, his very own, hand-picked earthly family, they had a terrible time remembering who he was and who he wasn't. Time and again he rescued them with spectacular acts of power, only to find that within a short time, they had completely forgotten his place in their lives. The cycle is frustrating to read. God intervenes. The people worship him. The people drift away. The people start worshiping other gods. God gets angry and punishes his children. The Israelites repent. And God intervenes again. Every time I read through the first few books of the Old Testament, I can't help thinking, "What is wrong with these people?!"

The truth is, the Israelites had a problem with idolatry. It's a theme that runs throughout their story. God was well aware of their propensity because when he gave the Ten Commandments to Moses, the first two speak directly to the issue:

You shall have no other gods before me (Exodus 20:3).

You shall not make for yourself an idol in the form of anything in heaven above or on the earth below (Exodus 20:4).

But the Israelites just didn't get it, as the scene in Exodus 32 describes. Forty days prior to this scene, Moses had been called up to the mountain top by God amidst a cosmic display of fire and clouds. We are told that "to the Israelites, the glory of the Lord looked like a consuming fire on top of the mountain" (Exodus 24:17). Apparently most everyone witnessed it. However, when their leader didn't return for several weeks, the people in the valley got restless. They got nervous. They forgot who they were, where they had come from and where they were going:

When the people saw that Moses was so long in coming down from the mountain, they gathered around his second in command, Aaron, and said, "Come, make us gods who will go before us. As for this fellow Moses, who brought us up out of Egypt, we don't know what has happened to him" (Exodus 32:1).

So Aaron had all the people bring their gold jewelry and he melted it in the fire, fashioning it into a golden calf. The people then built an altar in front of the calf, bowed down and worshiped it as the god who brought them out of Egypt, and threw a big party to celebrate! The revelry came to an abrupt end when Moses showed up. He was so angry that he smashed the two stone tablets with God's Ten Commandments before throwing the calf in the fire and melting it down. But he didn't stop there. He took the lump of gold, ground it into a fine powder, spread it over the water and then made the Israelites drink it (Exodus 32:19-20).

While Moses was being a "Presence seeker," the people were being "idol keepers." Moses was face to face with God, living an encounter with the great "I AM" that transcends description. The people, at the same time, were clinging to the past, grasping at security like a young child holding tight to a teddy bear. Moses was strong, resolute, wise and patient. The people were weak, gullible, immature and reckless. This is the difference between Presence seekers and idol keepers.

Although the Israelites had escaped Egypt and the tyranny of Pharoah, they couldn't seem to shake the influence of the pagan culture with its many idols and shrines. Without Moses' reassuring leadership, they quickly reverted to what felt safe and familiar. They built a god they could see, control and understand. They wanted to worship something that was more manageable—something that didn't threaten their lifestyle or fill them with fear. Let's face it; God's style of personal interaction up to this point had been pretty much terrifying.

Before you judge the Israelites too harshly, keep in mind that under the new covenant, we are also part of the chosen race formed from Abraham's seed (Galatians 3:29). And we are just as prone to idolatrous ways as they were. While we may not build golden animals to worship, we erect plenty of other idols in our lives and churches. We too get nervous, forgetful and restless. We too prefer a god we can see and understand. And we can be every bit as gullible and immature as the sheep that Moses was desperately trying to shepherd.

I love the way Phillip Yancey defines idolatry— "a

commitment of spirit to something that cannot bear its weight."[2] He also points out that when God rebuked the Israelites for their idolatry, he wasn't condemning their urge to worship, nor the other urges that drove them to the idols: the desire for fertility, good weather, or military success. What God detested was the fact that they were placing something above him. They were committing their spirits to things made of metal rather than to the God who loved them.

Idolatry can be defined as "a commitment of spirit to something that cannot bear its weight."

To what do we commit our spirits? What do we allow to exalt itself above the Most High God in our thinking? This is the pretension in the whole matter—the corporate carnal mindset "pretends" to know better than God. The "arguments" that the apostle Paul referred to in 2 Corinthians 10:3-5 are belief systems that disagree with God's perspective, or as we will see in the next section, with the mind of Christ.

The Bible repeatedly connects idolatry to "high places" and "Asherah poles," two different but equally offensive objects of pagan worship that the Israelites continually struggled with. High places were elevated altars or monuments where the people brought sacrifices and offerings to the pagan gods. The places were chosen for a variety of reasons, perhaps because some significant event, military victory or religious rite occurred there. Asherah poles were symbols of the sensual Canaanite goddess Astarte, and were basically sex symbols, most often made of wood.[3] Because many of the pagan cultures incorporated perverse sexual practices into their religious ceremonies, the Asherah poles were a blatant abomination to God.

Whereas we have already established that we no longer build graven images, we have in the body of Christ today our own forms of idols, high places and Asherah poles, and they are just as detestable to God. We idolize million dollar buildings and famous preachers. We glorify doctrines, traditions and achievements of men. We deify power, wealth, beauty and education, and even as believers we are yet seduced by the pleasures of sin, self and sensuality. We do not need gold idols; our spirits are overcommitted to the things of this world, none of which can bear the weight of that worship.

Every carnal stronghold involves an idol. It is the stronghold's energy source and rally point around which we the worshipers gather to rehearse our belief script and reaffirm its importance in our lives. In a carnal stronghold, we look to the idol for affirmation and identity. We think we are in control of the idol, but in reality, it has a strong hold on us. The idol can be a person, an ideal, a place, an event, an object—anything that competes in our minds for the allegiance we want to give to the Most High God.

We are created by God to worship. And nothing or no one is more deserving of our worship than the Most High God. As Graham Kendrick explains:

> Everybody worships. Whether it is a hero, possessions, success, pleasure, a political cause, a carved idol or oneself, the way we live and behave makes evident the things we love and give ourselves to. It is in our very nature to worship, and that inner drive is God-given; the disaster is that as part of a fallen race, we have replaced the object of our worship. To be converted to faith in Jesus Christ is to return to the worship of the true God, and to dethrone all rivals to His authority.[4]

The Bible says that we are spirit beings, and God is a spirit being, and therefore we are to worship him in spirit and truth (John 4:24). His pre-fall plan was for us to worship him alone, and be fully satisfied in him. We would enjoy his presence and he would take pleasure in our praise and adoration. But like the Israelites we are weak and reckless. We forget who we are, why we're here and where we are going. Our thinking becomes confused. When we allow anything to challenge God's place in our lives, stealing our devotion, we are under the curse of carnal thinking and in danger of living outside of his Presence.

Cognitive Closure

In the fortress of a carnal stronghold, a robust preservation instinct dictates that new ideas be treated as enemy fire. Incoming missiles are quickly identified, intercepted and shot down before they are allowed to breach the outer walls. And when one does slip in, it is quickly and skillfully disengaged. I call this elaborate defense mechanism cognitive closure.

In a carnal stronghold, those in charge work rigorously—sometimes going to great lengths—to seal the church off from any thought, suggestion or initiative that might alter the status quo. New visions and bold innovations pose a threat. Church consultant Bill Easum agrees:

> Controllers [in the church] not only do not want change; they also want to control everything that happens. If the new ministry is not what they want and need, they make sure it does not happen. They work so hard at keeping bad things from happening that nothing new ever happens. Paranoia over past mistakes and future errors have led to a highly controlled atmosphere.[5]

Redundancy is the name of the game. Anyone that might come along and try to shake up the established routine or ways of thinking may learn well the meaning of "ambush." I've said it before, sheep can bite. Christians can be mean. Sweet gray-haired ladies can grow fangs and blow fire if you mess with their choir music or change the Wednesday night potluck. In a carnal stronghold, pastors are puppets, leaders are gate keepers, and the people plod along like a mindless herd of cattle, each one following the tail right in front of his nose.

Susceptibility to Demonic Activity

Often times when people hear the term "stronghold" they assume that it must involve some kind of demonic oppression or possession. This is not necessarily true. As I have just described, a stronghold is a belief system made up of attitudes, expectations and thought patterns. When we give it permission, the stronghold will affect our behavior and can ultimately control our destiny.

Occasionally, a carnal stronghold offers Satan an open door—an opportunity to get a foothold in our midst—and he can assign a demonic spirit to take advantage of the opening and further the destruction. However, I firmly believe that in most churches, this isn't the case. The enemy can accomplish plenty just by fueling the curse of the carnal mind, and generally our twisted thinking is harmful enough on its own to keep us spiritually distracted and off-course. Satan has only to sit back and watch as we suffer the natural consequences of our misplaced affections.

Satan has only to sit back and watch as we suffer the natural consequences of our misplaced affections.

Furthermore, trying to identify whether a church does or does not have some demonic activity going on is not the purpose of this book as much as my purpose is to direct your attention to the mental structures that might be suitable housing for such uninvited guests. If you have a rat problem in your garage, you can launch an all out assault on the rats to drive them away, but they are likely to return. Or you can focus on identifying and cleaning out whatever might have attracted the rats there in the first place (like garbage) so that whether they starve to death or simply leave, they have no reason to come back. This is the approach I tend to take to spiritual warfare.

That is why it was important to me to define a stronghold as something that invites spiritual domination. When we breed a carnal stronghold, we are making ourselves vulnerable by creating an environment which could be a staging area for demonic activity, whether or not it actually is. We don't want to make the mistake of giving Satan more credit or attention than necessary because that's exactly what he wants. We do, however, want to be diligent about recognizing and taking out the trash.

DIVINE STRONGHOLDS

If you have ever observed a church or ministry that seems to have the "Midas touch"—everything they touch turns to gold—or one that grows exponentially for no obvious reason, or maybe one that always has a budget surplus, lives in a constant state of revival and regularly sees miraculous signs and wonders, then there is a good chance you have seen the effects of a divine stronghold. It can be an amazing thing to witness because so often it defies explanation and disregards accepted church management practices. If I had to pick one word to sum up a divine stronghold, it would be effortless. At least they appear that way.

It's not that people operating within a divine stronghold don't have to put forth any effort; they do. But it's a different kind of working atmosphere. It looks and feels empowered.

I was in the airport very late one night waiting to board a plane that had been delayed several hours by weather. It was nearing 10:00 p.m. and many of the gates were bringing in their last flights of the night and clearing out. I realized the terminal was about as empty as I had ever seen it, except for our little group of passengers camped out by our gate. We still had an hour to wait.

A young girl and her mother had been waiting also, and apparently decided to take advantage of the long, empty corridor to stretch, walk and kill some time. They started "race walking" each other up and down the terminal, one of them gliding smugly along on the moving sidewalk and the other trying desperately to keep up under her own power. One easy step on the sidewalk required three or four brisk ones just to stay close. Every time they reached the end, they would laugh at themselves, switch places, and take off again. I'm not sure why it was so funny—probably because we had been sitting at the gate for several hours already, and because it was getting late and because the airport had an eerie quietness about it. But the luxury of racing on a moving sidewalk was a picture that stuck in my mind.

That is a little how a divine stronghold looks and feels—like the whole thing is on a moving sidewalk powered by an unseen force. Effort is multiplied and a little goes a long way. One easy step takes you farther, faster than three or four hard fought steps in a carnal stronghold. Instead of groups of people within the church pushing and pulling in opposition, when a divine stronghold is in place, all the motion seems to flow in generally the same direction. Conflict is minimized and production is increased.

A divine stronghold is a state of total surrender to the mind of Christ in which he is the Most High God, and everything bows to the knowledge and experience of his Presence.

I defined a stronghold (of any kind) as a belief system that influences behavior. Now let me expand that definition for a divine stronghold by adding the following: **a state of total surrender to the mind of Christ in which he is the Most High God, and everything bows to the knowledge and experience of his Presence.** Notice that there is still a belief system in a divine stronghold, but it is rooted in the perfect mind of Christ. And the belief system still influences behavior in that we are totally surrendered to the lordship of Christ. We are mastered by the Master; governed in every way by his Presence.

So how does a divine stronghold form? It starts with a church that desires his Presence to be manifested in every possible way. They seek hard after God; it is the underlying rhythm of all they do. These Presence based thought patterns, when practiced over

a period of time, cut the grooves, which opens the way for the
Holy Spirit to work. He nurtures and feeds our hunger for God's
Presence, helping us form a belief system that reflects the mind
of Christ. Without the Holy Spirit, we couldn't think like Jesus,
but he is our divine helper and the part of God that lives in us to
conform us to his likeness. He works on God's behalf to establish
his kingdom rule where he finds believers waiting, worshiping
and welcoming his Presence.

Divine strongholds differ from carnal strongholds because
they are really two-pronged: one point is an element of the mind
of Christ that we choose to put on, and the other point is God's
response to that mindset, or what he gives of himself in answer.
To see divine strongholds grow in our midst, we must choose to
put on the mind of Christ; we must make conscious decisions to
tear down old ways of thinking and cut new grooves that reflect
kingdom thinking. However, as we do that, God responds. He is
able to establish divine patterns in our church. In other words,
his kingdom comes, and his will is done, right here on earth as it
is in heaven (Matthew 6:10).

It is really both of these prongs that make up the divine
strongholds, and you will recognize this as we examine them
more closely. We begin to conform our thoughts and attitudes
to those of Christ Jesus, and the door is opened for God to gain
control, working according to his will and purpose in us.

A divine stronghold can be expressed in a variety of ways
in a local church. I have identified six in contrast to the carnal
strongholds, which I will list here in relationship:

Religion—**Passion** (Presence)

Pride—**Humility** (Power)

Sedition—**Honor** (Favor)

Parochialism—**Unity** (Glory)

Judgment—**Grace** (Salvation)

Fear—**Faith** (Hope)

Just as with carnal strongholds, there are several common threads that run through each of these—worship, the mind of Christ and openness to the Holy Spirit—so I want to address those before we look at the strongholds separately.

Worship

Worship plays a primary role in the Presence based church, and also in the formation and maintenance of a divine stronghold. There are several reasons for this: 1) worship is the necessary protocol for hosting the Presence of God; 2) it sharpens our revelation of Jesus; and 3) it firmly establishes him as the Most High in our thinking. Therefore worship is the energy source that fuels a divine stronghold. The clearer our view of the savior, the more we welcome the Presence and exalt him in his rightful place, the more our thought life can conform to a pre-fall pattern.

The people of Israel whom God led out of Egypt were the first to experience a divine stronghold. God himself took up residence with them from his resting place over the Ark of the Covenant. The Ark was his own self-appointed earthly seat, and it became the center piece of the Israelite camp. God even chose for himself one tribe, the Levites, to be specifically assigned Presence seekers. They attended to the Ark and the tabernacle as God prescribed through Moses, waiting and worshiping day and night because this was the proper code of behavior in his Presence. From between the Ark's cherubim, on the Mercy Seat, God interacted with his children, ruling and reigning in every aspect of their lives. He led them, taught them, loved them and defended them. It was the epitome of a divine stronghold.

Worship is the energy source that fuels a divine stronghold.

While carnal strongholds are represented by a variety of idols that compete with God for our devotion, the divine strongholds all have this in common: Jesus is the focal point. As the new Ark of the Covenant, he is the high place in a divine stronghold, our source for approval and encouragement and direction. His name is above all names, and he is the starting point from which all plans and decisions are made. He is the beginning and the end. Worship sharpens our revelation of Jesus which only serves to draw us deeper and deeper into worship.

In the new covenant, Jesus is our rally point. He is the place we go to commit our spirits, be renewed and made alive. He is God in the flesh, and when we place him in the very center of our camp, he will rule and reign supreme in our lives. He will be our leader, teacher, lover and defender. His life will be expressed in us and through us for the world to see. All the "grooves" in our minds originate in him and lead back to him so that he is glorified in the life of the church.

But we know this—God is a jealous God, and he will not take up residence where his Son is not worshiped above all. This is the meaning of God's name "El Elyon," which translates as God, Most High.[6] El Elyon is used some 95 times throughout the Old and New Testaments, ascribing to him a status that is far higher than any other god. He is not just God, but El Elyon, the Most High God. In worship we acknowledge his eminence; he rises, and scatters his enemies before him (Psalm 68:1).

When we replace him with idols however, as the Israelites so often did, he backs away, turning us over to the consequences of our futile thinking (Romans 1:28). He doesn't settle for second place. That is why healthy, consistent worship is so key to courting his Presence and maintaining his stronghold in our midst. In worship we bow in submission to him, express our devotion to him, articulate our dependence on him and honor him as the Most High God, above all else. Our worship establishes his place on the throne in our minds and secures him there against the onslaught of would be insurgents.

The Mind of Christ

In the Garden of Eden, humanity sold out for the sake of knowledge, and in doing so, we opened our minds up to attack from self-absorption, sin and Satan. The battle for dominion was on and the playing field was our minds. We gave the enemy a viable strategy—confuse their thinking in order to control their behavior.

Fortunately, we are not defenseless. Jesus gave us a choice. What the first Adam forfeited, the second Adam reclaimed by paying the price at the cross for a new way of thinking. We read:

> They stripped him and put a scarlet robe on him, and then twisted together a crown of thorns and set it on his head. They put a staff in his right hand and knelt in front of him and mocked him. "Hail, king of the Jews!" they said. They spit on him, and took the staff and struck him on the head again and again. After they had mocked him, they took off the robe and put his own clothes on him. Then they led him away to crucify him (Matthew 27:28-31).

Jesus accomplished many divine purposes through his death and resurrection. No other single event in history comes close to the impact of the cross. In taking the scourging on his back, he bought our healing (Isaiah 53:4-5). By dying a criminal's death, naked on a cross, he took away our shame (2 Corinthians 5:21). But by willingly enduring the crown of thorns and the blows to his head, Jesus offered us a new way of thinking and a new mind—the mind of Christ. Paul explains this to the Philippians:

No other single event in history comes close to the impact of the cross.

> Let this mind be in you which was also in Christ Jesus, who, being in the form of God, did not consider it robbery to be equal with God, but made Himself of no reputation, taking the form of a bondservant, and coming in the likeness of

men. And being found in appearance as a man, He humbled Himself and became obedient to the point of death, even the death of the cross (Philippians 2:5-8, *New King James Version*).

Jesus came to earth to redeem, among other things, our minds. He came to break the hold of stinking thinking and the curse of the carnal mind. Just as we can trade our lives for his life in us, we can also trade our minds for his mind in us.

Volumes have been written about the mind of Christ—it's a big theological bite to chew. We know that Jesus and the Father and the Holy Spirit are one, yet we also know that Jesus put on human flesh and became fully man, experiencing the same emotions and physical sensations we do. So he must have had a thought life. He must have had thoughts about the people and places around him, the disciples, the Pharisees, his parents and his home. Maybe he even contemplated things like his job, his own appearance, his favorite food, or the weather. I imagine he might have thought about the millions upon millions of lives he would save, each one with its own unique story. And he undoubtedly thought about his destiny—the tremendous task he was sent to undertake.

Yet at no time did he sin. At no time did a single thought ever stray outside the perfect will of his Father. His mind, though capable of the same dishonest or unlovely thoughts that plague you and me, never went there. It was never even one degree less than perfectly righteous and satisfied. In other words, every one of his thoughts was in flawless harmony with God; the mind of Christ was totally surrendered.

We also know this about the mind of Christ; that we have access to it but it is up to us to "put it on." As Paul told the Corinthian believers, we have divine weapons that are capable of demolishing arguments and pretensions—thoughts that disagree with the mind of Christ—but it is our responsibility to use those weapons. He exhorts the Romans, "Do not conform any longer to the pattern of this world, but be transformed by the renewing of your mind" (Romans 12:2). We have to renew our minds through active engagement; we cannot just sit back passively and wait for God to do it for us. It is a choice we make day by day and even hour by hour. Paul alludes to this ongoing struggle when he says we must "take captive every thought to make it obedient to Christ" (2 Corinthians 10:5). Every thought. That is an enormous task.

If a stronghold is a belief system, then a divine stronghold in a church reflects some particular aspect of a corporate mind of Christ. When collectively a body of believers commits themselves to worship and to bringing every thought into the light of truth, then a shared mindset, patterned after the mind of Christ, takes hold. As a group, they begin to think like Jesus. Attitudes—like Jesus. Expectations—like Jesus. It can be said of a divine stronghold, "All the believers were one in heart and mind" (Acts 4:32). The end result is a communal "Presence of mind."

Openness to Holy Spirit Activity

The most visible and exciting thing about divine strongholds is the fruit. Kingdom results are the true confirmation of whether a stronghold is present and what its emphasis might be. If you cannot find discernable, quantifiable effects somewhere, either in the life of the church, the surrounding community, the individual lives of its people, or all three, then I would question whether a divine stronghold is really at work.

Fruit is a trademark of divine strongholds because where one is freely operating, the Holy Spirit has liberty to move. As I discussed before, the mental systems that form strongholds invite spiritual domination by creating an atmosphere that is conducive for it. I think of a stronghold as being like a nest which can be either inhabited or uninhabited. The stronghold establishes a particular environment, in this case, one that is welcoming to God's Presence, but then we must wait to see what will come to live there. The more favorable the conditions, the more likely God's Presence will take up residence.

This is the one area that I mentioned earlier in which divine strongholds differ from carnal ones: In the case of carnal thought patterns that form strongholds in a church of judgment, fear or pride, for example, I think the "nest" itself is so damaging that direct demonic possession or activity, while possible, is not generally the issue. On the other hand, when we lay out a spiritual welcome mat for God's Presence, he is faithful to come. It is not his nature to hide from us. Jesus says to the church, "Here I am! I stand at the door and knock. If anyone hears my voice and opens the door, I will come in and eat with him, and he with me" (Revelation 3:20). God is a gracious and loving Father who wants to heal, bless, restore, comfort and save. He desires to interact with his children, if only we will invite him. So as we make the choice to put on the mind of Christ, bringing every thought into submission, God responds and the stronghold is established.

We must be careful though not to fall into the deception that we can somehow manipulate God. He is completely sovereign and omniscient. We cannot put our trust in a formula or a book or something that worked in some other church and believe that we can guarantee his arrival. He is too big to fit in that box! We must simply ask, seek and knock and keep on asking, seeking and knocking because he promises to answer (Luke 11:5-10). Jesus tells us this parable about two neighbors to make the point that persistence pays off. "Which of you fathers," he reasons, "if your son asks for a fish, will give him a snake instead? Or if he asks for an egg, will give him a scorpion? If you then, though you are evil, know how to give good gifts to your children, how much more will your Father in heaven give the Holy Spirit to those who ask him!" (Luke 11:11-13)

When God is securely in his place as the Most High and our

worship and adoration are directed to him alone, we set the stage for him to come and live in our midst. And when he does, he releases the Holy Spirit to accomplish his purposes in and through our church. In a divine stronghold, everything is secondary to his Presence. Opinions of man step aside for his wisdom. Self-aggrandizing religion crumbles in the light of his glory. Fear is washed away by his limitless love. He is supremely exalted in our lives, and nothing or no one is greater.

When God gets his way, we truly experience the full and abundant life promised in John 10:10. It is only when we relinquish control and become completely surrendered to the lordship of Jesus Christ that we actually become free to receive all that God has for us. Being yoked to Jesus is not a position of bondage, but rather a place of infinite security and freedom from which we can fulfill every calling and maximize our gifts. Life in a divine stronghold is turbo-charged by the Holy Spirit.

Life in a divine stronghold is turbo-charged by the Holy Spirit.

In contrast to carnal strongholds where cognitive closure causes churches to stagnate and languish, divine strongholds are characterized by growth, innovation and even risk taking. The corporate mind of Christ is in tune to the Spirit and can therefore embrace the creative nature of God. Such thought patterns are open to new ideas and see risk as an adventure of faith. In a divine stronghold, the organism matures, strengthens, builds and changes.

Finally, divine strongholds, once established, tend to be self-perpetuating. As God is allowed to be fully God, the hunger for his habitation grows. His manifest Presence becomes the norm, and those who taste it will never again be satisfied with anything less. The intimacy of Presence based worship, the experience of his touch only energizes our desire to be totally conformed to his image and reflect the mind of Christ in all matters.

TWO DISCOVERIES

One of the exciting and sort of unsettling things about writing a book is that in the course of trying to communicate a message in print, I find myself scrutinizing every detail, every idea. In the process, I usually discover at least as much about the topic as I thought I knew to start with. It always makes me wonder why I thought I knew enough to write the book in the first place.

I had two such revelations while in the grips of this book, which I think are worth mentioning. First, a stronghold can look very similar to an anointing, or a special outpouring of God's favor. Both can produce inexplicable results. But an anointing is a different animal. In his sovereignty, God sometimes chooses to anoint a person or group of people to accomplish a specific kingdom purpose in the earth. The recipient does not do anything to earn or attract the anointing; it is given solely at God's discretion. And although it is possible for the person to not fulfill the purpose for which they were anointed, the anointing is still there. It cannot be revoked or lost.

For example, Moses was anointed by God for the purpose of leading the Israelite people out of Egypt and into the promised land. He didn't pray for the anointing; he didn't even want the job. But it wasn't his call. He was God's man, chosen and miraculously gifted to accomplish the task.

Strongholds, on the other hand, are something we can invite. Cutting grooves that are in line with the mind of Christ and welcoming God's Presence with worship will set the stage for a divine stronghold to occur. That also means that if we stop seeking and welcoming, and allow the enemy to gain a foothold through carnal thinking, then we can lose the divine stronghold over time.

I noticed as I observed and studied divine strongholds in churches that they often work in tandem with an anointing of some kind, but not always. They are two different works of the Holy Spirit.

My second revelation was that methods, ministries and models of "doing church" have very little to do with divine strongholds. Again, as I observed these strongholds operating in various churches around the country, I saw some patterns of methodology, which at first led me to believe that the methods were connected to the fruits of ministry. But that was not actually the case.

As I looked longer and wider, I realized that strongholds are a spiritual phenomenon and they bear spiritual fruit. When a divine stronghold is in place, and the Holy Spirit is free to work, the fruit of that stronghold will be evident regardless of what particular ministry or strategy the church decides to implement. In other words, if grace is flowing in a church, then people are going to be converted whether it's at special events, in small groups, through outreach programs...it doesn't matter. The Holy Spirit can and will do his thing anywhere through any means, as long as we have opened the door to him. That is why strongholds can be just as effective in big churches and small churches, traditional churches and contemporary churches.

That is also why, when churches see a great move of God happening somewhere, and they try to recreate it by copying the methods, they typically don't see the same results. The results weren't being rendered by the method, but because of a belief system that influenced behavior and invited the Presence of God to move. I think strongholds are copyrighted in heaven, and if you want one bad enough to pray the price for it, God will design one just for you.

Up to this point, I have been talking about strongholds in fairly general terms because I wanted to give you a basic understanding of what they are and how they develop and function. But now it is time to get more specific. Through the next several chapters, we will look individually at six carnal strongholds and six corresponding divine strongholds and how they function in real life churches.

Praise you my God that your eyes are on the righteous and your ears are attentive to their prayers. But your face is against those who do evil. Never let me do anything that would cause you to turn your face from me. How can I seek your face if you are looking away? In Jesus I am righteous and in Jesus I am delivered from evil (1 Peter 3:11-12).

2

RELIGION VS PASSION

Several years ago, while on a Holy Land tour, I visited a famous church site in Jerusalem. A line of people extended out the door of the church and into the courtyard area, so I got in line thinking that there must be something special to see inside. As I inched forward, my anticipation grew until I finally reached the door. With only a few people now in front of me, I saw what appeared to be a large rock under a table dressed in linen. One by one the visitors were crouching down close to the rock, pausing for a moment, and then leaving. I asked the attendant what they were doing.

In a serious tone he said, "Peter once stood on this very rock, so the people are laying their hands on the rock and kissing it to pay homage."

I looked at the rock. I tried hard to envision the apostle Peter standing on it delivering a powerful sermon, but all I could think about was how many hands and mouths had deposited germs there.

"It's your turn, sir. Kiss the rock and get out!" The attendant sounded agitated with me.

"No thank you." I think he was annoyed with me for slowing down the line, and also perhaps because I didn't drop an offering in the box that sat on the table.

Something about those people kissing that rock troubled me. I had gone to Israel because I wanted to see the places that I had read about and studied for so many years. I wanted to feel the land and experience some glimpse of the life Jesus lived while here on earth. It was my love for Jesus and the Bible story that drove me there, and I'm not sure what else I expected to see except historical sites and places where Bible heroes stood and walked.

But the rock kissing thing struck me as ridiculous. That rock didn't contain any residual particles of Peter's sandals. It wasn't powerful or life-giving and had no inherent value on its own. It was just a rock. A big, flat, dirty rock. Yet the people were treating it as some mysterious source of divine blessing, as if touching it with their lips was a spiritual act. The rock had become, in a sense, an idol, more real and sacred to many of those people than what it represented.

That's how the strong-hold of religion works. It confuses empty, meaningless scripts of behavior with genuine acts of worship.

That's how the stronghold of religion works. It confuses empty, meaningless scripts of behavior with genuine acts of worship. Those who are afflicted with it don't recognize it because they are deceived into thinking that their religious play-acting is real. The religious stronghold perpetuates programs, procedures and patterns year after year after year after year, long after they have lost any true spiritual significance they once had. Sincere Christians allow the real Jesus, who is alive and able to save and heal, to be replaced by a sentimental, storybook Jesus who was and did, but doesn't anymore.

I'm often amused by the way elements of the Christian faith

are played on the movie screen. While we all know that Hollywood can be blasphemous and licentious, it does have a way of
holding up the mirror to anyone and everything in society and
saying, "see, this is what you look like." Sometimes the images are
so dead on and so insightful that you can't run from them.

It was on that premise that I went to see the movie *Talladega
Nights: The Ballad of Ricky Bobby*, because I had been told it had
an amusing prayer angle. In the movie, Will Ferrell plays the part
of Ricky Bobby, a moronic yet good hearted race car driver, "with
two first names." Ricky always says a blessing before he eats, and
one of his most hilarious personality quirks is that he only prays
to the "baby" Jesus. Early in the movie when his family sits down
to eat, he prays:

> Dear Lord baby Jesus, we thank you so much for this boun-
> tiful harvest of Dominos, KFC, and the always delicious
> Taco Bell. I just want to take time to say thank you for my
> family. My two sons, Walker, and Texas Ranger, or TR as
> we call him. And of course my red hot smokin' wife Carley,
> who is a stone cold fox.

This draws an affirmative "mmm hmm" from his friend and
sidekick, and then Ricky continues his prayer, "Dear tiny infant
Jesus...."

When Ricky's wife interrupts his blessing to remind him
that Jesus did in fact grow up and that it's a bit strange to keep
praying to a baby, Ricky matter-of-factly answers, "Well look, I
like the Christmas Jesus best, and I'm sayin' grace. When you
say grace, you can say it to grown up Jesus, or teenage Jesus, or
bearded Jesus, or whatever you want." Throughout the movie he
prays on other occasions, "Dear 8 pounds 6 ounces baby Jesus,
new born, not even spoken a word yet," and, "I wanna thank little
baby Jesus, who's sittin' in his crib watchin' the Baby Einstein
videos, learnin' 'bout shapes and colors."[1] While I can't endorse
the rest of the movie as quality viewing from any perspective, I
laughed at those scenes until my side hurt.

How many people and churches I know that seem to relate only to the baby Christmas Jesus—that iconic, idyllic babe in the manger that represents the season of gift giving and glad tidings. How many church going Christians keep Jesus wrapped in his swaddling clothes and never let him grow up? Or what about churches that create their own favorite rendition of Jesus—a Baptist Jesus or a Catholic Jesus or a charismatic Jesus? I think many of us are guilty of making Jesus into our image so that we can understand him and think we have control of him. Instead of seeking after the true revelation of his glory, we accept a lesser characterization defined by our own experiences and convention.

The stronghold of religion can take on many forms. Traditions, denominational distinctions, even holiday festivities all have potential to support religious mindsets that want to protect and enshrine something of perceived or sentimental value. This tendency is evident in churches of all flavors—not just in the traditional mainline churches where you might expect it, but also in charismatic churches that can just as easily give idol status to trendy worship styles or high tech capabilities. Like the Israelites, we are decidedly prone to substituting that which is familiar for the real thing.

As you drive into the main entrance to Bush Intercontinental Airport in Houston, you can see several flight simulators where Continental Airlines trains its pilots. They look a little bit like an attraction you might see at a theme park—cockpit shaped capsules mounted on huge mechanical arms that are programmed to reproduce every possible movement that an airplane might experience while flying. In them, pilots practice emergency landings, routine take-offs, and procedures for dealing with unexpected turbulence or mechanical failures. The simulators are so good at creating the feelings associated with an actual flying experience (and I'm glad they are!) that it might be easy to forget they never really leave the ground.

The stronghold of religion can act much like a flight

simulator. It can create such an illusion of worship that people don't realize they're still on the ground. Man-made religion can be a moving, emotional experience, with a lot of motion and rhetoric that appears to be about God, even though it is completely devoid of his Presence. It can trigger all sorts of feelings and memories that are real, but it does not draw us any closer to the heart of God, it doesn't stir our spirits with compassion for the lost, and it doesn't compel us toward the goal of becoming like Jesus. Religion can look good, and it can even feel good, but it is a dangerous and hollow substitute for worship. It is, in Shakespeare's words, "full of sound and fury, signifying nothing."[2]

> *The stronghold of religion can act much like a flight simulator. It can create such an illusion of worship that people don't realize they're still on the ground.*

The Spirit of Legalism

The driving force behind the stronghold of religion is legalism, an overly strict adherence to a law or code. Even in a church that would never formally espouse a doctrine of salvation by good works, the legalistic spirit can be very strong. It keeps a tight reign on change or progress ("we've never done it that way before") and zealously polices every facet of church life with a long list of *dos* and *don't*s. It likes to keep control by issuing permits or denying permission. Legalism rewards those who stay in line, and punishes those who don't. It clings to convention, enforces rules and preserves traditions at all cost.

The sense of bondage and oppression in a church given to legalism can be stifling. Those with new ideas or fresh visions are met with harsh skepticism and can even be labeled as heretics. Sacred cows will always trump new milk dispensers. Cognitive closure protects the status quo and ensures that attitudes, thought processes and expectations foundational to the stronghold are preserved and passed down to new generations of militants.

Where legalism thrives and a religious stronghold is established, the laws and customs, rites and rituals, procedures and protocols that are part of a church's identity are the idols that have been set above the Most High God. They have become the objects of worship.

Jesus boldly confronted this legalistic spirit many times during his ministry, and in fact it was ultimately the religious stronghold that set the stage for his crucifixion. Of all the strongholds we will look at, this one solicited more of his direct attention and seemed to be the most repugnant to him. It was the Pharisees, the religious leaders and teachers of the day, that embodied and epitomized the religious stronghold, and Jesus seldom passed up an opportunity to publicly reprove them for it.

For example, in Mark chapter 7, a group of these Pharisees and teachers from Jerusalem had gathered around Jesus to listen to him. They were always trying to corner him with a difficult question or catch him saying something that might get him into trouble. On this particular day, the Pharisees noticed that Jesus' disciples were eating food with their hands without having first fulfilled the Jewish custom of ceremonial washing. This custom had nothing to do with sterilization or getting rid of germs; they didn't even know what those were yet. It was strictly a symbolic ritual.

The Pharisees themselves were known to be flawless keepers of every tradition handed down by the elders (and there were hundreds!) and they were fanatical in keeping the religious laws as well. No one surpassed them. They lived rigidly disciplined lives of fasting and prayer. So it was an affront to their belief system (egos) that Jesus did not rebuke his followers for failing to properly wash their hands. However, when they asked Jesus why his disciples weren't following the rules, he reprimanded the Pharisees instead:

> Isaiah was right when he prophesied about you hypocrites; as it is written: "'These people honor me with their lips, but

their hearts are far from me. They worship me in vain; their teachings are but rules taught by men.' You have let go of the commands of God and are holding on to the traditions of men."

And he said to them: "You have a fine way of setting aside the commands of God in order to observe your own traditions!" (Mark 7:6-9)

Imagine how infuriated the Pharisees must have been! They believed themselves to be shining examples of holiness, and they had just been called hypocrites in front of a crowd of people. The irony is that despite all their efforts to reach God, when finally they could touch him, they rejected him instead.

The Pharisees were so busy being prideful about how religious they were, that they did not have eyes to see Jesus, nor ears to hear the truth. Following the letter of the law had become their salvation, so that when Jesus came along to abolish the law and set in motion a new covenant of grace, their world was shaken to the core. They were at the top of the game, head and shoulders above the masses, but now someone was trying to change the rules—in essence to level the playing field. They just couldn't stomach losing their position, authority and control, so they dug in for the fight. They labeled Jesus a heretic and began plotting to have him killed.

Paul also confronted the religious stronghold fairly early in his ministry while in Athens. As he was waiting for Silas and Timothy to join him there, he was "greatly distressed to see that the city was full of idols" (Acts 17:16). The writer of the book of Acts, Luke, also makes it a point to mention that all the people who lived there "spent their time doing nothing but talking about and listening to the latest ideas" (Acts 17: 21). I find the connection between idolatry and the visual image of these philosophers discussing religious ideas interesting. The insinuation is that they sat around all day talking about religion but didn't actually do anything about it. They weren't discussing religious ideas in search of the truth; rather, they worshiped the idol of knowledge and therefore liked showing off their own educational prowess, like male peacocks strutting around with feathers held high.

Anyway, Paul did what Paul was so good at doing—he went to the synagogue and started telling the philosophers about Jesus, about his life and death and resurrection. He went right to the point:

> Men of Athens! I see that in every way you are very religious. For as I walked around and looked carefully at your objects of worship, I even found an altar with this inscription: to an unknown god. Now what you worship as something unknown I am going to proclaim to you (Acts 17:22-23).

He went on to share with them the good news of the Gospel.

Upon hearing Paul's message, while a few of the men did respond and become believers, many more were simply intrigued by this new, latest idea and wanted to discuss it some more. Others just sneered and dismissed him as a babbler. In the Athenian culture of academic religion, Paul experienced resistance and saw very few results.

A Form of Godliness

The religious stronghold looks much the same in churches today as it did in the New Testament. It still has "a form of godliness, but denying its power" (2 Timothy 3:5). It clings to the past, fiercely opposes change, and locks down churches in the impenetrable cages of their own time honored traditions. Let me give you just a few examples that I have witnessed first hand. Keep in mind that these are real churches, for which I could document names, dates and cities, but I won't here for obvious reasons.

In one church that I visited, the religious stronghold reared its head when a brand new sanctuary was completed, but the congregation refused to move into it. Despite the fact that they had voted for the building and given money for it to be built, when it came time to move, they couldn't leave the old one behind. It held too many memories. Their minds and spirits were completely committed to preserving the past and everything they held dear about their church, so they clung to the worn, tattered carpet and old wooden pews as though Jesus himself inhabited the place. The truth was, Jesus hadn't been there in a very long time, but they didn't notice and had long since stopped caring.

The truth was, Jesus hadn't been there in a very long time, but they didn't notice and had long since stopped caring.

Another example of the religious stronghold that I encountered was in a large, prestigious church where I was the guest preacher on Sunday morning. In between services I found an empty classroom where I could sip on a cup of coffee and sit quietly before the Lord. As I prayed and just worshiped there by myself, I lost track of time until I heard music trailing down the hallway. Because the style of this church was very traditional, I was supposed to have entered the pulpit area with the other members of the pastoral staff during the processional song, and had an assigned seat next to the senior pastor in the pulpit area. But because I had missed my cue, I just slipped into the sanctuary through a side door and sat in the front pew until I was introduced to preach.

After the service, I discovered just how legalistic the religious stronghold can be. In spite of the fact that many of the people that day responded to the message, and several even gave their hearts to Jesus, all the pastor could talk about after the service was his frustration over the fact that I had failed to follow their protocol. He was angry and offended, chastising me up one side and down the other for my apparent disregard of that which was most important to him.

Another church spent several thousand dollars to purchase a new Power Point system for the sanctuary. However when the system was installed, the large screen that the images were projected onto mechanically rolled down from the ceiling, obscuring the view of the organ pipes. A group of the members was so offended that the pipes were hidden by the screen that a massive church conflict ensued and the Power Point system was never used. As far as I know, it's still sitting in a storage closet.

And my favorite: in an aging downtown church where I recently spoke, the pastor pointed to a table in the altar area and said, "That table cost me several church members." He went on to explain that not long before that, they had moved the table from one side of the sanctuary to the other to better accommodate the worship team, and a small but significant group of people left the church. They were convinced that moving the table had opened the church up to demonic activity.

If you've ever encountered a religious stronghold yourself, then you know that strongholds are never required to make sense. These are real life examples from Bible teaching, mainline churches. Yet when you read them, they sound almost too silly to be true. That's the danger of strongholds. Because they are belief systems that develop in a congregation over time, the resulting behaviors can be difficult to self-diagnose. Twisted thinking becomes the standard, and the church forgets who she is. She is thrown into a crisis of identity.

> I believe that the greatest trick of the devil is not to get us into some sort of evil but rather have us wasting time. This is why the devil tries so hard to get Christians to be religious. If he can sink a man's mind into habit, he will prevent his heart from engaging God.[3]   —Donald Miller

THE STRONGHOLD OF PASSION

The opposite of a religious stronghold is a stronghold of passion. While religion perpetuates rules and rituals, passion pursues a deep and intimate relationship. Religion leads to bondage, but a love relationship like that between a bride and bridegroom results in freedom. Religion enshrines the past; the great "I Am" is about to reveal something new. Religion talks about God; passion experiences him. Religion is uncomfortable with miracles; passion is always looking for one. Religion makes the natural super, but the stronghold of passion welcomes the supernatural. Religion represents man's search for God, but in passionate pursuit of Jesus, we find ourselves completely captured by him.

The stronghold of passion is a belief system built on the idea that God is an emotional being, and that his desire is to have an intimate love relationship with each of us. Therefore this divine stronghold is characterized by a zealous pursuit of him—the full revelation of his nature, his glory and his heart. Rather than struggling to preserve man-made customs, the stronghold of passion grows out of an atmosphere that above all welcomes the Presence of God, whatever it might look like, and yearns for deeper communion with him, whatever that might entail. When passion has taken hold as a corporate mindset in a church, the evidence is easy to see: people seek beyond God's hand to his face, they are captivated by his beauty, they hear his voice, and they reflect and identify with the emotions of God.

Both Moses and David had a deep appreciation for God's face. The Bible says, "The Lord would speak to Moses face to face, as a man speaks with his friend" (Exodus 33:11). In David's Psalm of thanks he admonishes us, "Look to the Lord and his strength; seek his face always" (1 Chronicles 16:11). When we seek God's face, he draws near and turns his face toward us. As we noted in *The Presence Based Church*, the word "presence" is derived from the word paniym, which comes from the word panah, which means "to turn" or "to turn the face toward."[4] As he turns toward us, he reveals his identity.

A person's face is their identity. It is how we are recognized and distinguished from others. Therefore, to seek God's face is to discover his uniqueness. Moses was quick to explain this in

Deuteronomy 4, "Acknowledge and take to heart this day that the Lord is God in heaven above and on the earth below. There is no other" (4:39). God's uniqueness is also evident in his Old Testament names, which represent the various aspects of his character.

In a people based church, prayer is aimed primarily at God's hand; that is, asking him to give us what we need. We want financial provision, healing, a bigger house or an open door. And there is nothing wrong with this. Jesus told us, "Ask and it will be given to you; seek and you will find; knock and the door will be opened to you" (Matthew 7:7). He has helped me find lost keys, overcome obstacles and minister to hurting people. Countless times he has rescued me from despair and trouble. He has healed me and protected me, and done the same for my family. But prayer doesn't have to end there.

Prayer fueled by passion to know God and experience his Presence is life changing because when we catch a glimpse of God's splendor we are never the same. It leaves us overwhelmed and longing for more. When John saw the face of Jesus, he recorded this, "His face was like the sun shining in all its brilliance. When I saw him, I fell at his feet as though dead" (Revelation 1:16b-17). As you read the rest of Revelation, you can see that John never got over that one sighting.

When we press in to know God's identity, we also discover his incomparable beauty. David wrote often about the beauty of the Lord, as in this song that the Levites sang:

> One thing I ask of the Lord, this is what I seek: that I may dwell in the house of the Lord all the days of my life, to gaze upon the beauty of the Lord and seek him in his temple.... I will sing and make music to the Lord, hear my voice when I call, O Lord; be merciful to me and answer me. My heart says of you, Seek his face! Your face, Lord, I will seek (Psalm 27:4, 6b-8).

To say that God is beautiful is an understatement. Yet his beauty is a difficult thing to describe because he is a spirit being, and our vocabulary is limited to physical terms. Still, it is important that we acknowledge his beauty because we are made in his image. When we see brilliantly adorned flowers or listen to the musical genius of Mozart, something in us comes alive with a sense of wonder and fascination. The beauty we see around us in clouds hanging on top of a mountain or a rainbow stretching across the sky draws our attention to God, the artist and creator. We know that as beautiful as the natural world is, he is far more worthy of our gaze.

Where a carnal stronghold of religion has formed, it is a safe bet that the people have lost their wonder and appreciation for the uniqueness and beauty of the Lord. They surf through the church channels looking for something that piques their interest or even a good rerun, but they have ceased to be amazed by God himself.

The stronghold of passion keeps this awareness alive in us and holds us steady in awe of his loveliness. David's word for beauty meant "delight, splendor, suitableness, and grace,"[5] and God is all that and more. To be passionate in pursuit of him is to look more toward who he is than what he can do for us.

> To be passionate in pursuit of him is to look more toward who he is than what he can do for us.

God wants to be found. He's not going to hide from us any more than you would hide from your child or grandchild who was searching for you, calling out your name. So when we seek after him with passion and persistence, he responds. He draws near. He makes his Presence known. And he speaks. Where a people are truly seeking God's face, they tend to hear his voice as well.

John 10:4 says that "his sheep follow him because they know his voice." A Presence based church is voice activated—God's voice—acting when he speaks and waiting when he is silent. They know his voice because they live in the midst of an established pattern of listening. They expect him to speak and they expect to hear. It's not a surprise or a novelty, and it's not perceived as a threat. It's the norm. Every worship experience and every board meeting is an opportunity to hear God's voice.

It is wonderful to live in a divine stronghold of passion because there is a confidence in leadership and a discernable unity of heart and mind in regard to vision and direction. Since laity and leaders alike are seeking and hearing God, the whole body is moving forward with a surety that comes from everyone being on the same page. The corporate mind of Christ is the inner guarantee that his word, his "rhema" word is good and trustworthy. Those who seek his face are not prone to stalls or nose dives because they are anchored in the light of electrifying truth and resistant to lies of the enemy.

A word that is often used to describe a stronghold of passion is emotional. And it can be. But what many people don't realize is that the emotion is not a one-sided, fanatical expression, but a genuine interaction between a Father and his children. God is emotional—he is glad, sometimes angry or sad. He can smile and he can turn his face away. He likes what is good. He is jealous for what he loves. When the object of his love spurns him, he hurts; when they are abused, he grieves; and when they overcome, he rejoices. Zephaniah 3:17 tells us he sings with pleasure, and at times I believe he laughs. Filled with compassion and zeal, he is neither distant nor indifferent. If you have any doubt that God is a passionate being, emotionally involved in the lives of his creation, reread the stories of Adam and Eve and of the Israelites' exodus and journey.

All that God felt was expressed in the life of Jesus who assured us, "I have told you this so that my joy may be in you and that your joy may be complete" (John 15:11). He also added, "I am coming to you now, but I say these things while I am still in the world so that they may have the full measure of my joy within them" (John 17:13). Jesus didn't come into the world to condemn us (John 3:17) but that we might know the joy available to us. This was the true passion of Christ, that we would discover the richness of an abundant life in him.

Unfortunately, many churches are so afraid of feeling any-thing—they fear losing control or having to deal with extremes—that they have all but eliminated any possible emotional triggers. They have developed a business relationship with God that favors the definable, intellectual aspects of faith walking and steers clear of the more muddy, affective aspects of the relationship. Spiritual maturity is measured by head knowledge gained and emotions have little credibility in the growth process.

Perhaps that is why so many of us relate to the "try harder" approach to Christianity that drives us to study more and do bet-ter but leaves us feeling empty and worn out. The fullness of life in Christ Jesus invites us to engage both our intellect and our emotions, and to disregard one or the other abridges our personal relationship with him.

Divine Habitation

As I mentioned earlier, fruit is a trademark of divine strongholds, and the results of the stronghold of passion can be summed up as the discernable habitation of God's Presence. When people pursue him with passion and fervor, not just for gifts or provision, but to know his heart, he responds by coming, abiding and making himself known. This is the outcome of all that we talked about in the Presence Based Church, and it is to a certain degree the point of origin for the other five divine strongholds. His Presence is the key.

As you read through the rest of the strongholds, notice how each one followed Jesus and was evident in and around his ministry everywhere he went. He operated in them and left a trail behind of kingdom fruit. The divine strongholds radiated out from his Presence because each one is an expression of some aspect of God's nature. Through his actions and words, Jesus made them plain for us to see. As we take on the mind of Christ, we too can expect to reflect the character traits of God in similar fashion.

Remember that for a stronghold to exist in a church there must be a belief system in place that includes patterns of thinking, attitudes and expectations. And that belief system, forged over time, must be shared by a significant percentage of the congregation and must influence behavior. So a stronghold of passion is much more than just an occasional emotional outburst or an isolated time of desperate seeking in the face of a crisis. A stronghold of passion means that day in and day out, in worship services and in committee meetings, at church and at home in their personal lives, the corporate body is identified by a consistent lifestyle of passionate worship, passionate prayer, passionate seeking to go deeper with God.

IHOP

I know of no better example of a divine stronghold of passion than the International House of Prayer in Kansas City, Kansas. Founded in 1999 by a Vineyard pastor named Mike Bickle, the IHOP has become known nationwide as a model of authentic prayer and worship.

The passion for pursuing God seems to be in Mike's genes. For example, when they were both young men, Mike's brother, a gifted athlete, broke his back in a tragic diving accident. In the weeks and months that followed, Mike would sit for hours by his bed praying and reading the Bible to him, sometimes all day long. The more despair he felt, the harder he sought the comfort of the Presence of God. Later during his years of church ministry, Mike studied extensively the life of David as a worshiper and a leader. He was fascinated with the man that the Bible describes as one "after God's own heart," and he wanted to know personally that same kind of intimacy with the Father. Eventually, he would write several books about the heart of worship and the pleasures of knowing and loving God.

Somewhere along the way, something in Mike sparked. His passion for worship, his hunger for God's Presence, and his desire to see God move in response to intercession all came together in a radical decision to leave the pastorate and start a 24/7 place of worship and prayer.

At that time, not too many full time worship houses existed. And I recall that as word spread about what he was doing—leaving a 5,000 member church to start a perpetual "seeking" service in a little trailer somewhere with a ragtag group of musicians and no guaranteed salary—well, many of our prayer colleagues were skeptical. It seemed risky at best and somewhere in the realm of fanatical to those who didn't understand. Many probably figured it would fizzle out after a while when the novelty wore off and the reality of sustaining such a vision settled in. Even his sons, who were 18 and 20 at the time and who had loved and supported their dad through the ups and downs of ministry, had to cock their heads and ask the question, "Why?"

Read how Mike responded:

I want to fast more, pray more and worship more to release the Great Harvest. This may surprise you, but one reason I'm doing this is because I love pleasure.

I'm addicted to wanting to feel more of God's presence. I must have more, and I must feel it deeper. I am a total pleasure addict. That's one reason I'm going to rent that trailer, get a couple of guitar players, fast, pray, worship, and study what Scripture says about the emotions of God.

I'm not sure they understood then, but I did. I had a vision in mind, learned from years of study and experience with

God, and I was going to pursue it more aggressively than ever before. I had discovered that intimacy with God starts with the realization that God likes us and wants to enjoy with us the pleasure of spiritual encounters with Him. There is nothing more exhilarating for us than plunging into that river of pleasure.[6]

The skeptics didn't know Mike's heart. And they underestimated just how many young people would find their way to IHOP, eager to be a part of the emerging model. God was doing something new, and Mike was riding the crest of the wave, with a generation of radical worshipers right on his heels. It quickly became apparent that this wasn't just a flighty idea, but it was a movement born straight from the heart of God, calling his people back to a Levitical style of sold-out prayer and worship. And he had been raising up an army of young Davids who were ready to answer the call.

It quickly became apparent that this wasn't just a flighty idea, but it was a movement born straight from the heart of God....

Today, the IHOP has taken over an old downtown church in Kansas City that is open all the time for worship and intercession. At any given time, a worship band or individual worship leader may be singing in one part of the loft-inspired space, while a small group may be praying together in another area marked off simply by a circle of chairs. Sometimes the music is live; at others it is piped in through a sound system. The musical style varies. People come and go, prayer requests and scripture prayers scroll continually across TV screens throughout the building. The site is also home to Mike's school, Friends of the Bridegroom, where people come to be discipled in what has become known as "harp and bowl" ministry.

The stronghold of passion is physically defined at the International House of Prayer, and it jumps off of every page of Mike's books. All the desire I can muster in my being to seek after God doesn't seem to equal that which Mike contains in his little pinky finger. If a local church today, any local church, could catch just a whisper of that kind of passion, it would totally transform the entire congregation. Pursuing and experiencing the Presence of God is not just an add-on to the Christian life; it is the glory of our lives and God's greatest desire!

Lord, we welcome you to demolish all carnal strong-holds in our midst. Let waves of your Presence sweep over any areas of prideful thinking. Only a divine encounter with you can create in us the desire to think your thoughts. Meet us on the road to Damascus (Isaiah 55:8-9; Acts 9:1-31).

3

PRIDE VS HUMILITY

I was watching one of my grandkids play baseball not too long ago and witnessed many of the rites and rituals we have all come to know as part of youth sports: overzealous team spirit, questioning close calls, complaining about coaching decisions, taunting players on the opposing team. And this was all coming from the parents—educated, mature adults who apparently morphed into little league enforcers as soon as their child stepped onto the ball field. I listened to them, barking out instructions to their kids, muttering under their breath about why the other team seemed to be doing better. It was obvious that they were involved, connected in an emotional way to what was going on out there between the baselines. They were proud, or at least, they desperately wanted to be.

I noticed another team playing on a field next to us that was wearing "Longhorn" uniforms patterned after the University of Texas. Having pastored for 16 years in College Station, Texas, home of Texas A&M University, my first thought was, "I am so glad that my grandson doesn't play for that team! I could never bring myself to yell for the Longhorns!" But then I had to laugh at myself, because I realized that if he did play for the Longhorns, I would undoubtedly don the offensive burnt orange team color and wave the Longhorn sign in support. It's a team thing.

It made me wonder, why is it that team spirit can so easily and completely take over our emotions and secure our loyalty, whether we are winning or not? What is it about the very nature of competition that fuels pride in us?

Competition is one of the main characteristics of the consumer based church. A church that is catering to people tends to have a spirit of competition toward other churches, that is, the feeling that they are trying to outdo one another. It goes hand in hand with the consumer based mentality that your percentage of the market share is a direct reflection of your success. He who has the most customers wins.

We talked in *The Presence Based Church* about the danger of consumerism when applied to the body of Christ. As churches, we are members of the same family, different expressions of Christ's earthly bride, connected in heritage and purpose. Like the various members of one body, we are more effective when working together than any of us are working alone. We are designed to complete, not compete.

> *...in that spirit of competition, we as churches quite naturally circle our wagons and hoist the team banner and chant the team creed because it's us against them, and we don't like to lose.*

Consumerism, however, turns us into adversaries, pitting the Baptists against the Methodists, the Lutherans against the Episcopalians, and the mainliners against the charismatics. It creates jealousy between pastors where there should be partnerships. It isolates and divides by focusing on differences rather than similarities. And in that spirit of competition, we as churches quite naturally circle our wagons and hoist the team banner and chant the team creed because it's us against them, and we don't like to lose.

Pride can be very emotional, whether you are proud to be a Green Bay Packers fan, proud of your ethnic heritage, proud to be an American, or proud because your child has the lead in the school play. As individuals, we take pride in all kinds of things— our kids, a raise, a new car, a beautiful garden. We take pride in things we acquire, things we accomplish and things we are a part of. Corporate pride, the pride we feel as team members, can be especially strong because it is supercharged by the explosive forces of group dynamics.

So what does the Bible have to say about pride? Both the Old and New Testaments speak directly to pride in more than 100 references, primarily to warn us that pride is dangerous spiritual territory and that in general, God does not look favorably on it. It is associated with arrogance, evil and foolishness. The message couldn't be much clearer—prideful individuals will eventually stumble and prideful nations will eventually fall. God himself will see to it:

> In his pride the wicked does not seek him; in all his thoughts there is no room for God (Psalm 10:4).

> Though the Lord is on high, he looks upon the lowly, but the proud he knows from afar (Psalm 138:6).

> When pride comes, then comes disgrace, but with humility comes wisdom (Proverbs 11:2).

> Pride goes before destruction, a haughty spirit before a fall (Proverbs 16:18).

> But after Uzziah became powerful, his pride led to his downfall... (2 Chronicles 26:16).

> This is what the Lord says: "In the same way I will ruin the pride of Judah and the great pride of Jerusalem. These wicked people, who refuse to listen to my words, who follow the stubbornness of their hearts and go after other gods to serve and worship them, will be like this belt—completely useless!" (Jeremiah 13:9-10)

It's not hard to recognize a prideful person, someone so full of himself that he overestimates his own importance and conducts himself with an exaggerated sense of superiority. Many great scholars from Oswald Chambers to Andrew Murray have written about the dangers of egos run amuck. The prideful often define their own significance with salaries and titles, and have an inflated sense of entitlement.

The Bible gives us several examples of individuals who rose to positions of fame and power, only to eventually sink out of sight in the quicksand of pride. Saul, for instance, was a great warrior and was appointed king over Israel by Samuel the prophet. But when David, a young handsome friend of Saul's son Jonathan, began to rise in fame because of his own even more spectacular battlefield exploits, Saul became consumed with jealousy. Despite David's unmatched loyalty to the king, Saul's pride so twisted his thinking that he spent the rest of his life pursuing David to kill him. He was eventually wounded in battle and took his own life, disgraced and remembered not for his greatness, but his gradual demise.

Another example of a leader corrupted by pride is Solomon, David's son, and one of the greatest kings to rule over Israel. God bestowed unprecedented wisdom and wealth on Solomon, but as his fame rose, he eventually became wrapped up in his own grandeur. Against the Lord's warning, he took for himself hundreds of wives, many of them from the godless foreign nations around Israel. In order to keep them happy, he erected high places to honor their idolatrous deities. Despite God's warning that his wives would lead him astray, the Bible tells that "Solomon held fast to them in love (1 Kings 11:2). He couldn't give them up, and as a result, lost God's favor.

The corporate stronghold of pride is equally problematic in a church setting. It will blind a church to its own shortcomings and create conflict within and without. It often creates the delusion that we are doing something great for God when in reality he is watching from afar, wondering when we might consult or include him. When we are impressed with our own resourcefulness, we don't want someone telling us that we're missing God; after all, we're too busy serving him to listen. Ultimately, pride blocks his power from flowing because where man is elevated, he backs away. When we are in charge, he isn't.

Faces of Pride

The pride stronghold can take on several forms, the most obvious of which is pride in material things or possessions. If you live in a community similar to mine, you see evidence of this kind of pride all around you. It might be the building, or the steeple, the pipe organ, or the sound system, but churches, like people, are easily enamored with "stuff." Instead of keeping up with the Joneses, we're all trying to keep up with the Baptists. It's a sort of spiritual materialism.

In my travels around the United States, I have seen some unbelievable things in church buildings: a ceiling inlaid with gold, a pastor's "office" that resembled an upper end loft apartment, enormous steeples on tiny church buildings. Not that having a nice facility means your church is afflicted with insufferable pride, but millions of dollars are spent every year by churches of every size and kind on things that have no conceivable function in spreading the gospel, and can only be rightly called extravagant luxuries. If that's not materialism fueled by pride, then I don't know what is.

And it's not just big churches that are guilty of allowing this kind of pride to dig a trench and take over. I've met plenty of small town pastors who were mighty proud of their new sanctuary (it seats more than First Church) or of their family life center (it's the only one in town, you know). They say the right things: "We're really trying to reach out to the youth in this community." But the sparkle in their eyes and their brisk step as they take you on a tour from the techno-heavy gameroom, through the coffee cafe and into the multi-purpose gymnasium reveals the rest of the story: they've bought a shiny sports car and parked it in the driveway, and are deriving quite a bit of satisfaction in knowing that the neighbors are admiring it.

Along with stuff, the stronghold of pride in a church may also be associated with intangibles, such as programs, history, education or achievements. The "Martha" church is full of talented, industrious people who bring all their skills to the table and make a lot of good things happen. When Martha is given the latitude to work and the resources she needs to operate, she can generate activity, inspire involvement and serve many people in creative ways. Congregations in older churches may take a great deal of pride in their place in history. I have seen this especially in some churches in England, where many of their cathedrals have been tolling bells on Sunday mornings for centuries.

...they've bought a shiny sports car and parked it in the driveway, and are deriving quite a bit of satisfaction in knowing that the neighbors are admiring it.

When it comes to educational pride, I've met with many a pastoral staff that boasts a collective resume showcasing successful business tycoons, expertly trained technicians and innovative young theologians. In my own denomination as well as in many others, the qualifications of some our top church leaders today give us a lot to be proud of! We are capable, experienced, authorized and certified. We can do the job.

I have to moderate what I'm saying here. It is not "unspiritual" for a church to build a nice sheep shed or assemble an accomplished staff. It is good when we bless our communities through effective ministry in the name of Jesus. I think it's even alright that we like these things and enjoy the blessings of our heavenly Father. It's good to rejoice over successes. However, if our gratification is not tempered with a healthy dose of humility before God, we are cutting a groove that leads to an arrogant, independent belief system and a stronghold of pride.

We must go back to Yancey's definition of idolatry—a commitment of spirit to that which cannot bear its weight—to understand when we have crossed the line into the dangerous area of self-serving pride. When things or accomplishments become the objects of our affection; when they become our source of affirmation, then they have become idols, replacing Jesus Christ as the Most High God in our thinking. When the pleasure and delight of serving God with our whole selves turns into self-importance and satisfaction, we have thrown the door open for the stronghold of pride to rush in and take over.

With all of our competence and resources, it is easy to lose sight of our desperate need for God. Instead of seeking him, we seek the advice of experts. Instead of depending on him to come through, we study harder and advertise more. Instead of waiting on him and listening for his voice, we adopt the latest church growth strategy and pledge to work harder and faster. We may echo rhetoric we've either inherited or heard about the importance of prayer, but it is really an empty script motivated by nostalgia and it's all part of the image. The reality is that we don't need to pray because we are running the show and getting it right. Over time, this mindset produces patterns of behavior that weave their way into the life of the church and color the tapestry with shades of Christian humanism—serving the cause of Christ under our own power.

The Humanistic Spirit

The humanistic spirit is what drives corporate pride: man at his best, planning, managing and consulting the experts. The feats of human triumph shine and everyone marvels at the end result. We put up plaques and build a trophy case to display our accomplishments because we want to make sure that they are remembered for years to come. We're so clever, God should be happy to have us on his team!

I want to shift gears now and look at two other alternative expressions of the pride stronghold in a church that are not as easily recognized but are just as prevalent and damaging. First, pride can be a self-absorption with failure and loss just as with success and gain. A pity party can have the same effect as a winner's celebration when it's all about us. Either way our world is very small and our options are limited. We can be so focused on our own pain and deficiency that we are unable to think or reach outside of ourselves.

This form of pride paralyzes us to act or move forward in fulfilling our purpose as a church. It keeps us from being the light of Christ and from impacting the community in a positive way. Have you ever tried to cheer someone up who simply refused to feel better? It can be frustrating. Sometimes a victim's mentality—I always get the short end of the stick and it's always someone else's fault—causes a person or group to choose to remain depressed because being that way validates their belief that they are, in fact, a victim. The internal voice of pride says, "We didn't deserve the treatment we received, so we will choose to be despondent to ensure that everyone knows how much we have suffered."

In *Praying God's Word*, Beth Moore talks about this type of pride:

> Pride is not the opposite of low self-esteem. Pride is the opposite of humility. We can have a serious pride problem that masquerades as low self-esteem. Pride is self-absorption whether we're absorbed with how miserable we are or how wonderful we are.[1]

When a body of believers is dealt a hard blow, just like an individual, they must go through the process of picking up the pieces, dealing with the emotions, forgiving and moving on. However if, as a group, they continue to meditate on the injustice, the seed thoughts fueled by anger and resentment become deeply entrenched in the corporate belief system, and produce attitudes and expectations consistent with the victim mentality. They make excuses. They point the finger at anyone and everyone: other churches, the community, former members, denominational headquarters. They refuse to take responsibility for their own destiny. Arrested by the stronghold, the church becomes apathetic, resistant to help or change, and bitter.

Keep in mind that because strongholds form over a period of time, they become the new "norm" and go unnoticed by those in the bubble. They can be subtle or blatant, but those affected are blind to the consequences. We are talking about things that cannot necessarily be seen clearly on the surface—no one wears a sign. But the belief system drives behavior, and becomes evident when you enter the church environment.

Lastly, the stronghold of pride can be expressed as a commitment to being right, no matter what the cost. I might describe this as doctrinal pride—an attitude that says, "Our way is the only way." This kind of corporate pride means never being able to admit that you're wrong, or that you made a mistake. It creates conflict and difficulty reaching consensus because everybody has an opinion and no one will back down. It makes a church argumentative and defensive.

Cognitive closure is in full force in this stronghold, not so much to safeguard the past, but simply to defend our cherished point of view. If it's not in the "handbook," it's taboo. As in the stronghold of religion, cognitive closure seals us off from any outside voice, including the voice of God, and therefore keeps us from experiencing him. The need to be right can be so strong that we simply refuse to listen, refuse to think, and refuse to question any of our own ideas, even in the face of mounting evidence to the contrary.

I had the privilege of attending a very prestigious seminary known for its liberal views on many topics. Many of my fellow students and I were interested in seeing more conservative theologies being taught and discussed, so we decided to take the matter to the dean. We met with him one day and suggested several ideas and schools of thought that we believed should be presented in the curriculum, and we asked if he would consider opening the door. This was his answer: "I have already evaluated those doctrines and they are wrong. They will not be taught here." So much for a liberal education. Apparently "liberal" to him meant "blind commitment to a narrow way of thinking." That was corporate pride at work, protecting a treasured position.

> *The need to be right can be so strong that we simply refuse to listen, refuse to think, and refuse to question any of our own ideas, even in the face of mounting evidence to the contrary.*

Living in Houston, we all witnessed through media coverage a very literal exhibition of the ill effects of corporate pride when Enron, the energy company once high on the list of Fortune 500 success stories, imploded as a result of extensive, systemic accounting fraud. As the truth of that situation was uncovered, it reminded me of many of our churches today that are textbook examples of innovation and success on the surface, but underneath are rotting as a result of internal problems that no one will see or admit. Corporate pride brought down an industry giant because those on the inside were totally committed to overlooking or rationalizing the wrongdoing, while protecting the public image at all cost. They were on the top; making lots of money, growing exponentially. The leaders at the helm looked like geniuses. They weren't about to disclose the truth and forfeit all that.

Another example of corporate pride involves a church that is down the road from my house. They have one of those sign boards in the front, which they change regularly to boldly share their doctrinal beliefs with the neighborhood. One day I drove by and read the words, "Max Lucado is a heretic." What a positive, life-affirming message. I guess they had a problem with the fact that Max's ideas often varied from their particular denominational script. They wanted to make sure that everyone (at least in our subdivision) knew that Max was wrong and they were right. Period. End of discussion.

No Room for God

If the religious stronghold set the stage for the crucifixion, then pride drove in the nails. The Pharisees who plotted to kill Jesus were filled with so much arrogance concerning their religious education and achievements that they could not tolerate being challenged. They were so impressed by their own brand of holiness that they could not and would not bring themselves to consider the new gospel of grace that Jesus was bringing. Look again at Psalm 10:4, "In his pride the wicked does not seek him; in all his thoughts there is no room for God." The Pharisees' pride literally blinded them, and kept them from being able to recognize the Messiah. They had no room for him in their hearts, in their minds or in their lives.

Jesus warns the church at Laodicea about their own corporate pride:

> I know your deeds, that you are neither cold nor hot. I wish you were either one or the other! So, because you are lukewarm—neither hot nor cold—I am about to spit you out of my mouth. You say, 'I am rich; I have acquired wealth and do not need a thing.' But you do not realize that you are wretched, pitiful, poor, blind and naked.

Wow, what a rebuke to a church that has no idea of its destitution. And then he says, "Here I am! I stand at the door and knock. If anyone hears my voice and opens the door, I will come in and eat with him, and he with me" (Revelation 3:15-17, 20).

Jesus is standing at the door of his own church, barred from entering because of the pride and ignorance of the people. How many churches today could Jesus reprove in the same manner, calling from outside the door to the wretched and blind inside, "Here I am; do you have room for me?"

THE STRONGHOLD OF HUMILITY

Everything about the life of Jesus stood directly opposed to pride—the circumstances of his birth, his social status, the people with whom he associated, and ultimately his death. He labeled as "hypocrites" the most educated and spiritual teachers of the day, yet came to the defense of prostitutes. He challenged the wealthy, but had compassion on the poor. He spent most of his time not with powerful leaders, but with sinners and lepers and those whom society had discarded. Though he had every right to be proud; he was a living example of humility in its most absolute form.

Scripture makes it clear that while pride is an attribute that God rebukes, humility is one that invites his Presence to draw near. As Beth Moore observed, they are opposites, and godly humility has nothing to do with low self-esteem. In fact, through vessels of humility, God accomplished some of his greatest work. God chose the Israelites to be his beloved people. Descended from one elderly couple, they were a nation which lived in slavery for much of its early history. He chose David, a small shepherd boy who was the youngest of seven brothers and overlooked by his father, to defeat a giant and become a great commander and king. And he chose Mary, an innocent Nazarene teenager, barely old enough to wed, to bear and raise his holy son. Humility is one of the most consistent character traits possessed by many of the heroes and heroines of the Bible.

However, as noteworthy as the humility of these individuals may be, nothing can overshadow one of the greatest ironies of the

Bible—the humility of Jesus Christ. His life and ministry should teach us that the most amazing and powerful abilities of God are expressed through those who are completely yielded to him, free of all pride and ambition.

Every time I think about it, I marvel at what it means for God himself to be humble. To have come to earth in the manner he did, with all of his majesty wrapped in the cloak of a human body, and then to have endured what he did on the cross just for you and me, it's almost inconceivable. But it's true. When he could have called a vast army of angels to his defense, when he could have, with one word, struck dead his accusers or vanished into thin air, he instead chose to stay still. Silent. The spotless Lamb of God allowed himself to be scorned, ridiculed, spit upon and tortured. Though he had command of the seas and the wind and all the earth, he chose to surrender, not to the soldiers, but to the will of his Father. He "humbled himself and became obedient to death—even death on a cross."

With a sense of wonder, Paul explains what our response should be:

> If you have any encouragement from being united with Christ, if any comfort from his love, if any fellowship with the Spirit, if any tenderness and compassion, then make my joy complete by being likeminded, having the same love, being one in spirit and purpose. Do nothing out of selfish ambition or vain conceit, but in humility consider others better than yourselves. Each of you should look not only to your own interests, but also to the interests of others.

> Your attitude should be the same as that of Christ Jesus: Who, being in very nature God, did not consider equality with God something to be grasped, but made himself nothing, taking the very nature of a servant, being made in human likeness. And being found in appearance as a man, he humbled himself and became obedient to death—even death on a cross! Therefore God exalted him to the highest

place and gave him the name that is above every name, that at the name of Jesus every knee should bow, in heaven and on earth and under the earth, and every tongue confess that Jesus Christ is Lord, to the glory of God the Father (Philippians 2:1-11).

This passage gives us a wonderful starting place in understanding the stronghold of humility as defined in the life of Jesus. It provides us with a list of attitudes and actions that might indicate when it is operating in a church. In order for humility to truly be considered a corporate stronghold, the attitudes and actions would have to be dominant, and reflected both in the personal relationships within the congregation and in the church's relationship to other churches and the community:

- They would "do nothing out of selfish ambition or vain conceit."
- They would "consider others better" than themselves.
- They would look past their own interests to care about and invest in the interests of others, even other churches.
- Their attitude in all things would be "the same as that of Christ Jesus."
- They would take on "the very nature of a servant."
- They would be completely yielded and obedient to the Father's will, even to the point of dying to self.
- They would glorify and lift the name of Jesus above every name, even higher than the name of their pastor or their church. His name would be preeminent above all else.

That's quite a list! If implemented, it would certainly define a church and make it stand out as different. I think humility is something that we think we understand; but when we define it, or set the standard, in the person of Jesus, humility must take on a whole new depth of commitment. To read this passage literally challenges our assertive, self-entitled, ideals about justice, marketing, budgeting, goals, achievement and rewards. It pushes the concept beyond shallow proclamations of our own flaws and token gestures of acquiescence to real self-denial and sacrifice.

It seems to me that in general we embrace the idea of humility as a socially appealing quality. We admire the self-effacing MVP who refuses to take all the glory and instead gives credit to his teammates. We like an unassuming co-worker who shares praise for a job well done. But I don't really think we necessarily want humility to ask much more than that from us. We don't expect it to be painful. Yet for Jesus, humility demanded more than just casual, socially correct modesty. It insisted that he deny his identity and disallow his own power. It required that he give up his rights, both as God and as an innocent man condemned to die. How many of us are really willing to embrace humility to that degree in our own lives? Are we willing to give up what is rightfully ours, or even endure some kind of hardship, for the sake of others? The truth about what Paul is asking from us, if taken seriously, would make us uncomfortable.

True humility can only be achieved through the mind of Christ and the power of the Holy Spirit. If we want to tear down a stronghold of pride and replace it with a stronghold of humility, we must take steps to lay down our resources and rely on God's. We must surrender our will to his. We must decrease so that he might increase. But how do we achieve that?

Taking His Yoke

The Bible gives us a perfect symbol for the stronghold of humility. Look at these verses:

> Come to me, all you who are weary and burdened, and I will give you rest. Take my yoke upon you and learn from me, for I am gentle and humble in heart, and you will find rest for

your souls. For my yoke is easy and my burden is light (Matthew 11:28-30).

The yoke was an everyday tool used by many people whom Jesus would have been teaching, so it was a very familiar example. In fact, as a carpenter, Jesus would have even been hired to make yokes in his shop. When two oxen were yoked, they were harnessed together by a crossbeam of wood attached to their necks by a u-shaped oxbow. The yoke was then attached to a cart or plow or load to be pulled. When properly fitted, the yoke harnessed maximum power from the animals without creating sores on their necks or shoulders. However, an improperly fitted yoke or one that was poorly made could have injured a healthy ox quickly. William Barclay suggested that Jesus had a sign across the top of his workshop door that read, "My yokes fit well."[2] I'm sure the yokes Jesus made were both perfectly strong and perfectly gentle on the animals.

A "yoke" in the Bible was more than just a necessary work tool, however. It also became a common term used to describe the weight of bondage, oppression and slavery. It was the physical representation of subjugation and shame. Look up "yoke" in a concordance and you will find numerous examples of this usage, such as when God told the Israelites through Moses, "I will take you as my own people, and I will be your God. Then you will know that I am the Lord your God, who brought you out from under the yoke of the Egyptians" (Exodus 6:7). In other words, a yoke was anything but glamorous; no one would have hung a yoke over the fireplace mantle or worn a diamond studded yoke necklace. Jesus' suggestion that we take a yoke on ourselves to find freedom and rest would have seemed strangely contradictory. So what was he really saying in Matthew 11:28-30?

When Jesus suggested that we take up his yoke, he wasn't suggesting that we become slaves harnessed to a plow. To the contrary, he was describing a wonderful and mysterious relationship. He was offering us the opportunity to surrender the struggles of life and find security in him. He was offering us shelter in the perfect alignment of our will with his. He was saying, "Come and be tied to me. Get really close. Where I go, you will follow. What I feel, you can feel. We will be inseparable." Jesus changed the symbolic meaning by 180 degrees, just as he did with the cross. Once a symbol of dishonorable death; Jesus turned the cross into a lasting sign of resurrection life. And the yoke of oppression he declared an emblem of humility and safety.

Once a symbol of dishonorable death; Jesus turned the cross into a lasting sign of resurrection life. And the yoke of oppression he declared an emblem of humility and safety.

Jesus won't force his yoke upon us; we must choose to submit our lives to its discipline. We must choose to put it on. That is where humility is required on our part. Oswald Chambers wisely asserts that humility is not a virtue to be attained, but is a result of being in right relationship with Jesus Christ. And the right relationship is yoked with him. The closer we get to Jesus, the more humble our lives become. Humility is a direct result of being in his Presence. In the light of his glory, all forms of human pride simply turn to vapor.

As a church becomes more and more Presence based, humility quite naturally grows and spreads. The more time a congregation spends worshiping and seeking after God's face, the clearer the revelation becomes of his nature and our frailty. The corporate stronghold of humility forms when a church truly recognizes its dependence on God and submits as a body to the yoke of Christ.

When we do make the decision, the moment we slip under the crossbeam, and yield ourselves fully to its control, we immediately sense the safety, peace and assurance that come from being rightly connected with God. When we take his yoke upon us—the yoke of humility—we will discover four benefits: rest, power, direction and balance.

A Place of Rest

Serving God outside of his Presence is a tiring enterprise. To win the world with only a budget and a strategy is a burden. Relying on the resources of people to accomplish goals can be frustrating at best. Maintaining a polished image in the community is exhausting. Keeping everyone happy and entertained with new ministries and ideas year after year is not only arduous, it's impossible! In other words, pulling the plow alone is definitely hard labor.

Jesus' yoke is different. He tells us that his yoke is easy and his burden is light. He promises that we will find rest for our souls—not labor or struggle—when we submit to his harness. On our own, we toil and strain with every step. But in him, we find peace and relief in his strength.

Jesus' yoke is alive; it will impart to us everything we need. One of the words used for "rest" in this passage is the word "refresh," meaning that this yoke is more than just a coupling; it is a re-creational lifeline.[3] Through it, we can be refreshed or renewed every day. This is not just a relationship of self-help advice. Jesus goes beyond that. He says, "When you put on my yoke, you can die to yourself so that my life lives in you. Lay down your resources and pick up mine. Put your limited understanding aside and see things from my perspective." Taking up his yoke means that we can rest in all that he is and all that he has. We are not alone.

Paul wrote to the Galatians, "It is for freedom that Christ has set us free. Stand firm, then, and do not let yourselves be burdened again by a yoke of slavery" (Galatians 5:1). In other words, don't choose the world's yoke of slavery that says we must work harder to achieve perfection and then feel miserable all the time because we fail. No! Instead, bind yourself to Jesus and experience the freedom in this life that he wants to give you. He will clean out the old and replace it with all things new—new desires, new thoughts, new attitudes and new visions. He will re-create you every day in ever increasing love and acceptance. In his yoke you will taste his glory which far surpasses the pride and glory of men. Slip his crossbeam over your head and blend the divine into your mortal life. In his yoke, we can live life as he meant for it to be.

Watchman Nee says in his book *Sit, Walk, Stand*, that Christianity starts from a place of rest; God invites us to sit and rest in Jesus' finished work on the cross. The work has already been done.[4] Jesus did it. He lived it. He died it. He resurrected it. He tells us to take our seat next to him (Ephesians 2:6), and then walk in the work he does. "For we are God's workmanship, created in Christ Jesus to do good works, which God prepared in advance for us to do" (Ephesians 2:10). We find rest in his yoke because when we surrender to his will for our lives, he moves us forward by the Spirit and we can ride the train of his glorious Presence. As he told Moses, "My presence will go with you, and I will give you rest" (Exodus 33:14).

A Position of Power

Occasionally when flipping television channels, I come across a strong man competition. Men of enormous size and strength harness themselves to a large piece of machinery and see who can pull it the farthest down a flat road. It's an amazing display of power and determination. But the harness is the key. Without it, their Herculean brawn couldn't be applied to the tractor.

The yoke was an instrument of power transfer; it harnessed the brute strength of the oxen and transferred it into a plow to break up the earth. Likewise, Jesus' yoke of humility allows him to transfer his power through us and into situations and needs in our church and community. To put on the yoke of Christ as a church means to humble ourselves in a way that opens the door for God to show his hand through signs and wonders and displays of his power and authority. This is the fruit of the stronghold. In Acts 11:21 we read, "The Lord's hand was with them, and a great number of people believed and turned to the Lord." When we bow in submission, he can make his strength manifest in our presence.

One ox could pull a lot of weight, but two yoked together could pull more weight than the sum of that which both could pull separately. They were stronger in tandem. When we cease trying to pull the tractor on our own, and bow in submission before God, we discover the immense power in humility, that is, the power of the Holy Spirit. As an angel of God revealed to Zechariah the prophet, kingdom work will be completed, "'Not by might nor by power, but by my Spirit,' says the Lord Almighty" (Zechariah 4:6). In the yoke, we discover that he is far more adequate than all of our abilities combined.

In the yoke, we discover that he is far more adequate than all of our abilities combined.

When we are in the driver's seat, we ask God to anoint our efforts and bless our work. But as we discover how to humble ourselves and truly relinquish control to him, we slip into his harness and find that it is much more effective to simply apply our energy to that which he has already anointed. By being yoked to Jesus, we embrace our weaknesses in order to see his power flow through us. He tells us, "My grace is sufficient for you, for my power is made perfect in weakness." And Paul responds, "Therefore I will boast all the more gladly my weaknesses, so that Christ's power may rest on me. That is why, for Christ's sake, I delight in weaknesses, in insults, in hardships, in persecutions, in difficulties. For when I am weak, then I am strong" (2 Corinthians 12:9-10). The more yielded we become, the more God can rise up and show himself strong in our behalf.

This pattern of thought is pretty contradictory to the consumer based church environment, in which we do all we can to hide our weaknesses while putting our strengths out on display. Remember that the consumer based system is all about image, appearance, and attracting people. It's about using our gifts, resources and knowledge to market our church to potential customers. So the idea of corporate humility may sound easy to achieve, but in fact runs in direct opposition to many of the church management ideas circulating today. The key to establishing this stronghold, like all the divine strongholds, is the Presence of God.

An Instrument of Control

When yoked together, oxen could not wander off in opposite directions. They were tied to each other and connected by leads to a "driver." The one who controlled the leads controlled the oxen.

We talked quite a bit about control in *The Presence Based Church*, because control issues are somewhat of a hallmark of consumer driven thinking. When the church is all about people applying their time, energy and resources to make the church successful, the people inevitably begin to take pride in their accomplishments. And with pride comes a sense of ownership, and with ownership, control. In other words, when you cater too much to the desires and egos of people, they take over. And when people are in control of a church, God can't be. However, when a church yields together in agreement and submits itself to the yoke of Christ, the question, "Who's in charge here?" is answered. God himself has the reigns and he gets to steer the cart.

Pride wants to invest; humility tends to divest. Pride wants to own; humility wants to let go. The danger in ownership is the risk of being owned; but the freedom in humility is being owned and operated by the Holy Spirit. Perhaps that is why Jesus said we must become like little children to enter the kingdom, because little children do not own much and therefore are not possessed or driven by the desire for more, bigger and better. They simply trust and follow.

Pride makes us vulnerable to so many things; particularly

the opinions of people. When we are concerned about our image and appearance, we are easily pulled and pushed by fickle trends and relentless expectations dictated by cultural "norms." What people say about us, how they react to us, how we "measure up," where we fit it; so many things touch us and affect us. But when we are humble before both God and man, we become "untouchable." In the stronghold of humility, we are unaffected by outside forces because we are directed and controlled from within, by the power of the Holy Spirit. When a church puts on the yoke of humility, it is choosing to let go of the reins and instead trust and follow in faith.

A Posture for Balance

Because pride is rooted in self-absorption, it can be given to extremes. It may be high or it may be low, but it is seldom satisfied. When we are sharing the glory with God, we are struggling to stay atop the high place in our own minds.

The yoke of humility offers us a relationship with Jesus that stabilizes us by giving us his perspective in all matters. In fact, the word for yoke is "zugon," which means "balance." The yoke postures us in a way that rightly governs the limits and freedoms of life. Through the lens of humility, we can balance going out and coming in, giving and receiving, speaking and staying silent, acting and trusting, taking and letting go, fighting and making peace, serving and being served, being seen and being obscure, reacting and being patient, taking care of oneself and denying oneself, accomplishing something outstanding and being faithful to the very simple. I always have found it interesting that before Jesus walked out of the tomb, he took the time to fold the napkin that had been wrapped around his head! (John 20:7) What an amazing demonstration of balance.

This sense of healthy equilibrium is one of the reasons that divine strongholds are more characterized by longevity than depreciation—when life is in balance everything seems to work better and last longer. Where carnal strongholds cause wear and fatigue, the divine stronghold of humility allows us to walk in the rest, power and steady direction of Jesus. These are the fruits of, and God's response to, our decision to resist pride and live in humility before him and others.

The best example of the corporate stronghold of humility I know of is the Korean Christian church. In a culture given in many ways to gestures of respect and humility, numbers indicate that the church has thrived on the fruits of such an atmosphere. According to a recent posting on the *Christianity Today* website, the Christian community of South Korea doubles just about every ten years. It is growing at a rate of approximately 9 percent a year, which is four times the rate of population growth in the country as a whole. In addition, the ten largest denominational churches in the world are in South Korea, six of which are in Seoul.[5]

If you have ever visited Korea, and in particular a Korean church, you would probably agree that the people as a whole exhibit a kind and degree of humility toward their leaders and toward others that is not seen much in America. I believe this is at least partly responsible for the fact that the Korean church has always been characterized by very fervent, consistent prayer, the outward sign of a radical dependence on God. While they may be lacking in other areas, prayer is not one of them.

The evangelical Korean Christians often have and participate in several corporate prayer opportunities a day. One church I was in several years ago had morning prayer meetings several times during the week at 4:00 am, 5:00 am, and 6:00 am, and every one of them was full. Thousands of Christians flock to prayer vigils such as these daily, passionately seeking God on their faces, sometimes in reverent silence and other times with loud voices. They ask God to pour out his Spirit on their churches and families, never taking for granted that he will come uninvited.

When we humble ourselves, we are acknowledging Jesus as the "name above every name," the Most High God, and we are inviting the Holy Spirit to display his power in and through us. As we cultivate an atmosphere of yieldedness toward him and others in our church, he begins to take over. The more surrendered we can become, the more freedom he has to work. Over time, we can see a stronghold of humility develop in which everyone and everything bows to the knowledge and experience of his Presence.

Forgive us, Lord of the Sabbath, for our failure to honor the day of rest. Forgive us for filling our lives with so many things that we do not worship you as you deserve. We make idols out of sports, entertainment, pleasure, eating, toys and technology, all of which steal our focus from you. Have mercy on our foolishness. Deliver us in Jesus' name from idolatry and be Lord over every part of our lives (Exodus 20:23; 32:1-14).

4

SEDITION VS HONOR

Years ago when I was pastoring in a small Texas town, the kind of small town with four churches, two Baptist and two Methodist, one of the Baptist preachers across Main Street resigned. His church began interviewing to fill the vacancy. They quickly hired Brother Elmer, a man with outstanding credentials, a warm smile and a shiny bald head. Within a few days, he was easily recognized by just about everyone in town that had met him in the coffee shop or the post office.

On his first Sunday in the pulpit, however, a funny thing happened. Brother Elmer stood up to preach with a dark, thick head of hair, neatly groomed and combed to one side. It was impossible not to notice. A few of the ladies whispered. Several of the men shifted uneasily in their pews. It might have ended at that, but come Monday morning, Brother Elmer could again be seen around town, his head wanting for a single strand of hair.

As you might imagine in a small town, people started to talk. They talked on the phone and in the grocery store line. They whispered in hushed tones at the drugstore and at little league practices. "Either put it on or take it off!" was the collective public opinion, but no one really wanted to be the one to confront the issue "head on." It paralyzed the church and rendered Brother Elmer completely ineffective.

When Brother Elmer finally realized what a target of ridicule his "two-headedness," had become, he was devastated. In addition to being embarrassed, he was hurt that no one had talked to him about it. His confidence plummeted and within a year he had packed up his toupees and left the church.

This story seems funny in hindsight, but there is nothing funny about sedition, the destructive undercurrent of slanderous gossip, accusations, and negative words aimed at leaders and intent on provoking rebellion. Many good men and women have been forced out of the pulpit, or out of ministry altogether, by the methodical campaigns of one or two disgruntled church members. But that's just the tip of the iceberg.

If you could travel the entire nation, from church to church, interviewing pastors and their spouses in the safety of their own homes, you would find very few that couldn't share painful stories about wounds inflicted by sedition. Your pastor may seem happy (and maybe he or she truly is!), but I can almost guarantee that at some point, he or she has had to deal with unresolved hurt as a result of a church member's thoughtless or even malicious words or actions. Because of their role as spiritual leader, pastors often feel that it is their duty to humbly accept all forms of criticism without ever responding. They just "take it." As a result, even seemingly insignificant remarks or jabs can, over time, snowball into something that causes a lot of emotional harm.

When I am teaching or ministering in front of a mixed group of laity and clergy, I sometimes facilitate a time of corporate repentance. I ask the pastors and their spouses to come to the front of the room with me and turn and face the people. I lead the people in a prayer of repentance, allowing them to seek forgiveness for any unkind words they have spoken about their pastors, and take responsibility as a congregation for pain exacted upon pastoral families because of abuse, insensitivity and spite. Then I lead the pastors in a similar prayer of repentance for any harm or confusion they may have caused as leaders.

The exercise always makes it evident that as the church, we are being led by the walking wounded. Years of grief, silenced out of fear, erupt to the surface because for many of the pastors, it is the first time they have ever heard the words, "I'm sorry" from a parishioner. Not surprisingly, it is often the spouses, wives in particular, who are most affected, because they tend to absorb all the garbage their pastor husbands bring home, and they have nowhere to dump it. Pastoral wives are also inclined to discern or overhear more negative talk than their husbands simply because of the roles they generally take on in the life of the church. For many, the careless jokes and insults, comments and criticisms, get swallowed and stuffed inside, where they become a festering source of heartache.

The Rebellious Spirit

Sedition is killing our clergy. And it is crippling the church in the process. It is a stronghold born out of a rebellious spirit, originating from Satan himself, the "accuser of our brothers" (Revelation 12:10). When we bring accusation, or deliberately go about exposing the faults of others, we are acting in line with our sinful flesh nature. And when we have the barrel pointed at one of God's appointed representatives, he takes the offense personally.

Sedition is killing our clergy. And it is crippling the church in the process.

My favorite example of God's attitude toward sedition is in Numbers 16, a passage I've written about many times before. The Israelites hadn't been wandering in the desert for very long but had already found plenty to complain about. In this scene, three men in particular, Korah, Dathan, and Abiram, along with 250 followers, confronted their leaders, Moses and Aaron, questioning their authority. They said to Moses and Aaron, "You have gone too far! The whole community is holy, every one of them, and the Lord is with them. Why then do you set yourselves above the Lord's assembly?" (Numbers 16:3) They were jealous. Maybe they wanted to have bigger tents and special titles. They didn't want to leave the camp to start their own nation; they just wanted to disrupt the balance of power where they were.

When Moses responded, he made it clear to them, "It is against the Lord that you and all your followers have banded together" (Numbers 16:11). He knew the source of his authority, and he knew the source of the rebellion. Moses arranged for a censer showdown in front of the Tent of Meeting, saying, "...the Lord will show who belongs to him, and who is holy..." (Numbers 16:5). When all the men brought their censers before the Lord at the entrance to the Tent, God opened up the earth and swallowed the three traitors along with their censers, their households, and all of their possessions. Then the Lord consumed the remaining 250 followers of Korah with holy fire, leaving only a smoldering pile of ashes. When God anoints and appoints someone to do a job for him, he does not take lightly the actions of those who would rise up in opposition.

The stronghold of sedition, like the other strongholds, forms over a period of time and becomes part of the consciousness of the church. The foremost accuser loves to stir up dissention by fueling all kinds of finger-pointing and condemnation. Exposing other's weaknesses works in opposition to the gospel of grace and creates an atmosphere that is unsafe—not suitable for healing and restoration at all. Church families that are in the grips of this stronghold are mistrustful of each other and generally not effective in influencing their communities because they are too busy managing internal conflicts.

While all of the carnal strongholds have some control issue lurking underneath, sedition is especially fueled by the question,

"Who's in charge?" In fact, sedition bows to the idol of control or autonomy. The covetous, envious sin nature inside of all of us takes some kind of pleasure in finding and illuminating the faults of others, especially those in power. It's that same part of the sin nature that caused Korah to rise up against Moses. Our flesh does not like to submit, and the spirit of rebellion is always there to encourage thoughts of insurrection. Even our culture is much more likely to admire and applaud independence than obedience.

Forms of Sedition

In a church setting, sedition isn't limited to direct accusations aimed at leaders. It can take on several other forms as well, all of which are detrimental to the spiritual health of the body, and all of which invite the enemy to maintain a foothold. Sedition can include: 1) complaining and grumbling about circumstances in spite of God's past goodness; 2) rebellious or negative talk about God's calling or vision for the church; 3) doubts verbalized in the face of God's ability; and 4) regarding man's wisdom above God's wisdom.

The Korah rebellion certainly wasn't the only time Moses was forced to deal with insubordination; the Israelites were a chronically seditious group. Numbers 11:1 says, "Now the people complained about their hardships in the hearing of the Lord, and when he heard them his anger was aroused. Then fire from the Lord burned among them and consumed some of the outskirts of the camp."

Despite the dramatic fashion in which God had brought them up out of Egypt, and despite his 24/7 pillar-of-fire protection plan, the Israelites couldn't seem to remember from day to day how powerfully God had acted on their behalf. In blatant disregard for all his goodness toward them, they grumbled and complained all the time. About everything. When they were hungry, they complained about not having food. When God provided daily manna, they complained about not having meat. They complained about their living conditions and they complained about the weather. You would think that God's stern response (fire from heaven) would have curtailed all the grumbling, but it never really did. The Bible record indicates that the Israelites started complaining the day they left Egypt and never stopped, even after they entered the promised land. That kind of sedition has been wearing pastors out ever since.

...the Israelites started complaining the day they left Egypt and never stopped, even after they entered the promised land. That kind of sedition has been wearing pastors out ever since.

Consider another scenario: a young, new pastor is appointed to a declining downtown church. Embracing the challenge, he begins talking about inner city ministry, reaching the droves of 30 something's migrating to loft apartments, and adding a new contemporary service. What happens? A different kind of sedition kicks into high gear, the subtle (and sometimes not so subtle) negative comments about the church's vision or direction:

"I don't like the changes we're seeing..."

"Some of these new programs cost too much...they just aren't in the budget!"

"Next thing you know he'll be trying to move the church..."

"Our other pastor never would have done this..."

"We need to meet and talk about this, but let's keep it quiet..."

Change seldom comes easily, and pessimism is surely one of the most common forms of sedition. Conversation after church about the new building program shifts from neutral to negative when questions are posed about the site selection process and the handling of finances. We may not really mean to stir up distrust, but we can't resist letting a few skeptical remarks slide. We may even be in favor of the plan and generally supportive of the church's direction. But we don't want to appear too eager, or too naïve. Raising tough questions just makes for lively discussion, right?

This is just another example of how the seeds of sedition can be planted. It doesn't always require an angry church member or someone intent on subversion; negative talk of any kind can agitate others and then spread, escalating each time it is repeated.

Doubting God's ability is the third form of sedition, and another problem the Israelites struggled with over and over. Numbers 13 gives us a glimpse of this kind of rebellion, underscoring how costly it can be, and how much God dislikes it.

After Israel had been in the desert a while, God instructed Moses to send a group of men into Canaan, the land he had promised to give them, to secretly explore the area and report back to the camp everything they saw. So Moses chose 12 leaders, one from each of the ancestral tribes. He instructed them, "Go see how many Starbucks there are; check out the housing market; and see what kind of shopping is available. While you're there, bring back some carry out." Moses was also probably interested in knowing how they might be successful in driving the current inhabitants out.

The group did as they were asked, spending 40 days sightseeing all throughout Canaan. When they returned, the report was mixed:

> We went into the land to which you sent us, and it does flow with milk and honey! Here is its fruit. But the people who live there are powerful, and the cities are fortified and very large. We even saw descendants of Anak there (Numbers 13:27-28).

The men lost heart when they saw the Amalekites, Hittites and Canaanites. They told Moses, "We can't attack those people;

they are stronger than we are." They even compared themselves to grasshoppers because they were focused on the enemy instead of on God, and they were overcome with doubt. After their initial report to Moses, the Bible says they "spread among the Israelites a bad report about the land they had explored" (Numbers 13:31-32).

However, two of the 12 men, Joshua and Caleb, gave a different report. They believed God, and encouraged Moses and the people to go up and take possession of the land, saying, "The land we passed through and explored is exceedingly good. If the Lord is pleased with us, he will lead us into that land, a land flowing with milk and honey, and will give it to us" (Numbers 14:7-8). Their faith was strong because they were trusting in God, not in the circumstances. They believed in his promise, and they believed he was able.

The Lord made it abundantly clear how he felt about being doubted. He asked of Moses, "How long will these people treat me with contempt? How long will they refuse to believe in me, in spite of all the miraculous signs I have performed among them?" (Numbers 14:11). Because of their lack of faith, God sentenced the entire nation of Israel to wander in the desert until that whole generation died off. Only Joshua and Caleb, who had believed in his ability, would ever be able to enjoy the abundance of the land which they had explored.

When we speak with our lips doubts about what God can do, we are elevating the problem or circumstance to a high place in our thinking.

Our God is the creator of the universe. He hung the stars in the sky and formed everything from the vast expanse of the galaxies to the intricate inner workings of molecules and cells. I think his ability level so far surpasses our comprehension that we can't even fathom it. Scripture confirms that he is "able to do immeasurably more than all we ask or imagine..." (Ephesians 3:20).

When we speak with our lips doubts about what God can do, we are elevating the problem or circumstance to a high place in our thinking. In other words, we are in rebellion toward God. And to the degree that our own distrust causes others to doubt, we are helping strengthen the carnal stronghold.

Finally, intellectual self-reliance can interfere with the mind of Christ, and easily turn into another type of seditious rebellion against God as the Most High. One of the New Testament churches, the one Paul discipled in Corinth, struggled with this problem early in its growth. Paul's letter to the Christians there gives us an idea of what was going on in the new congregation. I especially like Eugene Peterson's language in *The Message*:

> I have a serious concern to bring up with you, my friends, using the authority of Jesus, our Master. I'll put it as urgently as I can: You must get along with each other. You must learn to be considerate of one another, cultivating a life in common.

> I bring this up because some from Chloe's family brought a most disturbing report to my attention—that you're fighting among yourselves! I'll tell you exactly what I was told: You're all picking sides, going around saying, "I'm on Paul's side," or "I'm for Apollos," or "Peter is my man," or "I'm in the Messiah group" (1 Corinthians 1:10-12).

Paul continues, and he does not pull any punches:

> But for right now, friends, I'm completely frustrated by your unspiritual dealings with each other and with God. You're acting like infants in relation to Christ, capable of nothing much more than nursing at the breast. Well, then, I'll nurse you since you don't seem capable of anything more. As long as you grab for what makes you feel good or makes you look important, are you really much different than a babe at the breast, content only when everything's going your way? When one of you says, "I'm on Paul's side," and another says,

"I'm for Apollos," aren't you being totally infantile? (1 Corinthians 3:1-4)

If Paul were to visit some of our churches today, I think he might have the same reaction. It seems that the Christians in Corinth were arguing over whose teaching they liked the best, or which pastor was their favorite. Instead of encouraging one another in the faith and working together to strengthen the body, they were bickering over insignificant theological details. Sound familiar? I know I've been in several churches that could be described the same way.

In the consumer based church, where everything caters to the opinions of people, all manners of sedition can thrive. Eugene's paraphrase went right to the heart of the matter when he said, "you grab for what makes you feel good or makes you look important." Control—keeping things running the way you want them to—becomes a high place in our thinking. Church consultant Bill Easum describes the many forms control can take on:

> Control takes many shapes: our insistence on controlling everything that happens in our congregations and denominations; our desire to coordinate everything that happens, or to know about everything before it happens, or to insist on voting on every new issue or ministry; a parlor that few people use; a gym floor that must be kept scratch free; a kitchen that no one can use but designated persons; money that belongs to the Trustees; an official body that has to approve every decision.[1]

Our carnal belief system says that our presence has value; therefore, we believe that the threat of our unhappy departure must carry some weight. If we aren't happy and in control, we threaten to leave. After all, we're so important, even God would probably be disappointed to see us go! As consumers it's so easy for us to buy into the idea that it's all about us.

But we really don't want to leave, we just want to pull the

strings and make the puppet dance. So we email. And we call. We grumble and complain. We let slip a negative word or an accusation, even while we smile and shake hands and keep filling our seat. We may even take aim at the pastor, convinced in our own way that we are just protecting what is ours. When fully operational, the stronghold of sedition will entangle a church in conflict, and will cause a church to forfeit its God given destiny.

THE STRONGHOLD OF HONOR

If there is an antithesis to sedition in the church, it would have to be honor, a concept unfortunately nearly lost, or at the very least distorted, in our society of free speech and entitlement. When it comes to our relationships with other people, the idea of giving honor may be confused with any number of things: tolerance, indulgence, envy, worship, approval, admiration. But the truth is, we don't have to agree with someone to honor them. Honor doesn't require that we necessarily admire someone, or that we indulge their sin. The kind of honor I'm talking about is the intrinsic value given to every human being by God, simply because he created us, and because we are important to him.

On my bookshelf is a book entitled *Honor* by Fawn Parish. It is the only book I know of dedicated to the topic of biblical honor. I have read and reread parts of it, and referred to it often in my own studies and preparation. It is such a foundational spiritual concept, and largely overlooked in Christian literature.

Fawn suggests that honor is one of heaven's preoccupations. She writes:

> In the book of Revelation, we see the Bride heaping honor on the Son, the Son on the Father, the Father back to the Son and the Son back to His bride. And then the whole process marvelously begins again and continues forever. It is one glorious circle that never ends.

She goes on to challenge her readers with this:

The wonder is that this glorious, honorable God does an astounding, heart-stopping thing. He also crowns us—tragic, shattered earthenware that we are—with glory and honor. In a sweeping display of His generosity he gives us what He alone deserves. And He invites us to give this marvelous gift to each other.[2]

God not only invites us to honor others, he instructs us through the apostle Paul, "Honor all people, love the brotherhood, fear God, honor the king" (1 Peter 2:17 NAS). It is interesting to me that he tells us to "honor all people," yet then makes it a point to emphasize again, "honor the king," referring to those in authority. Paul included a related message for the early Christians in his letter to Timothy when he wrote, "I urge, then, first of all, that requests, prayers, intercession and thanksgiving be made for everyone—for kings and all those in authority, that we may live peaceful and quiet lives in all godliness and holiness. This is good, and pleases God our Savior..." (1 Timothy 2:1-3). Honor all people, but especially kings. And pray for all people, but especially kings. Do you see a pattern?

These verses are giving us two different levels of the same mandate—to honor in spirit and with our prayers all people (I think this actually means all people, not just the ones we like or find agreeable), and to pay special attention to covering our "kings" and other key leaders in prayer. We can also glean one other very important truth from these two verses; that is, to pray for someone is one of the highest forms of honor we can give.

...to pray for someone is one of the highest forms of honor we can give.

As we have already seen, God takes sedition, especially when it is aimed at one of his called and appointed leaders, very seriously, which should give us a good indication of how he expects us to treat these spiritual leaders in our lives. Yet scripture also reveals that God expects us to give a certain level of honor to all those in authority over us, including such people as political leaders, employers or supervisors (Colossians 3:22-24), our parents (Exodus 20:12), and the elderly (1 Timothy 5:17). In God's economy, there is something significant about our willingness to revere and respect those who lead. In every arena, we are to "give to Caesar what is Caesar's" (Luke 10:25).

One of the first books I wrote over ten years ago is entitled *Preyed On or Prayed For.*[3] Throughout my years of ministry, it has continued to be one of the most meaningful messages God has given me to teach. It is simply a message about the importance of honoring our pastors by intentionally covering them with prayers of blessing and protection. It asks the question, "How can we honor God, whom we can not see, if we can not honor his chosen representatives, whom we can see?" As God is the source of all honor, he is also the most worthy of honor.

The book *Preyed On or Prayed For* is based largely on the scene in Exodus 17, when the Israelites faced a battle with the Amalekites. As the army commander, Joshua led the troops into the valley at Rephidim; Moses, who was both national leader and pastor, headed up to the top of a hill where he could overlook the fighting and pray. Two of his aides, Aaron and Hur, accompanied him. The Bible says that as long as Moses held up his hands, the Israelites prevailed. But when he grew weary and lowered his hands, the Amalekites would gain the advantage.

Noticing this, Aaron and Hur found a large stone and sat Moses down on it between them. Then with one on one side, and one on the other, they held up his tired arms so that he "remained steady until sunset" (Exodus 17:12). In this manner, honor and prayer secured the victory for God's people.

When a church is honoring its pastors and leaders, it is empowered to walk out the will and destiny God has established. However, when a church fails to honor its pastor, it fails to honor God. And as we learned from the Korah rebellion in Number 16, when a church fails to honor God, it often is forced to forfeit part or all of its God given inheritance. The reason is that where God is dishonored, he can not bestow his favor, a necessary ingredient to the health and vitality of the church. True to his nature, God will not impart all of what is in his heart to give where he finds his appointed leaders being abused and taken for granted.

Landing Strip

I fly somewhere just about every week, and I've noticed something—planes don't just land anywhere; they always land on a runway. Runways have been specifically designed, measured and lighted to be proper places for planes to descend. Likewise, honor is the landing strip for God's favor. When we live with an attitude of honor, valuing people in Jesus' name, the transport of God's favor is able to alight.

The consumer based church seeks the favor of man. Who is on our side? Do they have influence? What can they do for us? Certainly, to some extent people can be a source for money, ideas or promotion. But people won't always come through. They may change their minds. They may not agree. Or they may give with strings attached. Seeking the favor of people creates opportunities for disappointment and hurt feelings arising from control issues, the perfect backdrop for sedition. However, the Presence based church seeks only the favor of God.

I must be truthful; I do not understand all of the hows and whys of God's favor—how we can receive it and why he chooses to pour it out in one place and not in another. God is far too magnificent for me to pretend to have insight into his sovereign reasonings. But I do know this, I want it! More than anything, I desire to be favored of the Lord. I yearn for his favor on my family, my children and my grandchildren. I long for it in my own life as a husband, father, teacher and servant of the gospel. And I pray that his favor could be evident in every local church in every town and city across the nation. Nothing that man can give us or do for us; nothing on this earth can take us further or help us get closer to our own promised land.

When we have God's favor, we don't have to campaign for support from a political majority because we have God's support. We are his preferred. In his favor, we don't need to seek approval from the fraudulent spirit of cultural worth because we walk in God's highest esteem and acceptance. With God's favor, we don't have to sell out to men and their money in order to advance because we have complete access to all of his benefits. He helps us. He promotes us. He encourages us by his Spirit. He furthers our cause. In other words, he becomes our source for everything.

If we desire to attract God's favor, then we must be looking to him through Christ Jesus, and not people, for everything that we need. For his favor to gain a stronghold in our church, Jesus must become our corporate fixation, the Most High in our thinking. Where we look when we have a need reveals exactly what our source is. If you want to go on a road trip and you need gasoline, you go to a service station. If you need to feed your family, you go to the grocery store. Whatever our needs as a church—whether money or direction or protection—we must look first to him as our source for every good thing:

> How great is your goodness, which you have stored up for those who fear you, which you bestow in the sight of men on those who take refuge in you. In the shelter of your presence you hide them...praise be to the Lord, for he showed his wonderful love to me when I was in a besieged city (Psalm 30:19-21).

The Corinthian church that we talked about earlier in the chapter was divided into camps and locked in seditious mudslinging because they had forgotten their source: Jesus crucified. They had fallen back into patterns of thinking like the world instead of with the mind of Christ, bickering about trivial matters and boasting about their own "wisdom." Paul, their spiritual mentor, addresses their childish behavior by putting the very notion of man's wisdom into perspective:

> While Jews clamor for miraculous demonstrations and Greeks go in for philosophical wisdom, we go right on proclaiming Christ, the Crucified. ...[T]o us who are personally called by God himself—both Jews and Greeks—Christ is God's ultimate miracle and wisdom all wrapped up in one. Human wisdom is so tiny, so impotent, next to the seeming absurdity of God. Human strength can't begin to compete with God's "weakness" (1 Corinthians 1:22-25 *The Message*).

Paul elaborates further by reminding them that he never tried to impress them with polished speeches or trendy philosophies. His message was clear and simple: who Jesus was and what he did on the cross. He urges the church to quit relying on the latest ideas or the opinions of experts, and to look to Jesus himself as their source, so that their "faith might not rest on men's wisdom, but on God's power" (1 Corinthians 2:5).

We think we are pretty smart. But even the best and brightest Bible scholars throughout the centuries could not decipher the mystery that is God's wisdom except what was revealed to them by the Holy Spirit. For all our education and research, we can only guess at the heart of God. Yet in his favor, "No eye has seen, no ear has heard, no mind has conceived what God has prepared for those who love him—but God has revealed it to us by his Spirit" (1 Corinthians 2:9-10). When Jesus is our source, we look to him as our wellspring of ideas and he gives us his mind and his discernment in all matters.

If something is your source, you look to it often. If you say, "God is my source," yet you seldom go to him in private worship and prayer, then he is not really your source. Do you make time to spend in his Presence? Do you talk things over with him, listen for his voice, and seek his heart in every matter? Prayerlessness is a failure to recognize God as your starting point, the giver of all good things. On the contrary, pervasive patterns of worship and prayer are signs that you are looking first and foremost to him as the stronghold of your life.

This is not to say that people and earthly resources are not sometimes a part of God's favor and provision toward us. As we look to him as our source, he may, in his great love for us, grant us favor with men in order to accomplish his purpose. He may open and close doors, reverse circumstances, or supply us with a large sum of money. An amazingly "good deal," coincidentally perfect timing, or an unexpected breakthrough can all be evidence of God's favor at work. The key is that we must be looking to him and recognizing that he is the spring from which it all comes.

If you say, "God is my source," yet you seldom go to him in private worship and prayer, then he is not really your source.

The very first sermon I preached, which I still have a copy of, came from 1 Corinthians 1:26-30:

> For consider your call, brethren; not many of you were wise according to worldly standards, not many were powerful, not many were of noble birth; but God chose what is foolish in the world to shame the wise, God chose what is weak in the world to shame the strong, God chose what is low and despised in the world, even things that are not, to bring to nothing things that are, so that no human being might boast in the presence of God. He is the source of your life in Christ Jesus, whom God made our wisdom, our righteousness and sanctification and redemption; therefore, as it is written, "Let him who boasts, boast of the Lord" (*Revised Standard Version*).

At that time, I was the perfect model of everything these verses speak of—not powerful, not of noble birth, foolish, weak and low. Recently converted and called to ministry, I had gone straight from beer joints and pool halls to the pulpit after only a few seminary classes. I had never attended Sunday school, never said a prayer in public, and definitely never preached a sermon. I could overhaul a motor and referee a bar fight, but I really didn't know the first thing about printing a bulletin or conducting a funeral. But one thing I was confident about: God was my source. I knew that somehow through him, I could do what he had called me to do. I knew that if I looked to him, he would fill in the holes and make up for my inadequacy. I didn't really have any other choice.

When God is your source, he can cover all kinds of deficiencies and flaws—lack of education, lack of experience, lack of resources, character weaknesses. He is not afraid to use imperfect vessels for his purposes; in fact, it would appear from scripture that he prefers them. The Bible is replete with examples of men and women whose personal failures and poor decisions are clearly recorded right along with their kingdom accomplishments. Pretty much all of the Bible heroes that shaped God's salvation plan from the very beginning had well documented failings that could have disqualified them from such noble work (and from most church boards). Yet they became part of the gospel heritage anyway. The Psalmist understood this when he prayed, "May the favor of the Lord our God rest upon us; establish the work of our hands for us—yes, establish the work of our hands" (Psalm 90:17). What God's favor produces in spite of our shortcomings can have an impact for a very long time.

> *He is not afraid to use imperfect vessels for his purposes; in fact, it would appear from scripture that he prefers them.*

Consider a man like E.M. Bounds. I was in a grocery store the other day and noticed several of his books on a display. "Amazing," I thought. "Here's a man who has been dead for years, and still has a better marketing strategy than I do!" He lives on in this millennium because the wind of God is still in the sail of his life.

Motor boats can go very fast, but they can not go very far without fuel. Sailboats, on the other hand, can travel around and around the world with only the wind. When you have the favor of God, and he is your source, it is like having the wind in your sails.

A Favored Son

When I think of the favor of God as the unseen, driving force in someone's life, I think of one of my favorite Old Testament stories—the story of Joseph. The youngest of 12 brothers, he was unashamedly his father's favorite, which made him quite despised by the other 11. To further fuel his brother's hatred, Joseph had a habit of using his God-given gift for dreams and visions to humiliate his brothers by sharing dreams he had in which they, though they were older, would someday bow down to him. At 17 years old, Joseph was already favored of God and destined for great things, but he was nevertheless still typical for a young man on the brink of adulthood, with growing edges of arrogance and immaturity. His behavior toward his siblings was probably enough to provoke any big brother to anger, even today. However, in that culture, where the rights of birth order were strongly upheld, Joseph would have been wiser to have kept his mouth shut.

His brothers finally became so annoyed with Joseph that they conspired to kill him, but settled instead for selling him into slavery so that at least they could profit from the deal and not carry family blood on their hands. In a hastily constructed plan, they sold him for 20 shekels of silver to a traveling caravan, and then passed him off as dead to their heartbroken father.

God was with Joseph, however, and he ended up a slave in the home of Potiphar, the captain of the guard and one of Pharaoh's officials. Soon, because of God's favor, Joseph rose to the top, even as a lowly servant. The Bible makes it clear how God promoted him:

The Lord was with Joseph and he prospered, and he lived in

the house of his Egyptian master. When his master saw that the Lord was with him and that the Lord gave him success in everything he did, Joseph found favor in his eyes and became his attendant. Potiphar put him in charge of his household, and he entrusted to his care everything he owned. From the time he put him in charge of his household and of all that he owned, the Lord blessed the household of the Egyptian because of Joseph. The blessing of the Lord was on everything Potiphar had, both in the house and in the field. So he left in Joseph's care everything he had; with Joseph in charge, he did not concern himself with anything except the food he ate (Genesis 39:2-6).

But of course that's not the end of the story. Just when things appeared to be going pretty well for Joseph, Potiphar's wife tried (unsuccessfully) to seduce him and then flipped the table, accusing him of rape. With his hands tied, Potiphar threw his trusted servant in prison. Yet even there we read:

[T]he Lord was with him; he showed him kindness and granted him favor in the eyes of the prison warden. So the warden put Joseph in charge of all those held in the prison, ...because the Lord was with Joseph and gave him success in whatever he did" (Genesis 39: 21-23).

After several years, Joseph finally got another break when Pharaoh had some disturbing dreams which no one could interpret. Someone called for Joseph, who interpreted the dreams accurately, thus gaining the gratitude and favor of Pharaoh, the most powerful man in all of Egypt. His response was familiar:

Then Pharaoh said to Joseph, "Since God has made all this known to you, there is no one so discerning and wise as you. You shall be in charge of my palace, and all my people are to submit to your orders. Only with respect to the throne will I be greater than you" (Genesis 41:39-40).

With that, Pharaoh put his ring on Joseph's finger, his robe around his back, a gold chain around his neck, and a chariot under his feet. Joseph was put in charge of all of Egypt; no one was to come in or go out, stand up or sit down, without his command.

The best part of the story though, came several years later, when the entire region was suffering from severe drought, and Joseph's brothers traveled from Canaan to Egypt to buy food. They appeared unsuspecting before their younger brother, bowing low, and requested grain to take back to their households. Joseph recognized his brothers and eventually revealed himself to them, setting up one of the greatest "I told you so" opportunities in history. But Joseph had grown too much for that. He knew his source.

Rather than reminding his brothers of his dreams which had proven accurate, he comforted them:

> And now, do not be distressed and do not be angry with yourselves for selling me here, because it was to save lives that God sent me ahead of you. But God sent me ahead of you to preserve for you a remnant on earth and to save your lives by a great deliverance. So then, it was not you who sent me here, but God (Genesis 45:5, 7-8).

After years of waiting and suffering and probably doubting his own sanity, Joseph saw the big picture. He recognized how God's favor had directed his life.

Joseph was living out of a divine stronghold of honor in his life, and the fruit of God's favor was evident. In a moment that Joseph had probably imagined much of his life—his jealous, traitorous brothers bowing before him, completely at his mercy, and he with the power and authority to exact any kind of revenge he might dream up—Joseph instead was completely surrendered to the Most High God. He not only forgave his brothers, but he attended to their fear by reassuring them that he would provide for them. He fed them, gave them gifts, and sent them back home to bring his father and all of their families back to Egypt to live under his care. After years of forced labor, false imprisonment, lonely nights in a foreign land far from home, during which he must have wondered hundreds of times whether he would even live or die, Joseph certainly could have responded out of bitterness and hatred. Instead, he was full of love and compassion. Only a divine stronghold could produce such dramatic results.

While we know that God's hand was on Joseph from a very early age, I also believe that Joseph continued to invite God's favor because he continually lived out an attitude of honor, even under some very trying circumstances. He conducted himself with honor toward his master Potiphar, and also toward the prison warden, in such a way that he became a most trusted manager. He must have worked hard and with a spirit of humility to have earned such respect as a slave. When we honor those around us, especially those in leadership over us, the wind of God's favor can propel our lives.

When we honor those around us, especially those in leadership over us, the wind of God's favor can propel our lives.

In such a divine stronghold, we can find shelter from mean and spiteful people because we are not controlled by their actions or words. "For surely, O Lord, you bless the righteous; you surround them with your favor as with a shield" (Psalm 5:12). Where the mind of Christ reigns and he is worshiped and honored above all, the bad, the evil and the wrong will eventually bow to his Presence. His favor can turn acts of sedition and malice into opportunities for the outcome of our lives to bring glory and honor to God.

A Favored Friend

Another familiar name in the Bible gives us an idea of what a stronghold of honor and favor looks like: Daniel. We can draw several parallels between the life of Joseph and the life of Daniel.

Both were forced to live as exiles in a foreign land; both were conscripted into service to the king; and both had a gift for interpreting dreams and visions, which ultimately earned them the favor of their "captors" and high ranking positions in their respective lands. Furthermore, both were men whose lives of profound honor also merited for them the favor of God. Daniel 6:3-5 gives us a glimpse into how Daniel served an idolatrous king with loyalty and even affection, while at the same time remaining completely steadfast in his devotion to God:

> Now Daniel so distinguished himself among the administrators and the satraps by his exceptional qualities that the king planned to set him over the whole kingdom. At this, the administrators and the satraps tried to find grounds for charges against Daniel in his conduct of government affairs, but they were unable to do so. They could find no corruption in him, because he was trustworthy and neither corrupt nor negligent. "We will never find any basis for charges against this man Daniel unless it has something to do with the law of his God."

Daniel, well loved and highly respected by the king, was known as one consecrated to the Most High God, the God of Israel. So in an attempt to get rid of him, the jealous administrators craftily convinced King Darius to issue a decree carrying a penalty of death for anyone who prayed to any other god or man except the king himself. When Daniel heard about the decree, "he went home to his upstairs room where the windows opened toward Jerusalem. Three times a day he got down on his knees and prayed, giving thanks to his God, just as he had done before" (Daniel 6:10).

Of course, when the king was informed about Daniel's refusal to comply with the decree, and was thus forced by his own hand to throw him into the lion's den, God shut the mouths of the lions and spared Daniel's life. As a result, he became even more highly favored by the king, and those guilty of sedition were fed to the same hungry lions who devoured them. In addition, King Darius issued a new decree to the entire nation declaring the God of Daniel the true and living God (Daniel 6:28). What a great example of how honor became the landing strip for God's favor to overcome sedition!

God's favor does not always guarantee us wealth or positions of authority however. Sometimes, the stronghold of favor simply means that we are able to walk humbly in the path laid out for us in him. "For we are God's workmanship, created in Christ Jesus to do good works, which God prepared in advance for us to do" (Ephesians 2:10). Sometimes it means living in peace and contentment, despite meager surroundings. Sometimes favor is defined in the life of one like Phinehas.

A Favored Life

I met Phinehas in a slum camp outside of Hyderabad India. He was a pastor, called to love and minister to several hundred of the most poverty stricken, disinherited people I have ever personally encountered. They lived in make-shift tents constructed from various salvaged materials—families of four or five crammed into living spaces no larger than my closet. With no running water, no electricity, and no sanitation of any kind, daily life was reduced to tasks related to survival in its simplest form.

Phinehas was fortunate. On a salary package of one dollar per day, he and his family lived in a two-room house made of wood, although neither of the small rooms contained a piece of furniture. As he walked me around the village of tents, he introduced me to many of his converts—45 or more—all of whom smiled graciously and greeted me with such warmth that you would have thought they hadn't a care in the world. The honor and love that the people demonstrated toward me and toward one another in that community of believers made me wonder if perhaps sedition is directly linked to materialism. So many control battles in our churches ignite over things—building plans, new carpet, stained glass windows—seemingly the more we have, the more we feel the need to protect and direct. We want jurisdiction over some piece of the pie. These people had so little; they simply had nothing to fight over.

When we returned to Phinehas' home, he served me tea as we sat on the floor and visited. Face beaming with pride, he told me how his wife was teaching the women of the village to sew. He talked about Jesus, and about the families in his church, and about all that God was doing in their lives. It was an amazing thing for me to see.

I meet hundreds of pastors each year as I travel around the United States, many of whom seem to wear the signs of ministry stress visibly on their faces. Their shoulders droop, their eyes look glazed, and the corners of their mouths turn downward. By all accounts, they have more than Phinehas will own in a lifetime—more money in the bank, more food in the pantry, more lines in the church budget, yet they are miserable. And here was Phinehas, living in the most dismal circumstances I could imagine, and he was truly happy. He smiled all the time.

I could only explain it by the favor of God. Phinehas was an oasis of joy, walking in the good works he had been called in Christ Jesus to accomplish. God was truly with him in all he was doing.

Phinehas was an oasis of joy, walking in the good works he had been called in Christ Jesus to accomplish.

The process of establishing a stronghold of honor to invite God's favor in a church starts with the questions, "How are we treating our pastor? How do we talk about others in authority over us, such as our nation's leaders? And what is our attitude toward others in our lives, particularly those in our church family?" If we want God's favor over our church, then we need to be actively cultivating attitudes and behavior patterns of honor and respect. God's favor can not be manipulated, but it will not come uninvited.

Seeking his favor means seeking his face. As we press into him in worship and prayer, he gives of himself out of his great love for us. Those who enjoy the favor of God are so caught up in him that they are unaffected by it. He is the Most High. His name, his nature and his glory are the centerpiece, and worthy of all the honor we can give. As we wait in his presence, he turns his face toward us and smiles—his smile encompasses all that is the favor of God!

Therefore, as a church we must renew our minds in Christ to cover and not expose; honor and not disgrace; forgive and not accuse. For the enemy is the architect of rebellion, but Jesus came that we would be kings or slaves no more, but all children of the same Lord, and heirs to his throne.

Lord Jesus, we thank you for the people called Baptists; they are such an important part of the body of Christ. Be glorified in their preaching of the Word, their faithfulness to world missions, and their zeal for winning the lost. Lord, let the best of the Baptists be reflected in us, and may we bless and encourage them as we pray and worship you. Amen.

5

PAROCHIALISM VS UNITY

As a teenager, I spent a lot of time in pool halls and beer joints. My father followed the oil industry along the coastal towns of Texas, south of Houston, working on the rigs. He lived hard and drank hard, and as a young man with little motivation to be different, I followed his example. Tall and wiry, I was equally adept at replacing transmissions and fist fighting, so I found the camaraderie in the local taverns appealing.

That's why when my life radically changed course as a young man and I first entered the ministry as a United Methodist pastor, I was bewildered at some of my first encounters with clergy from other denominations. One friendly preacher in our small town invited me to lunch. Three bites into my BLT sandwich, he asked me if I spoke in tongues.

"What do you mean?" I asked.

He never really answered my question, but instead told me that if I didn't even know what that meant, then I wasn't really saved.

Not long after, I visited another pastor in his church. He led me through their grand sanctuary (it seemed grand to me at the time), and showed me a door in the floor that opened to reveal a baptismal. Apparently—and I was quite puzzled by this because I had been learning a lot about grace—only people who were baptized in that water were truly saved.

Then one day some young people came knocking on my door and wanted to know if I was saved. I told them I believed that I was (although secretly my sense of security had taken some pretty serious hits in the days prior). They proceeded to explain to me that there was only room for 144,000 people in heaven, and unless I was a part of their group, I wouldn't be able to get in!

I felt frustrated and confused. I had experienced God in a very real and personal way, and knew in my heart that he had done a salvation work in my life and even called me to serve him. Yet now I was being told that I needed to learn another language, be dunked in a special tank, and gain admittance to a very select fraternity if I really wanted to be saved. I was ready to embrace the calling of the gospel and my new teammates, but a lot of them weren't ready to embrace me.

I went back to one of my favorite "before Christ" hangout spots to visit some old friends and wondered if maybe they didn't have a better chance of going to heaven than I did.

Several weeks later I visited another church where I first bumped into a practice known as closed communion. I knelt at the rail to receive the elements, but the pastor skipped right over me like I wasn't even there.

I was surprised to discover that many churches, even those bearing the same denominational labels, refused to serve communion to anyone outside of their own church family. When the ushers passed the bread and the cup of the Lord's Supper, they would deliberately pass over visitors, even if they attended a similar church down the street! I thought it was a strange incongruity that the beer joint crowd, who heartily welcomed anyone to step up to the bar and share a drink, was far more accepting of new-comers than the Christians. In fact, they were far more accept-ing of the Christians than the Christians! And it was especially ironic since all the Christians in town would go eat hamburgers together after church on Sundays in the local café.

Closed communion basically says, "Since you are not one of us—not baptized in our water, not on our membership roll, not of the same church heritage—you are not worthy to partake of this sacrament of the Lord Jesus Christ. You are not accepted. We don't recognize you as part of the church body." I knew I was young and green, and had a lot to learn. But the stance, like oth-ers I had discovered, seemed cliquish, arrogant and even blasphemous. It was like they thought that the only people saved and going to heaven were of their own little flock, which made their view of the gospel and of salva-tion pretty narrow.

It was like they thought that the only people saved and going to heaven were of their own little flock, which made their view of the gospel and of salvation pretty narrow.

The sad result of closed commu-nion in that town was that there were many Christians living there who opt-ed out of church completely because of the way the churches treated each other. And if the Christians were offended, you can imagine how the non-Christians must have felt. They wrote the church off as hypocritical and irrelevant, and committed their tithes to the local bar where the food and drink flowed freely and no one was an outsider for long.

Practices such as closed communion fuel the stronghold of parochialism, or denominationalism, a people based stronghold that attempts to seal itself off from all others, even others within the body of Christ. I prefer the term "parochialism" to "denomi-nationalism," although they are similar, because this corporate mindset can exist between churches of the same denomination or in networks or independent churches that would not consider themselves to be a part of an official denomination. Simply put, parochialism is the narrow-minded attitude that those in one's own spiritual community are "in" and everyone else is "out."

I'm not suggesting that denominations are inherently bad. They are a diverse expression of the gospel, reaching out to many different kinds of people in all walks of life. Their uniqueness adds richness and color to the body of Christ and each one has made its own distinctive contributions to the faith. I have been in dynamic churches of many different flavors that were worshiping creatively and earnestly seeking his Presence. God is worthy of our most resonant diversity working in harmony to glorify his name.

Denominations are more than just brand names; they are legacies built on the lives and sacrifices of great men and women of God, on histories and memories of failures and accomplishments. They are defined by personalities, worship styles, movements and even buildings. When a person says, "I am Baptist," or "I am Lutheran," he is identifying with more than a label; he is connecting himself to a rich spiritual heritage. I think it would be revelatory for many Christians to learn more about the beginnings of the denominations of which they claim to be a part. Much can be gained from studying the lives of Wesley, Calvin, Luther and others.

Paul even urged us to cherish our Christian lineage, "So then, brothers, stand firm and hold to the teachings (traditions and doctrines) we passed on to you, whether by word of mouth or by letter" (2 Thessalonians 2:15, parentheses mine). Remembering where we came from—honoring our mothers and fathers in the faith—is good and keeps us grounded in our beliefs. Throughout the decades, the great Christian denominations have in many ways acted as guardrails which kept us from straying too far to the left or right as religious fads came and went.

So if denominations have value and place in the body of Christ, at what point does allegiance turn into a stronghold of parochialism? I would refer back again to Yancey's definition of idolatry—a commitment of spirit to that which cannot bear its weight—and say that denominationalism becomes destructive when our spirits are more committed to the institution than to Christ Jesus. When our own spiritual community, whether it be a local church or a larger denomination, replaces God as the Most High in our thinking and actions, then it has become an idol. It is our source for affirmation and identity, and the true object of our worship.

Parochialism, like the strongholds of religion and pride, clings to the precepts and practices that make a community of believers unique. It reveres the denomination or institution itself as the all encompassing representation of a familiar set of beliefs, traditions, doctrines, rules and procedures. The health of the "parish" is more important that the health of the larger body of Christ, and an attitude of exclusivity grows.

This exclusive attitude is the deadly poison of parochialism. The danger of the stronghold goes beyond the idolatry and misplaced affection to the idea that "our way of thinking is right and yours is wrong." The nasty truth about parochialism is that it supports doctrines like closed communion.

The Political Spirit

Parochialism is a consumer based stronghold which is driven by a political spirit, in other words, an atmosphere of partisan decision-making, side-taking, finger-pointing and even mud-slinging. We can draw several parallels between a parochial system and political system to help us understand how the stronghold of parochialism affects people and the churches they make up.

1. Political affiliations often dictate what we think.

If you are a Republican, you probably oppose abortion, same-sex marriage, amnesty for illegal immigrants and censorship of religious organizations. If you are a Democrat, you most likely oppose the war in Iraq, the proposed federal marriage amendment, government funding for faith-based organizations and abortion limits. The party we align ourselves with has a platform on many different issues and we tend to buy into the whole package, or at the very least, a majority of it.

Furthermore, political parties are frequently known more for what they oppose than for what they support. That's because the political atmosphere is combative and insular, us against them. The parochial stronghold is similarly opinionated, with established belief systems that dominate the thought processes of the group. Where such a stronghold exists in a church, you may find many members who either oppose or support something—it can be an idea, a person, a doctrine, a worship style—strictly because it's the "party platform," when in fact they really have never given the issue much thought for themselves. It is what some would call blind allegiance.

2. Our political bent determines who our friends are and who our enemies are.

Which party you support most likely governs which candidates you vote for. Political affiliation draws a clear circle around the good guys, branding everyone outside the circle an adversary. Likewise, where a parochialism stronghold exists, the boundary clearly defines who can be trusted, and who can't be. Some church groups actually claim that they are the only ones saved and going to heaven. Others, while they might not be that direct, target specific theologies that are deemed unacceptable, and anyone who holds to that particular belief becomes a threat. They are not to be trusted.

3. The political spirit impedes our ability to evaluate individuals apart from their group connections.

Consider this situation: You move to a new city. Within the first few weeks, you see the mayor interviewed several times on the news and he strikes you as an intelligent, sincere man. You find his personality to be likeable and his statements, answers and actions to be reasonable. Then campaign ads start surfacing for the upcoming election. You discover that he represents the political party you don't normally vote for. How does this information change the way you think about the mayor?

If you are like most people, the label would make you more skeptical and less likely to take what you observe at face value. Instead, you would begin to apply all that you know and feel about that particular political party to the mayor. You would no longer be seeing him as an individual but as part of a group.

Parochialism is very similar in that it brings party politics mentality to the church. Denominational labels influence how we relate to other Christians because we apply all the characteristics of the group to the individual. We meet a new neighbor who says she attends First Other Church and we smile and say, "How nice." But what we really think is, "Oh, she's one of *those*."

We meet a new neighbor who says she attends First Other Church and we smile and say, "How nice." But what we really think is, "Oh, she's one of **those***."*

True to the pattern of corporate strongholds, parochialism grows over a period of time and involves the development of thoughts, expectations, attitudes and beliefs. The patterns of thinking can develop in individual congregations or across entire denominations. What seems hard to believe though, is that many of those separatist attitudes originate from and are fed by the churches and institutions themselves, which often have policies or doctrines in place, such as the ones I discovered as a new pastor, that encourage spiritual prejudice. Of course they wouldn't explain it that way, but consider the following common practices:

- Many of the denominational structures pressure, either directly or indirectly, all pastoral candidates to attend only their sanctioned seminaries. I actually started my seminary education at one school, and was forced to move when leadership in my denomination tactfully informed me that I would put myself at a great disadvantage in the appointment system if I didn't reconsider my educational choice. The political spirit behind parochialism wants to keep business in the family, support its own programs and maintain control over its next generation of preachers. What better way to promote the party agenda and censor new or threatening ideas.

- Similarly, many denominations will not recognize the credentials or license of a clergy person ordained in a different denomination. If a Baptist preacher wanted to seek a position in a Methodist church for example, he would have to go through additional training and schooling to ensure that he would adhere at all times to the certified Methodist script.

- Another common practice is for denominations to forbid any kind of curriculum from being used—such as for Sunday school or small group study—that isn't distributed through the denominational publishing house or some other authorized source. Again, the purpose is to strictly control theology being taught and keep educational dollars circulating close to home.

As I explained in the introduction, strongholds boil down to the issue of control and the question, "Who's in charge?" Obviously, each of these practices is an attempt to sustain control over the denominational persona and preserve its cherished beliefs and time-honored traditions. Remember that cognitive closure is an attribute of all carnal strongholds, and so the flow of information is always under the microscope. After all, innovative ideas and fresh moves of the Spirit might upset the status quo. They might even violate the denominational handbook.

The problem with a church sealing itself off from outside influences is that while doing so may protect the people from deceptive or misleading ideas, it also robs them of life-giving moves of the Spirit. Eventually it will result in an atmosphere that is stale and ingrown. Just like a body of water, church systems need a current source that flows in and one that flows out in order to maintain a healthy, fresh environment. When the water is too still, the lake stagnates.

Even though it may feel risky, churches need to cultivate relationships with other churches that are different. They need to come into contact with new teachings and ideas to stay vigorous and strong. An occasional theological challenge strengthens our spiritual muscles, gives us an appreciation for other doctrines that we may not understand, and encourages us to continue seeking scriptural truths. Regardless of what church you attend or what your background is, I can safely say that you don't know everything there is to know about God. Neither does your church or your pastor. We all need opportunities to learn and grow.

I have a friend who pastors in Georgia. He is fortunate to be part of a network of pastors and churches in his area that sponsor several events together every year to benefit the whole community. They cooperate to host concerts, street parties, benefits and conferences. Their teamwork makes it possible for them to do far more than any of them could do on their own, and in addition to providing opportunities for the city-wide church to fellowship as one family, it's a great witness to the community.

He tells me that there are several churches, however, that simply refuse to participate with the network. They won't contribute anything to the planning of the events, nor will they support the efforts by attending. In fact, at times he tells me, it appears they almost go out of their way to oppose the group sponsored activities by planning, for example, events of their own for the same dates. Despite the pastors' best efforts to reach out, these churches remain aloof. As I travel around, I see similar situations in many cities and towns.

This is another example of the stronghold of parochialism at work. It keeps Christians hidden down inside of their denominational bunkers and keeps the family of God divided. It's a dangerous testimony to the non-believers in our communities who must wonder how we can possible love or care about them when we don't even associate with each other.

Keeping God Out

Parochialism not only excludes others within the body of Christ, it can also shut out Jesus himself. Like all the carnal strongholds, it can cause a church to lose sight of its need for the Presence of God. The walls and fences that parochialism builds in order to protect the institutional character don't discriminate; they simply seal the church off from the inside out. Consider the following several ways in which parochialism erects barriers to the genuine and manifest Presence of God.

First, because parochialism is all about upholding the party platform, it can prevent us from listening for and hearing the voice of God. Instead, we just listen to the voices being piped in from headquarters. Jack Deere explains:

> Some people don't hear the voice of God very well because they have overwhelming confidence in the religious traditions. They are so pleased with the guidance they receive from their tradition; they don't really feel a need for God's voice. Moreover, they are sure God agrees with their traditions and would never speak anything contrary to their beliefs or practices."[1]

Deere adds, "Blind adherence to tradition gives some of us control and makes all of us feel secure. But this kind of control and security comes at a great price. It produces a religious people who have a relationship not to God but to a religious system."[2] To be Presence based means to be Presence drawn, and to be Presence drawn we must be in tune to the sound of his voice.

Second, parochialism as a stronghold is an obstruction to

free and expressive worship. We may feel that we are worshiping by singing the prescribed songs at the appointed time in the service because that's what we've always done, but in truth there is very little worship happening. Following a script requires little of ourselves or our hearts. We are going through the motions, but our spirits are not engaged in loving God. Worship is confined to what we did last Sunday and the Sunday before that and the same Sunday one year ago.

A commitment to adhere strictly to the customary worship protocol may mimic an experience that was meaningful at one time, but has since waned mechanical. Such an approach shuts the door on any opportunity the Holy Spirit may have to move us toward a deeper intimacy with God. Jesus described a similar situation, "These people honor me with their lips, but their hearts are far from me. They worship me in vain; their teachings are but rules taught by men" (Mark 7:6).

"These people honor me with their lips, but their hearts are far from me. They worship me in vain; their teachings are but rules taught by men" (Mark 7:6).

Third, where the belief system of parochialism is tied to a physical church building, we can barricade ourselves into the thought pattern that whatever goes on inside the building equals worship. In other words, as long as we are regularly on the premises, then we are fulfilling our worship quota. After all, if God is in the building, and we are in the building, then we are fellowshipping with God, right?

It is so easy for us to allow the symbols of our faith—buildings, stained glass windows, pipe organs, multi-million dollar sanctuaries, state-of-the-art audio-visual systems—to become the idols of our faith, even substitutes for our faith. I touched on this in the chapters on the strongholds of religion and pride also. When the accouterments of worship become high places, God takes a back seat and eventually leaves the building altogether.

Jesus addressed this tendency of ours when he spoke to the Samaritan woman, declaring:

> Believe me, woman, a time is coming when you will worship the Father neither on this mountain nor in Jerusalem. Yet a time is coming and has now come when the true worshipers will worship the Father in spirit and truth, for they are the kind of worshipers the Father seeks. God is spirit, and his worshipers must worship in spirit and in truth (John 4:21, 23-24).

Finally, because parochialism celebrates the accomplishments of people, it can lull us into thinking that we are self-sufficient and self-contained, that we can be the church on our own, without interference from the outside. We can generate lots of activity and celebrate lots of successes and really think that we are doing great things for God, when in fact his Presence is completely void from the whole process. Parochialism builds a fortress around our feats, exploits and triumphs. God is outside the wall, waiting to be invited in while we are inside, marching in a self-congratulatory parade behind the team mascot because we are so proud to be carrying the institutional torch. This is the scene at many denominational conferences and conventions where boards and agencies brandish how much money they have raised or how many people they have helped, and the whole affair is a testimony to institutional prowess.

King David learned about flaunting his resources in 2 Samuel 24. During a time of peace, David decided to count the number of men in his army for no other reason than to take pride in his military might. Nine months later, no sooner than the numbers were in, David was "conscience stricken," saying to the Lord, "I have sinned greatly in what I have done" (2 Samuel 24:10). God reprimanded David and the people severely for focusing on their own greatness instead of on him.

From every angle, parochialism is a prison. The boundaries we draw in self-protection confine us, keeping us separated from the rest of the body of Christ and often the Presence of God as well. It not only insulates us, but isolates us. I believe this attitude of independence is what Paul was referring to when he addressed the Christians in Corinth regarding the Lord's Supper:

> Therefore, whoever eats the bread or drinks the cup of the Lord in an unworthy manner will be guilty of sinning against the body and blood of the Lord. For anyone who eats and drinks without recognizing the body of the Lord eats and drinks judgment on himself. That is why many among you are weak and sick, and a number of you have fallen asleep (1 Corinthians 11:27, 29-30).

Could it be that as the body of Christ we are "weak and sick," unable to transform our neighborhoods, because we are not properly "recognizing the body of the Lord?" Maybe we acknowledge certain parts of the family but disregard others because we disagree with their style of worship or are offended by some point of their theology. Perhaps we are afraid that somehow intermingling with others will threaten who we are or dilute our own identity. Actually, the opposite is true. As Christians we most reflect the glory of God that was so evident in Jesus when we are worshiping together, loving and serving in one accord.

The Stronghold of Unity

I was in Lauderdale, Mississippi not too long ago and visited a Civil War cemetery. On top of a hill overlooking the neatly arranged lines of gravestones was the site of a hospital that had treated the wounded from both sides of the battle. I was deeply impacted as I walked through row after row, realizing that Confederate soldiers and Union soldiers, who had fought bitterly while they were alive, were now buried there side by side. Death had brought them peacefully together.

Heaven has no fences—no flags to distinguish the north from the south, no railroad tracks to divide the haves from the have nots, no campaign slogans to set apart the Democrats from the Republicans.

Likewise, there are no separate worship sections around the throne for Methodists or Episcopalians, those who speak in tongues or those who don't, those who sprinkle or those who dunk. In heaven, all will bow to the magnificent glory of Christ Jesus. Side by side we will worship, even those who refused to take communion together in this life. In the light of eternity, our defense of time-honored traditions and denominational sanctities will have netted us absolutely nothing.

God did send his Son into the world to divide mankind; Jesus' life and message drew a clear line between those who would believe and those who refused to believe, those who would spend an eternity with him and those who would not. While his desire is that all men be saved (1 Timothy 2:4), the truth of the gospel demands that this distinction be made so that salvation is an individual choice. John the Baptist explained that Jesus' mission was to separate the wheat from the chaff (Matthew 3:12).

God's redemption plan contained only one crucifixion, one resurrection, one atonement and one covenant.

However, God's redemption plan contained only one crucifixion, one resurrection, one atonement and one covenant. That covenant was ratified through Jesus' blood and is available to all who receive it through grace. On the grace side of the line, there is no division for those in Christ. "For we were all baptized by one Spirit into one body—whether Jews or Greeks, slave or free—and we were all given the one Spirit to drink" (1 Corinthians 12:13). Again Paul writes, "There is one body and one Spirit—just as you were called to one hope when you were called—one Lord, one faith, one baptism; one God and Father of all, who is over all and through all and in all (Ephesians 4:4-6).

Parochialism must be an abomination to God because it

presumes to own exclusive rights to the covenant. Our attitudes of superiority with regard to institutional affiliation are foolishly arrogant when we consider how small our contribution to the covenant agreement, and how inconsequential our efforts would be were it not for God's willingness to contribute the other 99 percent. For us to receive the gift of a saving relationship with Jesus Christ, and then to imagine that we somehow are more worthy or deserving of that precious covenant than another, is audacious and imprudent.

Jesus' Prayer

The heart of God and the mind of Christ for the church under the new covenant is that we live out a stronghold of unity. We know this because Jesus outlined it clearly in his longest recorded prayer in John 17, shortly before his time on earth was drawing to a close.

Jesus starts the prayer from his own heart, just as a son looks to his father for strength and encouragement. He prays for himself regarding the excruciating ordeal he is about to undergo, "Father, the time has come. Glorify your Son, that your Son may glorify you" (John 17:1b). Then he turns his attention to the 12 men closest to him, those with whom he has shared most intimately throughout his life and ministry, his disciples. He asks his Father to protect them when he is gone, saying, "I will remain in the world no longer, but they are still in the world, and I am coming to you. Holy Father, protect them by the power of your name—the name you gave me—so that they may be one as we are one" (John 17:11).

Finally, Jesus concludes his prayer by praying for the rest of his bride, all believers:

> I pray also for those who will believe in me through their message, that all of them may be one, Father, just as you are in me and I am in you. May they also be in us so that the

world may believe that you have sent me. I have given them the glory that you gave me, that they may be one as we are one: I in them and you in me. May they be brought to complete unity to let the world know that you sent me and have loved them even as you have loved me. Father, I want those you have given me to be with me where I am, and to see my glory, the glory you have given me because you loved me before the creation of the world (John 17: 20-24).

This prayer should leave no room for us to question Jesus' intent about how we are to relate to our brothers and sisters in him. His desire is that we would live in complete unity and oneness of spirit, in the same way that he and his Father are one in spirit.

Think about the situation here. Jesus is about to be crucified and buried before returning to heaven. He is, in essence, saying goodbye to his closest friends after years of traveling and ministering together. He knows what faces them once he's gone—persecution, difficulty and the small task of saving the world. I can imagine that there might be a lot of things he could have prayed about, but I find it interesting that he focused so deliberately on one thing—unity. He didn't just mention it once or twice, but four times he asked his Father that his disciples, and all of his followers, be one. It must have been really, really important to him.

His glory in us is the fruit of the divine stronghold.

Notice also that Jesus prayed unity over us for a specific purpose—so that the world would believe in him, and believe that he was sent by God. He also affirms that our unity will be a testimony to the rest of the world of his love. The bottom line throughout Jesus' prayer is ultimately that we bring glory to him which in turn brings glory back to the Father.

He is the Most High God and the only one deserving of that honor and position. When we as believers truly act like the family of God, demonstrating his love among us, we become shining beacons of his glory. His glory in us is the fruit of the divine stronghold.

The apostle Paul reinforces Jesus' prayer by giving us a perfect illustration of how we should act toward one another:

> The body is a unit, though it is made up of many parts; and though all its parts are many, they form one body. So it is with Christ. If the whole body were an eye, where would the sense of hearing be? If the whole body were an ear, where would the sense of smell be? But in fact God has arranged the parts in the body, every one of them, just as he wanted them to be. The eye cannot say to the hand, "I don't need you!" And the head cannot say to the feet, "I don't need you!" But God has combined the members of the body and has given greater honor to the parts that lacked it, so that there should be no division in the body, but that its parts should have equal concern for each other. If one part suffers, every part suffers with it; if one part is honored, every part rejoices with it (1 Corinthians 12:12, 17-18, 21, 24b-26).

As part of the body, we are, whether we like it or not, related by rebirth to the rest of the body. We can not say to some part of the body, "We don't need you!" just because we may not understand or agree with some aspect of their worship to God. It is not our job to question or put on trial other parts of our own body—that is only for God to do. As the creator, he is the one who knows the inner workings of the body, and how the parts are intricately knit together. Compared to his, our perspective is trivial and incomplete. Our personal beliefs and small-minded thinking don't any more define the body of Christ than your big toe could define you by believing itself to be an entire person.

Bound by Covenant

So what does unity as a corporate stronghold look like? Let's return to the idea of covenant. As recipients of God's abundant covenant provisions, we are compelled by the grace we have received to extend the same covenant terms to other believers.

Biblical covenant was a serious thing, more profound in some ways than even a marriage commitment or a legal contract. In the Old Testament, we know that when two parties entered into a covenant relationship, it was binding until death. And to break a covenant vow, one might pay with his life (Genesis 15). Think about all that we have access to through the new covenant in Jesus, and how that should motivate us to take on the mind of Christ toward others.

The covenant ritual included several symbolic gestures. For example, the two parties exchanged coats as a symbol of taking on one another's identity. Their names became synonymous. No longer did they think independently, but as though their lives were commingled. This meant that no longer was either life more important than the other, and competition was no longer an option, because all that belonged to one, also belonged to the other. Their resources, their reputations, their property was all unified under the terms of the covenant.

As a church, "exchanging coats" with other churches means that we will not promote our own name above others in the community. We will lift up one name only—Jesus. Our identities are connected, so our hearts will rejoice over their successes and mourn over their hardships. We will no longer think as separatists, but as members of the team, equipped and commissioned to play a role in reaching our community with the gospel. If another church needs money to repair their parking lot, we will take up a special offering. If they need workers to help paint the building, we will roll up our sleeves and show up with brushes. In covenant, we are now one, so what affects one of us, affects us all.

Exchanging coats also leads to what I call the "open pantry" principle: whatever we have in our pantry as a church that is good, we want to share it with other churches. Likewise, whatever they have in their pantry, we want to make use of. Rather than locking the pantry door, the belief system of unity says that what's mine is yours and what's yours is mine. Combining our resources and talents only makes us more efficient and effective. As churches, we all benefit when the pantry doors are open.

Another part of the covenant ritual was to exchange weapons as a symbol of mutual protection. This act was a pledge to fight for each other, and to come to each other's defense against any enemy or adversity, no matter the cost. If one was attacked, the other would rush to join the battle. If one became weak or vulnerable, the other would offer shelter and help. Parties in covenant promised to defend each other as if they were defending their own lives.

When we "exchange weapons" with other churches, we vow to help and protect, not tear down or destroy. That means if another church in our community comes under some kind of verbal attack, we will be there to defend and support them. We will even put our own reputation on the line to help preserve theirs. If another church is damaged by fire or storms, we will be the first on the scene to help clean up and rebuild. Anything we have, we will give until they are back on their feet, fully recovered, strong and healthy.

One of the most repugnant things to me about parochialism is to watch churches prey like vultures on another church's hardship, self-righteously mocking their failure and then unscrupulously taking advantage of their vulnerability by stealing their sheep. Watching the headlines today and the way that Christian churches respond to and deal with pastors who fall into personal crises, I have concluded that we know very little about grace and even less about our job as members of one body, one baptism, one Lord and one hope that Paul wrote about. I have seen so much pain and destruction in this area, both for pastoral families and for the people they shepherd; church scandal just seems to be an accelerant to the carnal strongholds.

However, in a divine stronghold of unity, when we are in

covenant together, if another pastor in our community falls, we will cover him, encourage him, and support him in the healing process until he and his family are completely restored. He is our brother, one of the family, and also one of God's anointed, and therefore we will not turn our backs.

We will not exploit another church's weakness by luring in their members in the wake of a crisis. Instead, we will do all we can to see that the church and its congregation are renewed in the Holy Spirit and reinstated to their unique and valuable place in the body of Christ. When the world sees us guarding and upholding one another like this, they say, "God's love must be real; look at how the Christians love and serve one another!"

Another covenant ritual in the Old Testament was for the parties to cut their hands or wrists and then press them together so that their blood intermingled. This was one of the most important symbols in the covenant ceremony because the spilling of blood was very meaningful in that culture.

Blood represented and emboddied life; that is why the Jews did not eat the blood of animals. It was also the basis for the blood sacrifice of animals on the altar, and ultimately for Christ's blood sacrifice on the cross for our salvation. In order for a sacrifice to be effective payment for sin, blood had to be spilled.

The idea that the parties' blood was now mixed was a sign that they had exchanged lives; each one's life now flowed through the other. Nothing, no circumstance, no passage of time, no action on either one's part could reverse or cancel the blood covenant. The scars served as permanent reminders.

When we give in to parochialism and act like God's covenant is only with us and no one else, we are disputing the worth and reach of Jesus' blood sacrifice. Doing so invites a pall of spiritual lifelessness to rest on our church. I sometimes wonder if this kind of shroud of carnal thinking is what makes so many churches look, feel and smell the same—dark, musty and stale.

Parochialism is the death reaper. That's why Jesus was so passionate in prayer that his bride be unified; he knew that disunity would make her weak and crippled, a mere shadow of what she was designed to be.

As co-heirs in the blood covenant of the cross, we are living exchanged lives, each church an expression of the life of Jesus pulsing through its body. His scars should remind us that we are forever connected, each an inextricable part of the other, bound tightly together to the cross and all washed clean by the very same blood that trickled down Jesus' wounded head and side. It wasn't metaphorical blood; it was physically real, salty, red, warm blood which became the single and narrow gateway through which all of mankind could enter heaven.

...we are forever connected, each an inextricable part of the other, bound tightly together to the cross...

The final part of the covenant ceremony was a meal shared together, which brings us back to communion. The communion meal ratified the covenant, much like a notary's seal would validate a document as official and binding. The sacrament of communion that we practice in church now is both a reminder and a celebration of the miracle of redemption through the covenant. Our attitude toward it should be nothing less than total and sincere gratitude. There is simply no place for pride or discrimination at the Lord's table.

When the disciples met in the Upper Room for their last meal together, Jesus, knowing that Judas had already set his arrest in motion, still made a place for him at the table and even washed his feet, right along with the other disciples' feet. If anyone was unworthy to partake of that first communion meal, it was Judas. Yet Jesus knew that Judas's worthiness was not the issue; the new covenant that he was about to establish would be based on his worthiness. And he is most worthy. If Jesus could serve communion to Judas, that leaves little room for us to deny it to others.

When I was pastoring in College Station, Texas years ago, I became friends with one of the Catholic priests there, Father John. He was young and very appealing to the many Catholic college students in town; therefore his church was full of them.

After talking one day we decided to do something pretty bold—we would combine services on two different Sundays. He would bring his people over and preach in my pulpit one Sunday, and the following week I would take my congregation to his church and preach in his pulpit. For many of my members, it was the first time they had ever experienced a Catholic mass. And for many of his parishioners, it was the first time they had ever attended a Protestant worship service.

When I preached in his church, at the start of the service I had asked the ushers to distribute among all the people pieces to a puzzle depicting the face of Jesus. In my sermon, I explained that each of us had a small piece of what Jesus looks like, and told them that they should all mingle around and try to put the puzzle together.

They just looked at me. Some laughed. With hundreds of people in the room, each holding one small piece, there was no way they could have accomplished the task. So then I suggested that in order to form the picture, we would really need the Holy Spirit's help. He is the only one who can bring us together so that all the pieces fit just right and the picture comes through.

At the end of the service, in a profound gesture of unity and love, Father John and his associates served the entire congregation communion. I knew how significant it was for him to serve the covenant meal to non-Catholics. When he came to me and held out the bread and wine for me to take, I said to him, "Father John, you don't have to do this. You could face charges or disciplinary action." He just looked at me and asked, "Terry, what would Jesus do?" It was a powerful moment. To achieve unity as a stronghold within our churches and communities, we must ask that question.

Another remarkable experience I had of corporate unity happened during one of our prayer conferences in a large United Methodist church in Montgomery, Alabama several years ago. I was speaking on Friday night to a group of about 500 representing a wide array of denominations and ethnic backgrounds. It was one of the most diverse groups of that size we have ever had, in fact.

Toward the end of my message, I felt the Holy Spirit impress upon me to do something I had never done at a conference like that before—have a foot washing. The theme of the conference centered around city-wide prayer, revival and unity, so to wash a few of the pastor's feet seemed like a vivid way to demonstrate the kind of servanthood and humility necessary to bring down some walls and build bridges. So I asked a couple of ushers to get me some bowls and towels.

As I began to wash the feet of one of the African American pastors in town, publicly repenting and asking forgiveness for remnants of prejudice that still lingered there in Montgomery, even within the body of Christ, the whole thing broke wide open. Other pastors began seeking out colleagues with whom they had conflicts, and they washed each other's feet. Baptists, Charismatics, Lutherans, Episcopalians, Nazarenes, Pentecostals, you name it—so many got involved that people were lined up waiting to use the bowls. To this day, it is still one of the most moving ministry moments I've ever been a part of.

Spiritual Transformation

When it catches hold, the stronghold of unity can play a role in literally transforming entire cities and even regions with the gospel. As the body of Christ, particularly here in the United States, I don't think we have any idea just how powerful our influence could be if we were truly "one" as Jesus prayed. We don't know because we have never seen. And we have little vision.

George Otis Jr. and the Sentinel Group have done their best to give us a vision of large scale renewals through their series of DVDs on community transformation. In the sequence of documentaries, they relate several stories of areas that have been radically changed by the gospel message being transmitted through the body of Christ working and praying together. One region they turned their cameras on is the Fiji Islands; another is the nation of Uganda.[3]

I don't think we have any idea just how powerful our influence could be if we were truly "one" as Jesus prayed.

In the year 2000, at the height of a crucial social and political upheaval, the nation of Fiji began to experience an astonishing spiritual revival. It was astonishing to the locals who had suffered through more than ten years of ethnic tensions, violence, corruption, widespread drug addictions, even suicides. And it was astonishing to Christians from all over the world who heard the story, many of whom flocked to the Islands to see and hear for themselves the testimonies of signs and wonders that had turned hopelessness into joy.

In an address to the Transform World conference in Jakarta, Indonesia in May, 2005, Pastor Ratu Epeli Kanaimawi, Vice President of the Association of Christian Churches in Fiji, explained first hand how and why the revival came about. The following is an excerpt from his report:

> In this lowest point in the islands' history, the mainly Christian population turned to God for help, choosing 2 Chronicles 7:14 as their motto. Everyone prayed, from the members of Fijian high society down to the loneliest villager. Many prayer groups formed in government offices throughout the islands, and tribal leaders and chiefs encouraged their followers to pray. The whole nation prayed to God, and the leaders of the faith put aside their differences, seeking unity. By May 2001, fourteen church leaders followed the call,

joining the President of the Methodist Church on the Fiji Islands to discuss ways of cooperating.

Previously, the churches and denominations had kept each other at arm's length because of theological differences. The putsch in May 2000 created just the right atmosphere for the churches to approach each other, and was God's timing for making the impossible possible.

The Association of Christian Churches in Fiji (ACCF) was officially founded by President Ratu Josefa Iloilovatu Uluivuda on 8th July 2001. It has four aims:

- Uniting all churches
- Putting God's way of love into practice
- Establishing God-fearing leaders
- Reconciliation in Fiji, to create peace and prosperity

God answered his people's prayers, giving the Fiji Islands a new government and leadership. A new political party won a dramatic victory in the 2001 elections; all previous leaders disappeared from the political stage almost overnight, and a new government under Prime Minister Laisenia Qarase took over the reins.

Pastor Kanaimawi went on to explain how both the President and Prime Minister humbly and publicly repented for their actions, and began working toward national reconciliation and unity. The Prime Minister also boldly confessed his faith in God before a crowd of 10,000 people, dedicating himself and his ministry to the "King of kings." The nation is still reaping the fruit of the spiritual renewal in tangible ways including a growing number of jobs, decreasing unemployment and booming building and tourism industries. [4]

If it is difficult for you to believe that transformation can really happen on such a grand scale, just ask the people of Uganda. Victimized by decades of tyranny under such rulers as Idi Amin and Milton Obote, and oppressed by the raging AIDS epidemic, both of which wiped out countless thousands of their family members, friends and neighbors, they will tell you, "Yes, it can." Ugandan pastor, Jackson Senyonga, founder of the 22,000 member Christian Life Church in the nation's capital city of Kampala, shared his own testimony of how and why the revival came. It is a similar story:

> In Uganda, we got our revival through devastation. The suffering of the people was beyond description, and no one came to our rescue. But God used that opportunity to lead a nation from a spiritual coma to a transformation state.
>
> A remnant of believers went in to the jungle. They gathered in underground caves. In desperation they prayed, "Lord, we don't know what to do. But you know." These people prayed continuously. They prayed desperate, deep, consistent, groaning prayers that never took no for an answer. They prayed, not for one month, one year, or five years, but until they got a breakthrough.
>
> Today, researchers say Uganda is one of the most transformed nations on the face of the earth. We've seen God transform the political system, the marketplace, and the church. We have been enjoying the presence of God everywhere.[5]

In a Christian Broadcasting Network interview, Pastor Senyonga explained that they used to see spiritual breakthroughs on the church and community level, but as they came together in unity in the body of Christ, they saw national breakthroughs. It wasn't quick or easy; the pastors and their people had to refuse to be offended. He said, "Unity is more than having a crusade together; it takes a revelation of God to strike hearts in tangible ways, causing a need for each other. Because of the intensity of the spiritual darkness over a city, one man or one church cannot handle it. But when there is unity in the Body, the spiritual strongholds cannot withstand the combined strength."[6]

As evidenced in the revival stories of both Fiji and Uganda, spiritual transformation requires two ingredients: unity and prayer. By God's design, as individual churches we are simply not equipped to affect far-comprehensive change. We were conceived and fashioned to be part of a larger body, significant in our own way, yet interdependent with other parts.

> *We were conceived and fashioned to be part of a larger body, significant in our own way, yet interdependent with other parts.*

Unfortunately, the stronghold of unity is often the result of hardship. In both Fiji and Uganda, the churches were driven together through years of pain and suffering, during which minor theological differences lost significance in comparison to the widespread physical, emotional and spiritual anguish of the people. The more oppressive affliction becomes, the less energy is available to devote to causes other than the most basic needs of safety and survival. It is under these kinds of circumstances that unity often thrives.

Here in the United States, where religious freedoms are almost as limitless as our resources, we have little outside motivation to cooperate. As a result, for us, unity must be a conscious choice we make to correctly discern the body of Christ. We must change our systems of thinking to reflect the mind of Christ toward his bride. Once the stronghold of unity begins to grow in a church, it can become a "convening church" in its community, drawing other churches together and facilitating relationships between different parts of the body. This is how unity spreads, gradually pushing the edges of the stronghold out to encompass more and more congregations. The bigger the circle grows, the more far-reaching its influence can be.

Lord, we have sinned and we deserve the conse-
quences; we have been addicted to thinking that has
made us sick. Yet in your grace you looked on us with
compassion; you forgave, healed, and set us free. We
are saved by grace, and in its fullness, we have received
one blessing after another. Now make us a divine
stronghold of grace that the world may be saved.
(Mark 6:34; Ephesians 2:8; John 1:16; Luke 19:10).

6

JUDGMENT VS GRACE

I have told this story before, but it was an incident that so deeply affected me that it is worth repeating here. It was one of those experiences that left an indelible impression on my mind and forever impacted my most fundamental attitudes regarding ministry and church culture.

Years ago a young high school football player that my son knew was killed in a tragic car accident. The boy, whom I will call John, was driving to work, lost control of his car and flipped it over. He died almost instantly. The event shook the small Dallas suburb where the young man had grown up and gone to school. Since his family had lived there most of John's life, the boy had a lot of friends and was very popular.

Grieving and confused, the family began making funeral arrangements. They had never attended church regularly so they asked me if I would perform the service, and then began calling around to find a church. They were discouraged to find however, that every church they called in their hometown said the same thing: "We're sorry for your loss, but we can't offer the use of our building to non-members." Finally, they found a church about 40 miles from their home that would, for a fee, allow them to hold their son's funeral in their sanctuary.

When we arrived at the church, a maintenance person let us in, showed us where the thermostat was, and then left, saying he would be back in a couple of hours to lock up. No one else from the church was there. The family had not made any arrangements for a musician, but instead had brought a small portable stereo which crooned a couple of country songs—John's favorites— from the pulpit area.

As I stood up and looked out across a sea of several hundred teenagers, I felt burdened and embarrassed—burdened by their blank stares that told me many of them, like John, were not regular church goers and probably had never experienced the comfort of a personal relationship with Jesus Christ, and embarrassed as a representative of the church which had so shamefully pushed this family further and further down the road during the most vulnerable time in their lives. What an opportunity to minister love to a room full of lost and hurting people. How could so many churches have turned them away?

As William Temple once said, the Church is one of the only institutions that exists for the sake its of non-members.[1] Our mission and purpose on this earth is to reach out to people who aren't a part of what we do and who don't understand what we are all about. Church is not—or shouldn't be—a rotary club or any other kind of fraternity with a members-only philosophy that is content to keep outsiders on the outside.

Self-Righteous Spirit

While the stronghold of parochialism all too often defines our relationship to other churches and believers, the stronghold of judgment frequently sets the tone for our interactions with non-believers or those who don't attend church. While we should be welcoming the lost and seeking to share God's love with them, we often do just the opposite, shutting them out with disapproving looks and critical comments. Instead of simply listening and loving, we evaluate. Instead of offering grace, we offer advice. Instead of forgiving, we condemn. As a result, the unchurched in our communities feel tried and convicted instead of welcomed and accepted.

Judgmentalism masquerades as a lot of different things in church society: confronting sin, speaking the truth in love, discipling, sharing prayer requests and sometimes counseling. We don't like to think of ourselves as judgmental; we prefer the terms "discerning" or "perceptive." We have a hard time coming to grips with the truth. Like all the other strongholds, we can live in denial because the mindset has been there so long that it feels justified, even spiritual. We think we are right, and it feels so good to know so much and be so mature in our own walk with the Lord that we can readily see the faults of others. Since we are so wise in our own eyes, we dub ourselves quality control agents, dedicated to protecting the image and reputation of our church congregation from contamination.

...it feels so good to know so much and be so mature in our own walk with the Lord that we can readily see the faults of others.

It is this self-righteousness spirit—our delusion that we are less sinful than the people "out there" just because we fill a pew on Sunday mornings—that drives the stronghold of judgment. We focus attention on the flaws of other people because it makes us feel better about ourselves. And we're really good at it! Just consider how we can minimize our own weaknesses by creating a "sliding scale" of sinful behaviors:

"I know I yell at my kids sometimes, but I would never hit one."

"I probably look at some images on websites that I shouldn't, but I would never be one of those pornography junkies."

"I occasionally spend more money on my credit cards than I should, but I would never run our family into serious financial debt."

"I may be a little overweight, but at least I don't smoke. I would never do that."

"Sure, I flirt a little at the office, but I would never actually cheat on my wife."

"I admit I'm not always completely honest on my tax returns...after all, it's just the IRS. But I would never embezzle money from my job."

Until I started writing about this, I had never really noticed how often I hear that phrase "I would never," and how often I say it myself. But one evening recently, as I sat in a busy restaurant watching the people around me, I became acutely aware of some of my own judgmental attitudes. I realized I was making some pretty "unspiritual" evaluations based on people's appearance, the company they were with, and their social habits. If I'm capable of passing judgment in a restaurant, I know I'm just as capable of doing it in church, even from the pulpit. Lord, help me.

What is your "I would never"? I think that phrase is a key identifier to the belief system behind the stronghold of judgment. As we go through life and see all kinds of abuse, perversion, dishonesty and violence around us, it's so easy to use the yardstick of comparison to keep us from feeling uncomfortable with our own faults. The self-righteous spirit enables us to look around and conclude, "I may not be perfect, but I sure am better than him, so I'm not going to worry about it much."

The Control Tower

At the George Bush Intercontinental Airport in Houston, there are two control towers: the active one, which is one of the tallest ones in the country, completed in 2004, and the old one, which is now vacant, that sits at Terminal A. From the new tower, air traffic controllers manage the routes of the hundreds of planes that take off and land every day in Houston. Their weighty responsibility is to keep traffic flowing smoothly and efficiently, and to keep passengers safe. As soon as the newer tower was completed, the old one was shut off and locked, because one could only imagine the confusion and danger that would be caused if someone were to sneak in and occupy the controls of the second tower, sending conflicting information to the pilots.

When we set ourselves up in the Christian community as judge, we are actually setting ourselves up as idols because we are asserting equality to God. In doing so, we not only foolishly challenge God's sole authority in that role; we also create chaos and confusion on the landing strips of grace and mercy. When we judge, we are canceling the effects of the cross and imposing our own invented criteria of acceptance. We approve of only those who meet our requirements, and in doing so, usurp the mind of Christ with our own belief system. Judgment is a mental high place that competes with God as the sole and final adjudicator, making idols of human standards and beliefs that are esteemed in church systems and revered as sacred.

Our job is to reach out to non-believers in love and compassion. God's job is to render judgments. When our self-righteous attitudes become such a high place in our thinking that we lose sight of that, we are in danger of sabotaging the church's mission, bringing the full wrath of God's judgment on our own heads.

Our natural tendency to judge is energized by the flood of information we see on the news and internet every day because sin makes the headlines. And the juicier the story, the more we like to hear it. We are inundated with images and stories of the sordid lives of lawbreakers, criminals, liars and cheaters. A junior high coach is accused of molesting students. The university chancellor is accused of using school money to buy his home. A major corporate CEO is accused of lying to shareholders. We sit in front of the television and mentally stamp people guilty and deserving of punishment because they are so bad and it makes us feel good to be better (or at least know that we haven't been caught).

The stronghold of judgment is a corporate mindset in the church that controls who is acceptable and who is not, who gets in and who stays out. If you want to gain access, you have to qualify or at least pay the dues which we will determine based on our own biases, and which are subject to change at any time.

The stronghold of judgment is a corporate mindset in the church that controls who is acceptable and who is not, who gets in and who stays out.

We will ask you where you work (because it's nicer than asking how much you make) and whether or not you are married. We may notice any of, but not limited to, the following: how you are dressed, the length of your hair, the body parts you have pierced or your accent. And we might even check around to find out if you drink, smoke, cuss or bite your fingernails, or have any other undesirable habits which might reflect poorly on our membership, before we are willing to issue you a parking sticker.

Judgment is about exclusion—excluding all but those whom we choose—to ensure that there is at least one place in our world where we feel "in." It is insecurity in action. Yet the gospel theme of grace would say that there are no "outsiders" to God; it is his desire that all people should come to a saving knowledge of Christ Jesus and have the joy of living in relationship with him. Setting ourselves up in judgment diminishes that truth and is costly to God's purposes. Eugene Peterson states:

> The terrible price we pay for being insiders is a reduction of reality, a shrinkage of life. Nowhere is this price more terrible than when it is paid in the cause of religion. But religion has a long history of doing just that, of reducing the huge mysteries of God to the respectability of club rules, of shrinking the vast human community to a "membership."[2]

God's Elect

Nowhere do we see a clearer example of the corporate stronghold of judgment than in the Jews attitudes toward Gentiles in the Old Testament. As God's chosen people, the direct descendants of Abraham, Isaac and Jacob became the first recipients of his redemption plan. God entered into a special covenant relationship with them, and set them apart as a "kingdom of priests and a holy nation" (Exodus 19:6). The Bible tells us that God chose the Israelites not because they were more talented or more deserving than any other people group, but simply because he loved them (Deuteronomy 10:15).

The Gentiles, on the other hand, were the nations outside of Israel. As the Israelites lived out the covenant with God, the lines between them and the nations around them became clear. They were the "circumcised" and the "uncircumcised" (Exodus 34:10; Leviticus 28:24-25; Deuteronomy 25:6), the worshipers of Jehovah and the worshipers of idols. As the Israelites struggled to keep their identity in tact, falling often into temptation by the immorality of neighboring people, they tried to draw the lines even sharper. This sense of separation caused the Jews to look with disdain on Gentiles or anyone who was not circumcised and living according to the Law of Moses.

So great was their contempt, in fact, that it was said that if a Jew saw a Gentile woman giving birth, they were not to render aid because that would only serve to bring one more Gentile into the world. Jews were forbidden from associating with Gentiles in any way, which would explain why the Jewish religious leaders were appalled when Jesus entered their homes and even ate with them. By the time Jesus came, the Gentiles' social standing had reached an all time low. They were basically looked on as little better than criminals or wild animals.

But God's intent all along had been to extend his salvation covenant to every person on earth. When Peter went up on his roof to pray and God gave him the vision of sharing the gospel with Cornelius and his family (Acts 10), the lines between Jews and Gentiles were erased, although the stigma would not easily fade. The stronghold of judgment was so strong and entrenched in the minds of the Israelites that it was hard for them to accept the notion of the uncircumcised, pagan Gentiles being converted and sharing in their covenant inheritance. The stronghold of judgment likewise makes it difficult for us today to welcome and accept "pagans" into our church culture with a genuine spirit of love and compassion.

3-D

Where church life rubs up against the mores of our degenerate society, the belief system of judgment that kicks in is 3-D, or three dimensional: 1) lost people **deserve** to be where they are; 2) they are just too **different** from us to gain approval; 3) and meeting their needs would **demand** too much of our time and resources. These three D's could be described as the seed thoughts on which the stronghold of judgment forms.

As a pastor, I spent many counseling hours working to undo the damage done by Christians who had passed judgment on a non-believer by basically saying, "You wouldn't be in the mess you're in if it weren't for the sin in your life." Some take it a step further, rationalizing, "Why should I help you out of this situation that you've spent many years creating for yourself?" The general attitude is, "You get what you deserve and you deserve what you get." When we think this way, we can practice exclusivity without taking responsibility for it.

This facet of judgment is pretty easy to buy into because we are big on personal responsibility. We expect the people around us to be accountable for their actions, and we hope to instill that value into our children. But when it comes to the gospel and our witness to unbelievers, we have to have the mind of Christ, "But God demonstrates his own love for us in this: While we were still sinners, Christ died for us" (Romans 5:8). Jesus did not wait for us to be holy or cleaned up or deserving of his love; he loved us while we were still dirty and trapped in our sin. He made the ultimate gesture of love and acceptance before he ever knew whether or not we would respond. The grace and compassion of God must be extended with no strings attached.

Sin has consequences, but God does not give a baby cerebral palsy because the parents conceived out of wedlock. He does not allow a young wife and mother to be killed by a drunk driver because she has an addiction to prescription drugs. We have to be so careful with the "you brought this on yourself" philosophy, or worse yet, "God caused this to happen to you to teach you a lesson." These are dangerous attitudes that produce only negative results. None of us who are in Christ get what we really deserve; that is the beauty of mercy, grace and forgiveness. In him we are free from judgment and condemnation.

...without the conviction and guidance of the Holy Spirit..., life is just a dangerous and haphazard journey for which there is no map.

Until a person invites Jesus to be his personal savior, he really has no reason or motivation or even reference point for accountability. There is a reason why we call lost people lost— because without the conviction and guidance of the Holy Spirit and some God-centered foundation, life is just a dangerous and haphazard journey for which there is no map. Our judgmental attitude—pointing out their sin and saying "you brought this hardship on yourself"—does nothing to invite them into the Presence of God so he can show them the way.

Another seed thought that fuels the stronghold of judgment is our belief that unchurched people are just too different from us to be accepted. We size up someone who looks very different and dresses very different and lives a completely different lifestyle from us, and we assume that we have nothing in common.

We don't want to make the effort to relate, because it just seems too difficult. Besides, we wouldn't want to compromise our own reputation.

Not long ago Hollywood Presbyterian Church was in the news for starting a new service in a Los Angeles bar to try and reach out to a group that was pretty much on the cultural fringe. Advertising "Body Piercing for All," the service quickly drew over 300 people. On any given Sunday the pastoral staff had the opportunity to minister to drug addicts, abuse victims, prostitutes and the likes who found their way to the bar. The dress code was loose, the music was loud, and the teaching was radically simple.

Things seemed to be going well except for one thing: the two lead pastors had underestimated the influence of long-standing attitudes that thrived beneath the surface of his prestigious congregation. Some of the traditional membership simply couldn't handle being associated in any way with such riff raff, and they had them put on leave. The mindset had such a stronghold on the church and was so deeply ingrained that they undoubtedly prevailed in the argument by listing several logical sounding reasons why the service was detrimental to the church's overall vision. The people being reached out to were simply too different to be included in the elite Hollywood Presbyterian circle.[3]

Finally, judgment can grow from the idea that to welcome sinners in would simply demand too much. We look at the addiction or financial need or the messed up family situation, and we mentally calculate the cost of rehabilitation, concluding that the expense of time and resources wouldn't be worth it. We don't really want to have to sacrifice anything on their behalf, especially if it might make us uncomfortable in any way. The result is that we focus all of our assets as a church on each other; we invest ourselves in making sure that our church meets all of our needs. And those on the outside stay out.

The 3-D seed thoughts are supported by one of the characteristics shared by all the carnal strongholds—cognitive closure.

Just as we resist new ideas that might stretch our theology, we resist bringing in too many sinners that would stretch our grace comfort zone. Instead of opening the doors and reaching out to the lost, we retreat into lock down mode, shutting out anything and anyone that might disrupt the routine.

Let me summarize by highlighting what the Bible says about judging:

- It is not safe. "Do not judge, or you too will be judged. For in the same way you judge others, you will be judged, and with the measure you use, it will be measured to you. Why do you look at the speck of sawdust in your brother's eye and pay no attention to the plank in your own eye?" (Matthew 7:1-3).

- We are not qualified. In John 8, a woman caught in adultery is brought to Jesus to be sentenced and stoned. The law said she deserved to die for her sin. Jesus, however, had a different perspective. "If any one of you is without sin, let him be the first to throw a stone at her" (John 8:7). One by one, all the accusers walked away.

- It is not our job to judge. "Brothers, do not slander one another. Anyone who speaks against his brother or judges him speaks against the law and judges it. When you judge the law, you are not keeping it, but sitting in judgment on it. There is only one Lawgiver and Judge, the one who is able to save and destroy. But you—who are you to judge your neighbor?" (James 4:11-12)

- It gives the enemy a foothold. "Therefore each of you must put off falsehood and speak truthfully to his neighbor, for we are all members of one body. 'In your anger do not sin.' Do not let the sun go down while you are still angry, and do not give the devil a foothold. Do not let any unwholesome talk come out of your mouths, but only what is helpful for building others up according to their needs, that it may benefit those who listen. Be kind and compassionate to one another, forgiving each other, just as in Christ God forgave you" (Ephesians 4:25-27, 29, 32).

I believe that the corporate stronghold of judgment in the church today is a primary hurdle to our effectiveness in ministry, and the main reason we are doing more sheep shifting than we are soul-winning. As the church, we have acquired a reputation for throwing stones instead of offering grace. Those on the outside see us as unforgiving and snooty, if not self-righteous. Philip Yancey agrees:

> Mark Twain used to talk about people who were "good in the worst sense of the word," a phrase that, for many, captures the reputation of Christians today. Recently I have been asking a question of strangers—for example, seatmates on an airplane—when I strike up a conversation. "When I say the words 'evangelical Christian' what comes to mind?" In reply, mostly I hear political descriptions: of strident pro-life activists, or gay-rights opponents, or proposals for censoring the Internet. I hear references to the Moral Majority, an organization disbanded years ago. Not once—not once—have I heard a description redolent of grace. Apparently that is not the aroma Christians give off in the world.[4]

THE STRONGHOLD OF GRACE

"If I hadn't have come here I would probably be in jail by now still involved in gangs." That's what 17 year old Manuel said when asked what the Dream Center means to him. After being in and out of jail several times, and eventually getting kicked out of his public high school, Manuel realized he needed to make some changes in his life or face a very dismal future. Like hundreds of others, he found his way to the Dream Center and discovered acceptance, help and hope.

Founded in 1996 by Pastors Tommy and Matthew Barnett, father and son pastoral team, the Dream Center was established in the heart of the Los Angeles inner city in the abandoned Queen of Angels hospital. The 360,000 square foot facility with over 1,000 rooms in nine buildings sits just two miles from Hollywood. The mission of the center is to meet the physical and spiritual needs of some of LA's most disadvantaged residents by providing food, clothing, shelter, drug and life rehabilitation, education and job training. And with over 200 different outreach ministries, the effects are dramatic.

The mobile food truck delivers up to 4 tons of food each week to feed over 30,000 people. The Adopt-a-Block program sends 600 volunteers out each Saturday armed with rakes, trash bags, footballs and smiles to reach out to another 30,000 people with tangible, servant-hearted love. Due in part to the relationships developed through this ministry, thousands of men, women and children are bused in for each of the center's 40 weekly church services.

The Dream Center's Hope for Homeless Youth ministry reaches over 2,000 hurting youth who live in abandoned buildings and dumpsters throughout the city, with more than 30 different outreach efforts that operate weekly. Every afternoon, Metro Kidz holds sidewalk Sunday school in both English and Spanish in neighborhoods across the area. And currently over 500 men, women and youth are housed at the center in the Discipleship Program, an intensive one-year, resident, work-discipline program for those serious about escaping the pattern of destructive choices and turning their lives around.

As a result of the Dream Center's commitment to ministering grace and compassion in inner city Los Angeles over the past decade, prostitution, rape, gang activity and homicides have all decreased dramatically, earning recognition and praise from the mayor, city council and President Bush.

The big numbers and remarkable results are impressive, but

the real testimonies to what the Dream Center means are in the lives of people like Manuel, and 16 year-old Ana. Ana had the potential to be a good student at Reseda public high school until she too was drawn into a gang. The gang ties led to fighting and drugs, and Ana's grades started to plummet. She often skipped school, and on the days when she did go, she seldom lasted through half the day before a fight erupted and she was sent home. Her father was desperate and decided something had to change.

He had heard about the Dream Center, which accepts individuals into their programs even if they can't afford to pay, and he enrolled Ana in the center's Academy. Though she struggled with the drastic change in lifestyle at first, she eventually adjusted and is now one of the Academy's top students. The stable environment of grace, acceptance, discipline and love helped Ana develop a new and meaningful relationship with Jesus Christ and redirect her life. The Presence made the difference for Ana.

The Presence made the difference for Ana.

The Dream Center is a shining example of a church living out of the stronghold of grace. It embodies everything that I have defined a corporate divine stronghold to be—exemplifying an aspect of the mind of Christ to such a degree that they are totally surrendered to it, and everything they do flows out from it.

The stronghold didn't happen by accident. What started as a typical local church grew to what it is now because of a vision God had placed in Matthew Barnett's heart to impact an entire city. He wanted the Dream Center to be a place where people would find a relationship with Jesus through very tangible, hands-on outreach. He wanted to offer grace. On the wheels of that vision, the church grew rapidly from 39 members at its conception to the thousands it has today. From the beginning, Pastor Barnett established patterns of thinking, attitudes and expectations consistent with the grace and compassion of Jesus, and the deep ruts of that belief system are etched into the very identity of the Dream Center and its people.[5]

In a Presence based atmosphere, where grace flows freely out from a church to non-believers, the visible fruit is salvation:

"For the grace of God that brings salvation has appeared to all men" (Titus 2:11).

"...it is through the grace of our Lord Jesus that we are saved..." (Acts 15:11).

Saving Grace

Grace is the open, no-strings-attached invitation to sinners to come as they are into the Presence of God where they can be helped and healed. Grace does not judge, exclude or calculate cost; it opens its doors without reproach to anyone who will come. By its very nature, grace has nothing to do with the recipient, and everything to do with the giver. It was seen and experienced in its purest form in Jesus Christ, who personified grace as it is in the Father's heart—boundless, unconditional and radically blind.

The stronghold of grace is a resounding trumpet that bids humanity into the spacious lap of God, and to a divine moment of repentance and salvation orchestrated by the Holy Spirit. This type of grace—saving grace—is open-ended, meaning that the recipient has the freedom to enter or pass by, stay or leave, accept or reject. It is offered without expectation and given without restraint.

The story of the prodigal son's return home is a word picture of the manner of grace God wishes to extend to the lost:

But while he was still a long way off, his father saw him and was filled with compassion for him; he ran to his son, threw his arms around him and kissed him. The son said to him, "Father, I have sinned against heaven and against you. I am no longer worthy to be called your son."

But the father said to his servants, "Quick! Bring the best robe and put it on him. Put a ring on his finger and sandals on his feet. Bring the fattened calf and kill it. Let's have a feast and celebrate. For this son of mine was dead and is alive again; he was lost and is found." So they began to celebrate (Luke 15:20-24).

The lovesick father didn't make his lost son explain why he smelled like pigs, or where he had been since he left home, or even what had happened to all the money he had obviously squandered. He didn't demand an apology or a promise of lessons learned. He simply placed the best robe around his neck, a ring on his finger, and sandals on his feet—all indicating his status in the household as master as opposed to slave—and then prepared a feast and celebration.

If there was a time for reckoning for the young son, it was later, after the party guests had gone home, and after he was cleaned and rested and settled back in with the family. I wouldn't be surprised if at some point his father sat him down for a father-son talk about choices, responsibility, consequences and commitment. With any loving parent, this would have been expected. But the boy's homecoming, the moment that he came walking up the road dirty, hungry and destitute, was marked with grace, unconditional and extravagant.

You see, grace is not to be confused with discipleship. They are two different things. Discipleship requires commitment and sacrifice; it costs the recipient something. It is the process we all embark on as Christians by which we are molded to the likeness of Jesus. And the church plays a big role in that process by providing a safe place for teaching, training and accountability. Discipleship, like grace, can be either accepted or rejected, but when we accept it, we must be willing to pay the price for it to be effective in our lives.

Grace, on the other hand, costs the recipient nothing. It is a free gift from God to us, his creation. It is the fishing line of salvation, undeserved, unearned, yet offered unreservedly to all who will partake. Grace gives liberally and asks nothing in return. Can it be taken advantage of? Most certainly! And for that reason many churches excuse themselves from extending grace to non-believers, fearing that their generosity might be exploited. But Jesus never taught us to feed only those who could afford to pay, or clothe only those who would be grateful in return. No, his example shows us that if a man asks for our shirt we should give him our coat too (Luke 6:29-30). He showed the world pure grace—compassion, acceptance and forgiveness beyond measure—especially to the least, the last and the lost.

Churches have a way of distorting grace sometimes, offering a counterfeit that looks like the real thing, but in fact is a form of judgment cloaked in religious platitudes. This kind of "grace" says, "We will help you, but only if you can first prove that you are really in bad enough shape to deserve our investment, and that you will immediately get saved, join the church and start coming to Sunday school. However, if we find something about you that we don't like—you smoke cigarettes, have a live-in girlfriend, listen to country music or go to night clubs—we can't help you because we wouldn't want to condone your sinful lifestyle or waste discretionary funds on a lost cause."

If you're not edging your way out toward the end of the limb, putting yourself in a position of vulnerability..., then you're not offering pure grace.

I think this kind of help is no help at all, and it sends the wrong message about grace and Jesus' heart for the disenfranchised. If you're not edging your way out toward the end of the limb, putting yourself in a position of vulnerability to be hurt or taken advantage of, then you're not offering pure grace. The kind of grace Jesus demonstrated time and again isn't safe or logical; it's risky business. Sometimes it backfires. Yet when freely given, grace has the power to melt the hardest of hearts and draw men to repentance.

Gracepitality

Rudy Rasmus didn't grow up in church. In fact, he didn't even become a Christian until he was 34 years old. At that point in his life, gun-toting and street-wise, he was running a hotel in downtown Houston that rented rooms by the hour.

Just one year later, after a salvation experience that changed his life completely and a few seminary courses, Rudy knew he had been called to ministry. After 15 years of being a "purveyor of pain," he felt compelled now to help people. His pastor at the time sent him on a mission: go check out an abandoned church in downtown to see if it had any potential. When Rudy drove up and saw the worn old building casting its shadow on countless homeless people wandering the streets, he knew he was home.

With his pastor's support and blessing, Rudy and his wife Juanita began pouring themselves into St. John's United Methodist Church which quickly grew to be a lighthouse in the poverty and crime ravaged inner city. Their hearts were passionate to minister to modern day lepers, reaching out with the grace and compassion of Jesus. Rudy explains the church's vision in simple terms, "So now we have this church, and we serve the homeless and people with HIV. We don't try to fix 'em. We just love 'em. It's a heartwarming gig."

What goes on at St. John's every day is more than just heartwarming though. Like the Dream Center in Los Angeles, St. John's distributes nine tons of fresh produce each week to hungry families, in addition to serving over 6,000 hot meals to the homeless each month. The St. John's Academy is an early childhood education center that currently serves 125 children who were born infected with HIV/AIDS, developmentally delayed, and/ or pre-exposed to alcohol or drugs. And throughout the week, the church operates dozens of other outreach ministries that include counseling, addiction treatment, education, job training and medical services.

The unique atmosphere of equality and authenticity that

Pastor Rudy maintains has attracted thousands of members ranging from the very wealthy to the very poor. In fact, the church has grown to the status of megachurch, and is the spiritual home to members ranging from pop star Beyonce to the homeless.

Rudy describes his role as a "diversity manager." He says:

Imagine one of the wealthiest people you know sitting next to one of the poorest people you've ever met, and that's the picture. Entitlement doesn't stop at church doors. Folk who have a real sense of entitlement sometimes believe that influence should transcend the mission of the church. What I've found is that those folk don't hang around me long. That's the reality when they find that there is no special seating.

Not only is there no priority treatment for his wealthy or influential members, Rudy also attributes much of his success at bridging the class divide to the mandatory hugging that goes on in every church service. That's right, hugging. In his book, *Touch: The Power of Touch in Transforming Lives*, he explains that many homeless people go through every week without being looked in the eye by another person, much less touched. So when they come to church, he wants to make sure they experience that sense of touch and connectedness, in addition to the Presence of God. "Yeah, it's uncomfortable for a lot of folk," he admits, "but it has real meaning and real purpose."[6]

If I had to choose one word to sum up the missions of St. John's in Houston and the Dream Center in Los Angeles, and what they are doing in their respective communities, I might start with the word hospitality—the friendly, welcoming and generous treatment offered to guests or strangers. But there's more to these churches than just a hot meal or a warm bed. What they are offering is gracepitality—hospitality that begins with intercession, is fueled by the compassion of Jesus, and offered in the atmosphere of his Presence. Gracepitality isn't content to just meet physical needs; it desires to have a lasting effect by meeting core spiritual needs as well.

As divine strongholds are rooted in the mind of Christ, the grace stronghold especially has the mind and heart of Jesus for the lost, hurting and disenfranchised segments of society. It is characterized by compassion, kindness, humility, gentleness, patience, forgiveness and love.

"Therefore, as God's chosen people, holy and dearly loved, clothe yourselves with compassion, kindness, humility, gentleness and patience. Bear with each other and forgive whatever grievances you may have against one another. Forgive as the Lord forgave you. And over all these virtues put on love, which binds them all together in perfect unity" (Colossians 2:12-14).

Compassion

Compassion is God's love expressed through us to sinners. It is not motivated by a person's value or status, but by God himself. In Mark 1:41 Jesus looked on a leper and was "filled with compassion." The origin of the word compassion in this verse is actually "righteous anger" or "indignation;" Jesus was angry that a person made in the Father's image could be so burdened by disease. In another instance in Mark 10, Jesus was approached by a rich young man who asked what he must do to be saved. The Bible says, "Jesus looked at him and loved him" (Mark 10:21). Jesus felt compassion for the wealthy man because he knew that his material possessions were great, and that he could not part with them in order to receive true riches in heaven.

We most love others when we intercede for them.

The highest form of compassion we can show toward nonbelievers is to pray for their felt needs, and that through the answers they would discover the amazing love of God. We most love others when we intercede for them. Ed Silvoso explains why some

Christians hesitate to offer this kind of gracepitality:

> The main factor that keeps us from praying consistently for the felt needs of the lost is our inability to distinguish between acceptance and approval. We are afraid that if we pray for a cure to be found for AIDS—which afflicts and is spread largely by homosexuals and IV drug users—somehow we will be condoning a highly objectionable lifestyle. Likewise, we are afraid that if we pray for a corrupt politician, we will be compromising the pristine nature of the gospel. So we choose not to pray. Through our verbal and nonverbal communication, we demonstrate judgment and condemnation, rather than love and acceptance. Though Christ died, the ultimate sacrifice for us when we were still sinners, we, His followers, refuse to extend grace to those in the same condition. What a contrast!.[7]

Kindness

This characteristic of the grace stronghold can readily be seen in the testimonies of the Dream Center and St. John's churches. Performing acts of kindness with no strings attached is a Presence based philosophy and draws attention to the saving grace of God. This is how Jesus lived—he did kind and thoughtful things for people with every day needs, without demanding that they join his movement or even show their gratitude. He didn't see people as projects or potential members, but as lost souls in need of a savior. When he healed a blind man, raised a young girl from the dead and turned water into wine for guests at a wedding party, he did so out of sheer love and pleasure. Jesus afforded people space and freedom because he trusted that love would always have its way.

When I was pastoring, a mechanic in my church spent a lot of time in the prayer room worshiping and listening for God's voice. As a result of that time, he got a creative idea one day to reach out to single moms by offering to do oil changes and other routine auto maintenance jobs. So on Saturday mornings once a month we provided oil and filters, and the cars would line up in our parking lot. Several other men volunteered to help out, and for hours we worked on cars for free. No questions were asked and no payment was accepted.

Some of the women who came by were church members; others were not. Some would leave and then return later with a friend. Though we promoted it primarily as an outreach to single moms, we didn't turn anyone away. Screening applicants wasn't the point. It was great to be able to provide such a helpful service out of pure obedience to the Presence. It was grace in action, reaching out to people just so they might experience a taste of God's love for them. And the men enjoyed it. It gave all the closet mechanics in our church, and the ones like me that loved to fiddle with cars as a hobby, a chance to roll up their sleeves and put their hidden skills to good use. The side benefit was the true male bonding that went on under all those hoods.

Humility

While we talked about how humility can be a divine stronghold in itself, it can also be evidence of a grace stronghold in action. Just as Pastor Rudy Rasmus has a "no priority seating" policy for the wealthy and influential members of his downtown church, there is no room for elitism or entitlement in the corporate stronghold of grace. Gracepitality as a mindset requires a servant's heart.

None of us is worthy to receive the gift of grace that Jesus paid for with his own flesh and blood—that is what makes it amazing.

This humility is due, at least in part, to the realization that were it not for the grace of God toward us through his son Jesus, we would all be spiritually destitute, condemned by our sin to an eternity of separation from God. None of us is worthy to receive the gift of grace that Jesus paid for with his own flesh and blood—that is what makes it amazing.

Gentleness

The very nature of gracepitality is easy and tender. It does not demand or pressure, but welcomes others in to a place of nurture and safety. It always gives its guests the freedom and room to be completely themselves without judgment.

Jesus' life is a good exampl of how it is possible to be strong and confident, yet still remain gentle. He never shied away from the truth, or from confronting sin as sin, yet he was never violent or forceful when ministering to sinners. Even with the religious leaders of his day, who were constantly antagonizing him and harassing his followers, Jesus turned away wrath with gentle answers.

Patience

Have you ever been a guest in somebody's home, or maybe even in a Bed and Breakfast, where you felt totally at ease and relaxed? If so, you were experiencing the peace and patience of gracepitality. Patience isn't just about being tolerant, or not being in a hurry. We sense patience in an atmosphere that is serene and tranquil. The stronghold of grace not only has staying power, but a spirit of quietude which invites guests to relax, kick their shoes off, and be content.

At one point early in my pastoral ministry, we saw the dramatic conversion of nearly all the employees of a brothel that had been operating on the edge of town. Because our church had reached out to these young ladies, we felt compelled to offer homes to some of them who had no other place to go while trying to turn their lives around. One couple in our church took in

Susan, whose steely eyes and street language made her seem much older than her tender teenage years. The couple loved Susan from the start, showering her with love and gracepitality.

Susan seemed to be responding quite well for several months, until one day the couple came home after a night out to find Susan gone. Not only was her room cleaned out, but they also discovered that most of the wife's valuable jewelry was missing.

Over the next few weeks, the couple continued to pray for Susan. They never spoke unkindly about her and never expressed anger or bitterness over having taken her in. They were even diligent to encourage the other girls who were Susan's friends and they remained optimistic that somehow, they had made a difference in her life.

Then one day they received a package in the mail. It was from Susan. She had returned all the missing jewelry with a note explaining that she needed the money, but simply couldn't keep the jewelry because they had shown her more real love than anyone in her life. She assured them that she was alright, and that she hadn't forgotten about the commitment she had made to Jesus. She thanked them for believing in her. Grace laced with patience had planted a deep seed in Susan's heart.

Forgiveness

Sometimes reaching out to the lost, or new Christians like Susan, requires an extra measure of forgiving grace. Just as Jesus often sought out the unlovables of his society to spend time with, the stronghold of grace looks beyond the dirty, stinky outward appearance of today's unlovables to the wounded and wanting souls on the inside. To do that, we must have an attitude of forgiveness.

The epitome of forgiving grace? Jesus on the cross, "Father, forgive them, for they do not know what they are doing" (Luke 23:34).

Love

As Colossians 2:14 stated, love is the virtue that binds all the others neatly together into the perfect expression of grace. The stronghold of grace is simply God's unrelenting love for his lost sheep, and his deep desire for them to come home, all flowing through our church and into the community we serve.

Saving Grace

Of all the Presence based strongholds, grace maintains particular importance because it is the foyer of salvation. Eternity is at stake. Jesus said, "It is not the healthy who need a doctor, but the sick. But go and learn what this means: 'I desire mercy, not sacrifice.' For I have not come to call the righteous, but sinners" (Matthew 9:12-13).

When Peter received the vision to visit the home of Cornelius and share the gospel with his family, the stronghold of grace was ignited. But because judgment had been in control for so long, the new attitude raised eyebrows at first. Acts chapter 11 describes what happened as word spread that Peter had baptized some Gentiles, and he suddenly found himself having to explain his actions and this different way of thinking: "The apostles and the brothers throughout Judea heard that the Gentiles also had received the word of God. So when Peter went up to Jerusalem, the circumcised believers criticized him and said, "You went into the house of uncircumcised men and ate with them" (Acts 11:1-3).

Understanding their confusion, Peter gave a detailed account of the vision he had received on the roof, probably assuring them that he too was skeptical at first, being a devout Jew. He told them how God himself had insisted that he had "changed the rules" regarding clean and unclean things, thereby opening the door for Peter to preach to the Gentiles. Then he described the moment of his own convincing: "As I began to speak, the

Holy Spirit came on them as he had come on us at the beginning. Then I remembered what the Lord had said: 'John baptized with water, but you will be baptized with the Holy Spirit.' So if God gave them the same gift as he gave us, who believed in the Lord Jesus Christ, who was I to think that I could oppose God?" (Acts 11:15-17).

When they heard how the Holy Spirit had moved just as they had experienced, they knew that they were seeing a new move of God, so they worshiped him, saying, "So then, God has granted even the Gentiles repentance unto life" (Acts 11:18).

Sometimes, divine strongholds have to be explained because they reflect a radical departure from the comfortable or current belief system. They may seem strange, perplexing or even threatening. Because church strongholds are usually deeply embedded and have a "strong hold" on the group psyche, tearing down the old, carnal ones and establishing new ones is a process that requires patience, persistence and the help of the Holy Spirit. You will need to keep this in mind as we look at the last pair of strongholds, and then explore a strategy of action.

All praise and honor to you Lord Jesus for breaking the curse of stinking thinking. Thank you for enduring the crown of thorns so that we might have hope through the renewing of our minds. We lay our own self-made "crowns" at your feet. Now let your mind reign in us. (Matthew 27:29; Galatians 3:13)

7

FEAR VS FAITH

I have a terrible habit of rescuing lost dogs. I know it sounds like a noble thing to do, and in moderation, it is. But mistreated and abandoned dogs—the kind that are handsome and so sweet natured that you wonder how in the world anyone could dump them on the side of the road—these helpless creatures seem to intersect my life far too frequently. Fortunately, I have a fairly understanding wife, although less so after one of my rescues knocked over a heat lamp and burned down our garage, and a very cooperative vet who helps me deal with the consequences of my addiction. I'm really trying to learn how to just drive on by.

About six months ago I found Doogie. A young, strong, beautifully colored chocolate lab-vizsla mix, he was actually in one of the kennels at my vet's office when I took one of my other dogs in. Dr. Angel (isn't that a perfect name for a veterinarian?) told me his story. Doogie had been picked up off the street by a woman who already had too many dogs and she wasn't able to keep him. She had kenneled him there at the vet while she was out of the country for two weeks, hoping that someone might adopt him. Upon her return, the woman planned to take Doogie to the shelter if he was still there.

I already had two labs at home, and I knew I didn't need a third. But I couldn't stand the thought of such a striking animal being sent to the pound and possibly euthanized. He was so shiny and well-muscled. And obviously terrified. I figured I'd take him home where a little TLC would bring him back to life, and then I'd find him a home.

Of course it didn't work out exactly that way. I got Doogie home only to realize that he was imprisoned by a host of phobias that tormented his mind. He wanted so badly to come close and let me pet him, but life had apparently taught Doogie to be very frightened of just about everyone and everything. He jumped at the slightest noises, barked nervously every time he saw me, and would regularly hide behind plants or under furniture. For a while, I couldn't coax him to come close to me even with food. I've seen dogs that have been mistreated who respond quickly to a safe, loving environment, but Doogie was different. His level of psychosis was deeply engrained.

Needless to say, Doogie is part of the family now. And while he's made a lot of progress, he still barks at me sometimes, almost as if he's forgotten who I am, he still retreats to one of his favorite hiding places at the slightest provocation, and he still won't wag his tail or wiggle much (universal sign of canine happiness) around anyone other than me. He's a work in progress.

Fear is so debilitating. And it is so hard to undo.

Fear is so debilitating. And it is so hard to undo. Few things are more tragic than opportunities wasted, blessings forfeited, and otherwise promising lives crippled by illogical, unfounded fear.

Before Adam and Eve disobeyed God by taking a bite of the

apple, they experienced something no other human beings have ever enjoyed—a life free from negative emotions. Can you imagine what that would be like? I don't think any of us really can imagine it, because living in the post fall world, we are sentenced to do battle with these feelings such as worry and inadequacy from the day we are born until the day we die. Adam and Eve, on the other hand, were lucky. They were allowed to taste life as God intended it—in perfect harmony with the earth, each other and their Creator.

No sooner had they swallowed that first juicy bite, however, than the sin nature sprang forth into the garden like a nasty weed, shooting off an array of condemning, poisonous emotions:

> When the woman saw that the fruit of the tree was good for food and pleasing to the eye, and also desirable for gaining wisdom, she took some and ate it. She also gave some to her husband, who was with her, and he ate it. Then the eyes of both of them were opened, and they realized they were naked; so they sewed fig leaves together and made coverings for themselves. Then the man and his wife heard the sound of the Lord God as he was walking in the garden in the cool of the day, and they hid from the Lord God among the trees of the garden. But the Lord God called to the man, "Where are you?" He answered, "I heard you in the garden, and I was afraid because I was naked; so I hid" (Genesis 3:6-10).

Fear was one of the first new and terrible thoughts Adam and Eve had after the fall. Along with it came shame, guilt, anxiety, and mistrust. It immediately took root in Adam and Eve's spirit, and has been an intrinsic part of our DNA ever since. We fear everything—death, loss, embarrassment, failure, people, governments—we even fear fear itself. Like Doogie, we get locked inside our own impenetrable cages of anxiety and trepidation.

Today, fear has big ramifications. We spend millions of dollars a year on insurance to help ease our fears about getting sick or losing material possessions. And we spend millions more dollars on counseling to help us deal with our fears of everything from terrorists to public speaking. We even have names for hundreds of phobias which are defined as irrational fears, yet they are so strong they can interfere with people's ability to function normally in life, and in some cases render them completely debilitated. Can you believe there are people who actually suffer from alliumphobia (the fear of garlic), pogonophoia (the fear of beards), chorophobia (the fear of dancing) or lachanophobia (the fear of vegetables)? Two more common phobias would be triskaidekaphobia (the fear of the number 13) and claustrophobia (the fear of confined spaces).

Since fear is such a natural part of our sin nature, it is easy for it to take hold in a corporate setting and become a subtle part of the belief system. And fear spreads like wildfire. More, perhaps, than the other strongholds, it seems to be highly contagious, very combustible in the atmosphere of group dynamics.

Fear and Rebellion

Consider, for example, the story we looked at previously in Numbers 13 when God instructed Moses to send the spies into Canaan to survey the land. The stronghold of fear is what drove the Israelite people into sedition. When ten of the 12 spies came back and reported that the inhabitants were too large and powerful for the Israelites to defeat, and the cities were too heavily fortified for them to overtake, fear raced through the Israelite camp like a wildfire through dry brush land. Only Joshua and Caleb, the two dissenting spies, had faith that Moses and the people could take the land as God had promised. They read their fellow countrymen perfectly, trying to hearten them, "Only do not rebel against the Lord. And do not be afraid of the people of the land, because we will swallow them up. Their protection is gone, but the Lord is with us. Do not be afraid of them (Numbers 14:9).

While ten of the spies had their eyes fixed on the strong,

well-trained fighting men and the well-fortified cities, Joshua and Caleb had their eyes fixed on God. They undoubtedly saw the same things—the same powerful inhabitants, the same defenses—but Joshua and Caleb had a different perspective. They knew what God had promised, and they chose to agree with him rather than the circumstances. They chose to have faith.

Unfortunately, the Israelites listened to the ten, and not the two. Upon hearing both reports, they were seized with fear and started doing what fearful people do...they got angry, complained and grumbled among themselves (confessing their belief script of fear), and lashed out against the voices of faith, Joshua and Caleb, and their leaders, Moses and Aaron. They talked of stoning Joshua and Caleb, and they whined:

> "If only we had died in Egypt! Or in this desert! Why is the Lord bringing us to this land only to let us fall by the sword? Our wives and children will be taken as plunder. Wouldn't it be better for us to go back to Egypt?" And they said to each other, "We should choose a leader and go back to Egypt" (Numbers 14:2-4).

Because of their lack of faith, God was so angry with his people that he wanted to wipe them all out with a plague and start over. He didn't comfort or reassure them. No, he said, "Move over Moses, and let me smoke them right now!" After all he had done for them, leading them out of Egypt and performing miracle after miracle, he expected more from them. He expected them to believe. It took Moses' fervent intercession on their behalf to avert a massive wilderness barbeque. When he chose instead to simply banish the entire generation from the Promised Land, he explained through Moses:

> So tell them, "As surely as I live, declares the Lord, I will do to you the very things I heard you say: In this desert your bodies will fall—every one of you twenty years old or more who was counted in the census and who has grumbled against

me. Not one of you will enter the land I swore with uplifted hand to make your home, except Caleb son of Jephunneh and Joshua son of Nun. As for your children that you said would be taken as plunder, I will bring them in to enjoy the land you have rejected. But you—your bodies will fall in this desert. Your children will be shepherds here for forty years, suffering for your unfaithfulness, until the last of your bodies lies in the desert. For forty years—one year for each of the forty days you explored the land—you will suffer for your sins and know what it is like to have me against you." I, the Lord, have spoken, and I will surely do these things to this whole wicked community, which has banded together against me. They will meet their end in this desert; here they will die (Number 14:29-35).

It was as if God was saying, "OK, since you chose not to believe, then you won't receive. Since you've got it all figured out, we'll do it your way." The Israelites may have escaped from their lifestyle of captivity in Egypt, but they still were in bondage in their thinking. They remained slaves to the corporate belief system that terrorized them worse than any task master—the stronghold of fear.

> *The Israelites may have escaped from their lifestyle of captivity in Egypt, but they still were in bondage in their thinking.*

Fear has consequences. It keeps us as churches from realizing and receiving all that God has for us, and it gives the enemy a foothold from which to operate. I think it is one of the weapons he uses most to steal our serenity, kill our credibility, and destroy our destiny (John 10:10). Fear is a thief that robs us of the very joy of life, living and serving him.

Fear is also the great paralyzer. It prevents us from moving forward by either binding us right where we are or keeping us in an ongoing pattern of retreat. When the stronghold of fear is in control, we do nothing. We may wish for change and we may long for something better, but we fail to act because our fear keeps us frozen in the now. Churches oppressed by fear often appear apathetic, simply unable to make a decision or move in any direction.

The Poverty Spirit

The driving force behind the stronghold of fear is what I call the poverty spirit. As the name suggests, it has something to do with lack and deficiency, however, even very wealthy churches can be afflicted with it. The poverty spirit simply perpetuates the belief that what one has is not enough. It urges us, "Hold on tight to what you've got! Don't lose it! Don't let anyone take it! You need more!" It keeps us yearning for what we don't have and anxious about protecting what we do. It locks us in tight, and we are afraid of making a mistake, being victimized, or losing. The spirit of poverty makes a church a submarine instead of a rocket, a storage place instead of a distribution center, a fortress instead of a launching pad for social action.

As in all the carnal strongholds, it is easy to see how cognitive closure plays a big role in keeping the toxic attitudes in place. When someone comes along and says, "Let's take the land that God has promised us," cognitive closure holds a magnifying glass up to the obstacles and then makes us stick our fingers in our ears to block out any voices of hope or change. We don't even want to hear it.

And if you happen to be that voice of hope, we may even circle up and stone you because we feel secure with the way things are (even though we know things really aren't that great) and we don't want anyone pushing us out of our comfort zone because then something bad might happen (or something good, but probably something bad). So we'd just prefer it if you leave us alone. Cognitive closure might even be characterized as "cenophobia," or the fear of new things or ideas.

We have said that carnal strongholds are built on a foundation of idolatry—placing more value on something or someone than we place on the Most High God himself. In doing so, we commit our spirits to a false god that can not bear the weight of our devotion, and can never be our true source for affirmation, strength or joy. When fear is our defining mindset, we make an idol out of safety or sense of security. We erect a boundary around the current conditions, including all of our possessions, and then we devote ourselves to protecting and maintaining the "bubble." We aim all of our energy at defending that comfort zone and all that it represents.

I see churches all the time that are playing "safe church," hunkered down inside their four walls, afraid to even open the windows. However, worshiping the idol of safety is incongruous with the nature of God. God is not safe, and he will ask us to do things that are not safe. As I have said before, he will violate our theology, our tradition, our self-assurance, our reputation, if it pleases him and furthers his purposes. He called us to take up our cross and follow, and he warned us, in fact, he assured us, that the way would be narrow and difficult. He never promised that we would not endure hardship or be called to make great sacrifices in his name.

If we become obsessed with security, employing safe-church tactics to maintain the status quo, then we are easily controlled by fear and confined only to what is. We forfeit everything that could be. Every board room discussion starts with the question, "Have we ever done that before?" and if the answer is no, then it's on to the next item. The main goal is meeting the budget and not making mistakes. Taking a risk or trying something new is just not done, and as a result, God's destiny for our church is put on the shelf in a box labeled "hazardous." It is in this manner that the stronghold of fear cheats us out of realizing all that God wants to do in and through us.

Nothing to Fear

You have probably heard the most famous and often repeated quote about fear. But until I looked up its origin, I admit to not remembering who said it and on what occasion. I also had never seen, that I could remember anyway, the entire quote, which really is far more meaningful than the more popular abridged version. In his First Inaugural Address on March 4, 1933, Franklin Delano Roosevelt opened his speech with the profound statement, "So, first of all, let me assert my firm belief that the only thing we have to fear is fear itself—nameless, unreasoning, unjustified, terror which paralyzes needed efforts to convert retreat into advance."[1]

When FDR took the oath of office for President that year, the country had already been suffering under three years of the Great Depression, a term that might well be applied to the state of many mainline churches today. And it was on a collision course, along with several other nations, which would lead to Pearl Harbor Day a short seven years later, and Roosevelt's official declaration of war on December 8, 1941. Faced with an economy in full blown crisis, and a people out of work and in despair, it was fitting that Roosevelt would recognize the pall of fear that lay over America like a shroud. He was facing the daunting task of leading a nation in the vice of not only financial collapse but also of a collective mental stronghold.

As I alluded to in the introduction, understanding how corporate strongholds form, how controlling they can be, and how they affect behavior in a group may give us some idea

People trapped in a stronghold of fear are often too fearful to even trust the rescue team.

of how the stronghold dynamic might be at work in certain areas of the world today. In nations that have existed for decades with totalitarian dictators for example, the stronghold of fear would almost assuredly be deeply fixed in the communal psyche. The result is a group of people who, when given the option to leave their past behind and enter into a new, more hopeful future, may very well surround the cavalry that has come valiantly to their aid, and throw stones. Fear breeds all kinds of other emotions such as hostility, anger, shame and mistrust, making the stronghold an especially difficult one to challenge with force. People trapped in a stronghold of fear are often too fearful to even trust the rescue team.

Stranglehold

The stronghold of fear in a church can take this kind of aggressive stance, or it can manifest itself in a much more cognitive, subtle way. This is perhaps how I encounter this stronghold the most. It goes something like this: After I speak, a pastor approaches me at the end of a session animated and energized about some new idea that I've just shared which he wants to take home and implement in his church. It's not necessarily a radically revolutionary idea, but a creative ministry that he believes will really strengthen his congregation's current prayer life and enhance some of their other efforts. We talk for a few minutes, exchange information, and set a time to follow up on the phone.

Later that week, I get a call from the same pastor who is still somewhat excited, but since arriving home, has thought of several more questions about the new initiative. We visit some more and he tells me that he will present the idea at their next board meeting and then call me back.

Several weeks later, since I haven't heard anything from him, I call. But instead of getting a return call, I receive an email from the pastor explaining that a) the budget is really tight and the finance committee has a lock on new programs until further notice, or b) a crisis has erupted in the church that is requiring all of his attention so the new idea is on hold, or c) the board listened to the idea, but felt like more discussion was needed to alleviate some concerns, or d) all of the above. The tone of the email is a familiar mixture of discouragement, embarrassment and an attempt at detachment. He thanks me for my time and prayers.

Translation: the fear based belief system and cognitive closure in control of his church has a strangle hold on both his finance committee and his board. As soon as he got home from the conference with enthusiasm and fresh revelation, they went to work. Within a short time, they had squelched his optimism and secured the comfort zone. Change was just too risky.

If I had kept them, I would have enough emails just like that one to make a book—a mournful anthology eulogizing the creative ministry ideas that were aborted before ever having the opportunity to live. It is a pattern that is played out over and over in churches of all shapes, sizes and varieties, and it is very coupled with the consumer based mentality of the Martha church. The consumerism approach wants to get everything just right because success depends on keeping the people happy and entertained. If the people's needs are not being sufficiently met, or if they become bored, they leave. And any financial support they may supply goes with them. In the Martha church, at the end of the day, it's all about giving the shoppers what they want.

That kind of mindset in the leadership ranks of a church creates an atmosphere of over-analysis, indecision, and fear. The fear may be of making a mistake, of rocking the boat or of stepping on toes. With the pressure to please all those people comes all sorts of debilitating worries. The fear-induced pattern of thinking, whether it resides in the finance committee, the choir, the deep pocket givers or some sub-group of parishioners, contributes to what I call "church cholesterol." If you want to get anything done, you must figure out a way to bypass it.

Fear can also be a factor that serves to energize the other five strongholds. For example, the stronghold of religion can be energized by fear of the Holy Spirit, fear of emotionalism, or possibly the fear of losing identity or control. That is why religion clings to the rules and traditions of the past. The stronghold of pride can be intensified by fears of failure or loss. Pride is about looking good, having the right building in the right location with the right qualifications and endorsements. The fear of coming up short or not measuring up drives many churches to focus more on material acquisition and superficial goals than on their true calling in the body of Christ.

Likewise, the strongholds of sedition, parochialism and judgment can also be accelerated by fear. Sedition can be driven by a fear of being controlled. It often vocalizes fear at the expense of someone else's reputation. Parochialism and judgment both involve fear of relating to others and dealing with people who are different. As a general rule, we prefer to interact with people we understand, people who are like us. Embracing those with dissimilar beliefs or lifestyles challenges our grace boundaries and puts our spiritual maturity to the test.

The enemy hovers about churches looking for an opening— the tiniest seed of doubt, rebellion, pride or judgment—through which he can gain entrance into our minds and begin to work. He knows that if he can gain a foothold, he has the opportunity to manipulate us into a thought pattern that will ultimately keep us from receiving all that God has for us. Fear is a form of faith in reverse that keeps us in retreat and robs us of our joy and fullness of life in Christ. Perhaps that is why the Bible has over 300 verses that say, "Do not be afraid."

THE STRONGHOLD OF FAITH

Imagine for a moment how the Israelites story might have been different had the whole assembly chosen to listen to Joshua and Caleb rather than the other ten spies. What if they had chosen faith over fear? After all, God had already promised to give them the land; it was earmarked just for them. And he had brought them out of Egypt in spectacular fashion, which should have left little room for doubting his determination and dependability.

If the Israelite people had simply trusted and believed, might they have marched into the Promised Land 40 years earlier instead of wandering in the desert until everyone in their doubting generation died off? Obviously we will never know the answer to that. But in hindsight, I can't help shaking my head as I read about that moment they made the decision to turn left, when in fact the shorter, easier road was surely to the right.

In many ways, faith is the converse of fear. It stirs us to action instead of entangling us in indecision. It pushes us forward instead of holding us back. It says yes instead of no. Yet, faith and fear are not completely mutually exclusive. Had the Israelites chosen to act in faith and march into Canaan, I'm pretty sure they would have done so despite some nagging fear of the current inhabitants. Having faith doesn't necessarily mean the absence of all fear.

Having faith doesn't necessarily mean the absence of all fear.

For some, faith means choosing to get on the airplane despite being afraid of flying. It might mean choosing to launch into a new career despite fears of failure. For a church, faith might mean continuing to give full support to missionaries even when tithes are down. Or it might mean reaching out to help another church in spite of harsh criticism. The key is that faith involves a choice—an act of will—sometimes in the face of conflicting feelings or circumstances.

We have talked about how the divine strongholds in a church reflect some particular aspect of a corporate mind of Christ. We have also seen that putting on the mind of Christ, or taking every thought captive as Paul urged us to do, requires intentional effort on our part. And that is no more true than when our faith is shaken and tested by life. We must choose to walk in faith, even when the enemies look like giants and we seem like grasshoppers in our own eyes.

The author of the book of Hebrews offers us a candid description of biblical faith, starting with a definition, "...faith is being sure of what we hope for and certain of what we do not see" (Hebrews 11:1), and then giving us several dozen biographical models of faith through a who's who of Old Testament heroes. He reminds us through these examples that faith is not a magic formula for an easy life, nor does it guarantee everything we want: "These were all commended for their faith, yet none of them received what had been promised" (Hebrews 11:39). However, God was "not ashamed to be called their God" (v 16) because they trusted and believed, for better or worse.

Read the inscriptions under some of the champions' pictures in the Hebrews faith hall of fame:

"By faith Abel offered God a better sacrifice than Cain did" (v 4).

"By faith Noah, when warned about things not yet seen, in holy fear built an ark to save his family" (v 7).

"By faith Abraham, when called to go to a place he would later receive as his inheritance, obeyed and went, even though he did not know where he was going" (v 8).

"By faith Isaac blessed Jacob and Esau in regard to their future" (v 20).

"By faith Moses, when he had grown up, refused to be known as the son of Pharaoh's daughter" (v 24).

"By faith the people passed through the Red Sea as on dry land" (v 29).

"By faith the walls of Jericho fell, after the people had marched around them for seven days" (v 30).

The author apparently didn't have enough room on his scroll to record details about all the faith heroes: "I do not have time to tell about Gideon, Barak, Samson, Jephthah, David, Samuel and the prophets, who through faith conquered kingdoms, administered justice, and gained what was promised; who shut the mouths of lions, quenched the fury of the flames, and escaped the edge of the sword; whose weakness was turned to strength; and who became powerful in battle and routed foreign armies" (v 32-34). That's an impressive list.

In the commentary notes of Zondervan's *Student Bible*, authors Philip Yancey and Tim Stafford describe the "by faith" passage in Hebrews like this:

> Sometimes faith leads to victory and triumph. Sometimes it requires a gritty determination to hang on at any cost. Hebrews 11 does not hold up one kind of faith as superior to the other. Both rest on the belief that God is in ultimate control and will indeed keep his promises—whether in this life or in the next.

> Faith, concludes the author, most resembles a difficult race. The runner has his eyes on the winner's prize, and despite temptations to slacken the pace, he refuses to let up until he crosses the finish line.[2]

Based on that, I might define faith as the deliberate choice to trust in who God is and believe in his promises. For faith to become a stronghold in a local church, that complete trust and belief in God must be shared by a significant percentage of the congregation and must be a pattern of thinking that influences actions. Just as in the case of the Old Testament heroes, corporate faith doesn't always guarantee a positive outcome, but it does help ensure a positive outlook.

Consider some other quick facts about faith that we can glean from scripture:

1. Through faith we are justified, or put in right relationship with God. In other words, it is a key to salvation:

> "Therefore, since we have been justified through faith, we have peace with God through our Lord Jesus Christ, through whom we have gained access by faith into this

grace in which we now stand. And we rejoice in the hope of the glory of God" (Romans 5:1-2).

Jesus said to the woman, "Your faith has saved you; go in peace." (Luke 7:50).

2. Faith is necessary to please God: "And without faith it is impossible to please God, because anyone who comes to him must believe that he exists and that he rewards those who earnestly seek him" (Hebrews 11:6).

3. Jesus often acknowledged the role of faith in receiving healing:

Then he said to her, "Daughter, your faith has healed you. Go in peace." (Luke 8:48).

Jesus said to him, "Receive your sight; your faith has healed you." (Luke 18:42).

By faith in the name of Jesus, this man whom you see and know was made strong. It is Jesus' name and the faith that comes through him that has given this complete healing to him, as you can all see (Acts 3:16).

4. With faith, we can see signs and wonders when we pray: "I tell you the truth, anyone who has faith in me will do what I have been doing. He will do even greater things than these, because I am going to the Father" (John 14:12).

5. Faith doesn't have to be big to be very powerful: "He replied, 'If you have faith as small as a mustard seed, you can say to this mulberry tree, 'Be uprooted and planted in the sea,' and it will obey you'" (Luke 17:6).

6. Sometimes we can lose faith: "But I have prayed for you, Simon, that your faith may not fail. And when you have turned back, strengthen your brothers." (Luke 22:32).

7. Faith, or the lack of it, influences God's plans: "And he did not do many miracles there because of their lack of faith" (Matthew 13:58).

Like all the other divine strongholds, the stronghold of faith is able to develop in a place of prolonged exposure to the Presence. Where Jesus is worshiped as the Most High King, and everything is subject to his supremacy, the belief system of faith is fed and nurtured. It is easier to trust and believe God when we are experiencing his Presence in a real and intimate way.

A church living in a stronghold of faith is constantly moving forward, building and creating. They make mistakes, and not everything they do is successful, but they never stop reinventing and going again. This is because where God finds a mindset of faith, he pours out hope. Supernatural hope is his response to our steadfast faith.

The Gift of Hope

It's really a wonder that I haven't dropped all my ideals, because they seem so absurd and impossible to carry out. Yet I keep them, because in spite of everything I still believe that people are really good at heart. I simply can't build up my hopes on a foundation consisting of confusion, misery, and death. I see the world gradually being turned into a wilderness, I hear the ever approaching thunder, which will destroy us too, I can feel the sufferings of millions and yet if I look up into the heavens, I think that it will all come right, that this cruelty too will end, and that peace and tranquility will return again.[3]

These poignant words of hope, written by Anne Frank just weeks before being discovered by the Nazis, have been read by millions of people since they were first published in 1947, just after the war's end. Anne's father, Otto, was the only member of her family to survive the horrors of the concentration camps where they were subsequently sent, yet her words have remained alive to inspire generations. As we look back on *The Diary of Anne Frank*, set against the backdrop of surely one of the darkest periods in human history, we can only conclude that the courage, faith and hope of this young teenage girl were both a determined choice and a divine gift. Her innocence is enchanting. Her insight is remarkable. And her optimism is heartrending:

> I've found that there is always some beauty left in nature, sunshine, freedom, in yourself; these can all help you. Look at these things, then you find yourself again, and God, and then you regain your balance. And whoever is happy will make others happy too. He who has courage and faith will never perish in misery![4]

What a word for the church! I have been in countless Sunday morning services when I stood up in the pulpit, looked out over the faces, and would have done well to put away my sermon notes and echo Anne's words, "whoever is happy will make others happy too. He who has courage and faith will never perish in misery!" It is amazing how many Christians look absolutely despondent in church, which must have something to do with the fact that so many of our churches, not to mention the lost, are perishing in misery! We have access to the most glorious source of hope there can be, yet we are wretched because we are deficient in his Presence and anemic in faith.

We have access to the most glorious source of hope there can be, yet we are wretched because we are deficient in his Presence and anemic in faith.

Freedom Writers

I can not help remembering, when I think about Anne Frank, the movie I saw not too long ago called *Freedom Writers*. It is the true story of Erin Gruwell, a high school teacher in Long Beach, California, who used Anne's diary to inspire dramatic transformation in her very first classroom of students. The Freedom Writers Foundation website explains how the book changed the

a constant expectancy for what God is about to do. Hope is willing to take risks, willing to try something new, willing to think outside the box, knowing that God is never still and he is always generating and innovating.

Whom Shall I Fear?

From very early in his life, David was a stronghold of hope. Sense the fervor of his song: "The Lord is my light and my salvation—whom shall I fear? The Lord is the stronghold of my life—of whom shall I be afraid? Though an army besiege me, my heart will not fear; though war break out against me, even then will I be confident" (Psalm 27:1, 3). David definitely had plenty of reasons to be afraid, yet he did not live in fear or allow himself to be overcome by it because God was the Most High in his life. From the time he was a young boy watching sheep until he ruled over Israel as a great commander and king, David was a worshiper. Therefore, no matter what his circumstances were, his hope was anchored in the Presence, and it yielded three attributes in his life—creativity, boldness and victory over enemies.

David's endless creativity in worship can be seen in many of the Psalms which he wrote for the Levites to sing in the temple. They comprised the very first hymnal! David also provided the Levites with musical instruments to play during daily worship, something which had never been done before: "Four thousand are to be gatekeepers and four thousand are to praise the Lord with the musical instruments I have provided for that purpose" (1 Chronicles 23:5). For David, nothing was too good or too beautiful or too extravagant for the Lord. And he was willing to do new things, things which had never been done before, just to pour his love out on God.

This creativity is a wonderful aspect of the divine stronghold, and we see it at work even in the very nature of God in Exodus 31:1-6:

Then the Lord said to Moses, "See, I have chosen Bezalel son of Uri, the son of Hur, of the tribe of Judah, and I have filled him with the Spirit of God, with skill, ability and knowledge in all kinds of crafts—to make artistic designs for work in gold, silver and bronze, to cut and set stones, to work in wood, and to engage in all kinds of craftsmanship. Moreover, I have appointed Oholiab son of Ahisamach, of the tribe of Dan, to help him. Also I have given skill to all the craftsmen to make everything I have commanded you.

The formation of the Tent of Meeting, and later the temple, at the specific direction of God himself, was gloriously creative, rich in color and intricate in detail. The divine stronghold of hope is a center of artistic expression and innovative design.

The divine stronghold of hope is a center of artistic expression and innovative design.

The Vineyard Community Church in Cincinnati, Ohio is an excellent example of a church living in a stronghold of hope-inspired creativity. Founding pastor Steve Sjogren, author of the book *Conspiracy of Kindness*, built the church based on his vision of creative outreach and radical servant evangelism. As a result, the 6,000 member congregation has been bombarding Cincinnati with acts of kindness since 1985 when they held their first free car wash. Other efforts include giving away soft drinks, planting flowers, gift wrapping, and scrubbing toilets, all for free.

Although some outreach ideas have been more successful than others (although it's hard to be unsuccessful at giving away free stuff!), the church has never stopped looking forward, and never stopped reaching out. Not unrelated is the fact that the church has exploded in size and been listed among the top 50 churches in the United States. That is the result of faith and hope, and the blessing of walking in God's promised destiny.[6]

Another manifestation of hope that was evident in David's

life is holy boldness, the courage to step out and use his creativity to do something new or inspired for God, even at the risk of harm, failure or embarrassment. While David accomplished countless remarkable things in his life as military leader and king, few demonstrate his boldness more in my opinion than his handling of Israel's most sacred artifact, the Ark of the Covenant.

We talked extensively about the Ark in *The Presence Based Church*, and how Israel gained a healthy sense of fear of its unique force. As God's self-chosen earthly seat, the Ark had enough voltage that it could, just by its presence alone, crumble false gods, wipe out opposing armies and execute anyone who approached in an unworthy manner. The Ark was dangerous, and its purpose and power were not to be taken lightly. God had given the Levites, his Presence keepers, a protocol to follow, and failure to do so was deadly.

Yet read what David did as the Levites carried the Ark from Gibeah into the city of Jerusalem:

> David, wearing a linen ephod, danced before the Lord with all his might, while he and the entire house of Israel brought up the ark of the Lord with shouts and the sound of trumpets. As the ark of the Lord was entering the City of David, Michal daughter of Saul watched from a window. And when she saw King David leaping and dancing before the Lord, she despised him in her heart (2 Samuel 6:14-16).

David danced! In a grand parade through the middle of town, wearing what would have been considered something of an undergarment for a priest or man in David's position, the king leaped and skipped and twisted and turned with expressive abandon. He danced to the glory of the Lord and probably to the surprise of many of his loyal subjects. Not only was David "uncovered," but the ritual he was performing would traditionally have been at the forefront of a female choir and was usually done only by women with timbrels.[7] No wonder his wife Michal was embarrassed and angered by the sight; it should probably have been her leading the procession. When it came to worshiping, David was so bold that he cared little for his own honor (or anyone else's), and thought only of the honor and majesty of God.

Another interesting thing about this event is that it marked the beginning of a new religious era in Israel. David was bringing the Ark to his newly established capital city, Jerusalem, rather than taking it back to Gibeah where the old tabernacle still stood. This tabernacle continued to be visited regularly by the people, even though the Ark had not been there for many years (it had been in captivity with the Philistines and then had stayed in the home of Abinadab at Kirjath-jearim, about 7 miles from Jerusalem after being returned), and Zadok the priest ministered there.

David, though, decided that the Ark should be placed in a new location. What led him to this decision, we don't really know. However, it must have been divinely inspired because David had just witnessed first hand the peculiar and specific wrath of God through the death of Uzzah, and he was not eager to experience it again. Nevertheless, David felt confident that relocating the Ark would be acceptable. As a man after God's heart, he apparently knew God's heart. He pitched a tent to house it, and then carefully set in order all the rituals of divine worship, appointing Abiathar high priest (2 Samuel 6:17-18). This new tabernacle was the birthplace of praise as a part of public worship.

David's determination to move the Ark, and his very public dance of worship were bold declarations of David's faith in God. His Presence orientation guarded him from the fear that might otherwise have overtaken him. David's commitment to maintaining the tabernacle's centrality in Israel and his many innovations in music and worship are evidence that hope was more than just passing thought for David. It truly was a stronghold in his life.

JJ Ramirez

I have a friend who exemplifies a David like boldness. We tell part of his story in a book called *Encounter: A Blueprint for the House of Prayer*. His name is JJ Ramirez. JJ was a drug dealer who was radically converted and then called to preach and evangelize in the streets where he had once sold. He has stories to tell that would curl your hair, and he has helped literally thousands of young people find their way from the hopelessness of drugs and gangs to a new hope in Jesus.

One of the most amazing things about JJ's ministry is the access to and freedom he has within the public schools in his area. If you were to ask several teachers you know if they are able to share the gospel with students in their classroom, you would likely get some funny looks and maybe the response, "Yeah, right." Yet JJ not only talks openly about Jesus in public schools, he fills up gymnasiums, preaches the gospel, gives altar calls, and sees dozens, sometimes hundreds of kids, at a time make decisions for Christ. All while the principal and faculty look on.

How does he do it? A combination of the inexplicable favor of God and a holy boldness that simply won't stop short of the truth. Years ago, when JJ received his first invitation to speak in a school, he initially declined, explaining to the principal that he really only had one message, which was Jesus, and he didn't think he would be allowed to talk about that, so he would have nothing else to say. But the principal

He expects doors to open; he expects God to show up, and he expects kids to respond. As a result, they do.

had heard of JJ's effect on kids. He knew the impact he was having on violent gang members and young drug addicts, and he was willing to take the risk in order to see if JJ might be able to reach his many troubled students. Nothing else had worked.

So the principal gave JJ free reign, and JJ has never looked back. The stronghold of hope in his life has given him a boldness to do things that others would never even attempt. His belief system runs along deep grooves of faith. He expects doors to open; he expects God to show up, and he expects kids to respond. As a result, they do.

The last characteristic of hope in David's life was the victory he enjoyed over his enemies. David was overwhelmingly victorious in the literal sense. As a warrior and military commander he led armies to success on the battlefield time and again because God was with him. The people celebrated David as a national hero, "As they danced, they sang: 'Saul has slain his thousands, and David his tens of thousands'" (1 Samuel 18:7).

What would end up being David's most famous battlefield victory actually took place when he was just a young boy, too young to even be a soldier in Saul's army like his big brothers. When he arrived at the camp one day to deliver food, David happened upon the scene of Goliath the Philistine taunting the Israelites. He was incredulous. Not even fully grown, David couldn't understand why the soldiers were allowing themselves to be made fun of like that. Why didn't someone teach this wise guy a lesson? So David went to Saul and volunteered.

Saul protested (although not very hard). After all, David wasn't even big enough to wear armor, and how would that make him look as the commander, sending a little kid out to defend his honor? Yet David's unreserved faith and total trust in God were evident, even then:

> But David said to Saul, "Your servant has been keeping his father's sheep. When a lion or a bear came and carried off a sheep from the flock, I went after it, struck it and rescued the sheep from its mouth. When it turned on me, I seized it by its hair, struck it and killed it. Your servant has killed both the lion and the bear; this uncircumcised Philistine will be like one of them, because he has defied the armies of the living God. The Lord who delivered me from the paw of the

lion and the paw of the bear will deliver me from the hand of this Philistine."

Saul said to David, "Go, and the Lord be with you." (1 Samuel 17:34-37).

David's unlikely victory over Goliath set a pattern in place for the rest of his life. He knew that no matter what the circumstances might look like, as long as he had God's Presence in his camp, he would never really be an underdog. His faith was so resolute that it became the overriding stronghold of his life, and he walked in the divine hope of God even through some tough times.

David's more significant victory was this—that he lived transparent before both God and man, leaving behind an extraordinarily personal account of his faith journey in the book of Psalms. What a treasure we have in David's Psalms, the intimate thoughts, questions, doubts and declarations of a man after God's own heart:

> He rescued me from my powerful enemy, from my foes, who were too strong for me. They confronted me in the day of my disaster, but the Lord was my support. (Psalm 18:17-18).

> The Lord lives! Praise be to my Rock! Exalted be God my Savior! He is the God who avenges me, who subdues nations under me, who saves me from my enemies. You exalted me above my foes; from violent men you rescued me (Psalm 18:46-48).

> You are my hiding place; you will protect me from trouble and surround me with songs of deliverance (Psalm 32:7).

> I sought the Lord, and he answered me; he delivered me from all my fears (Psalm 34:4).

> The salvation of the righteous comes from the Lord; he is their stronghold in time of trouble. The Lord helps them and delivers them; he delivers them from the wicked and saves them, because they take refuge in him (Psalm 37:39-40).

He ransoms me unharmed from the battle waged against me, even though many oppose me (Psalm 55:18).

When I think of churches that are living testimonies of victory, my mind scrolls through dozens of pastor friends I know who have personally overcome everything from critical health issues to bizarre legal problems and are still at the helm of healthy churches today. I think of several churches I know that have battled through financial difficulties, changing demographics, moral failure in leadership or catastrophic natural disasters and somehow survived and even thrived in the wake of the crisis. But the one church that keeps coming to mind when I think of the stronghold of hope is the church I talked about earlier outside of Hyderabad, India in the slum village. If ever there was a church that exemplified faith, hope and the creativity, boldness and victory they yield, it would be that one.

In my time there with Pastor Phinehas, I don't even remember that the church had a name. It certainly didn't have a building or a budget. Yet simply by existing in an overwhelmingly Hindu nation, amidst a quality of life that we can't even comprehend, Phinehas's church was a wellspring of life, an oasis of anticipation. Like the fire of God emanating brightly from the tabernacle in the desert, his Presence illuminated the lives of Phinehas and his fellow believers. With the unified mind of Christ, they trusted in who God is, and they wholeheartedly believed in his promises.

When we make the decision to renew our minds with faith, taking on the mind of Christ in agreement with the Father, he will bless us with the gift of divine hope. His promises are real and his word is true. We can trust him with our present and our future. When God is our rock and our security, and when our hope is in him, we don't have to be locked down by fear and worry. We can embrace the new things that he wants to do both in our church and on the earth.

*The weapons we fight with
are not the weapons of the world.
On the contrary, they have divine power
to demolish strongholds.
We demolish arguments and every pretension
that sets itself up against the knowledge of God,
and we take captive every thought
to make it obedient to Christ
(2 Corinthians 10:4-5).*

8

GET A (WORSHIP) LIFE

I think I'm in love with Tom. He is my constant travel companion now days and I can't imagine life without him. He is steady and dependable, but never overbearing. He is quiet, yet confident, and I've grown totally dependent on his wisdom. Just being around him has brought clarity and direction to my life. Not too long ago, I had to make a weekend trip without him and I felt completely lost.

Tom is my navigational device. Sometimes I call him Bonnie or Jane or Richard, because Tom has several personas to choose from, each of them friendly, patient and informative. But mostly I just call him Tom, short for tomtom. He is far more reliable than any convenience store clerk and easier to read than a Google map. He has taken me to places Rand McNally doesn't even know exist. When I get off the plane and throw my bags in a rental car, and it's dark and I'm tired and I need to find my hotel, I can not tell you how comforting it is to plug Tom in and let him guide me. He always knows the best way to get me where I need to be.

The very first Global Positioning System (GPS) is mentioned in the Old Testament, "By day the Lord went ahead of them in a pillar of cloud to guide them on their way and by night in a pillar of fire to give them light, so that they could travel by day or night" (Exodus 13:21). The Israelites didn't need a map or directions; they were guided by the pillars of fire and cloud throughout their 40 year trek in the wilderness. His Presence was their navigational device. When the pillar moved, they followed. When it stopped, they camped.

As churches we need the Presence of God to lead us. Of everything we can do to try and reach more people, be more effective, have more impact or be more relevant, learning to be completely dependent on God's Presence for direction is the most important. Being Presence guided means we operate within the covering of his divine purpose, and we don't waste time and resources chasing misinformed ideas or visions. If we can somehow get to that point of singularly following God's voice, not the latest trends or church growth gurus, I think it would revolutionize what it means to be the church.

The next two chapters are designed to be a sort of repositioning system. I want to give you some tools that will help you influence your church in the direction of a mental makeover. I also want to give you the confidence and belief that you can turn things around and start cutting some new grooves, all without too many casualties.

Through lifestyle worship and carefully crafted thematic prayer, you can welcome the Presence of God to inhabit your church, and you can begin seeing layers of crusty belief systems fall. Thought patterns can change, but it takes time. Those toxic attitudes and expectations didn't take root overnight, and they won't be erased by any singular effort either. Change requires a process.

As you have read through each of the strongholds, you may have recognized some areas in which your church is already experiencing the negative effects of a carnal stronghold, or perhaps you simply see signs that things are headed in that direction. If so, you are probably wondering, "So what now? What can I do? How do we get from where we are to where we want to be?" You may be thinking that one person alone can't possibly have much affect on a church's corporate identity.

But as we learned earlier, strongholds, and the thought patterns that feed them, are not legislated from the top down; they are formulated in your mind, and the minds of every other individual in your church, and then multiplied through the myriad of relationships and social networks. They are not voted on by the board, deacons or elders, but in the arena of group dynamics and interactions. New ideas and attitudes must start somewhere, with someone. That someone might as well be you.

Dismantling carnal strongholds and establishing divine ones is not quick or easy work. As we have seen, the carnal strongholds by nature are closed-minded and defensive. They fiercely resist change, and if you try to fight one with hand to hand combat, you will lose. In fact, everyone will lose.

The natural reaction to a stronghold is to set the crosshairs on the person (or persons) that seems to be at the leading edge, and then launch an all out verbal assault. But no amount of convincing or campaigning will turn the tide. You can't fight a stronghold with argumentation or persuasion—the belief systems are too deeply entrenched. They have been rehearsed and validated and acted on over and over again to the point that the thought patterns are no longer considered negotiable. This kind of combat will only cause both sides to dig their heels in further, and you will find yourself sucked into the nastiest kind of conflict—a church fight. Christians can be stubborn. And mean.

If you want to contain a stronghold, you must understand two things. First, the church controllers that are wreaking havoc and causing strife are not your real enemy. I know they may look like the enemy. And they may act like the enemy. On more than one occasion I have prayed, "God, isn't that one ready to go home? Why not just beam her up right now!" But you need to keep in mind that the real enemy is Satan, who is waging war for our minds, doing everything he can to keep the church squabbling like pre-schoolers over a toy in the nursery, totally oblivious to the world outside. He knows that if he can keep us imprisoned in mental strongholds and fighting with each other, then God won't be able to use us as the instruments he called us to be. We will all forfeit our destiny and forfeit our blessings too. People are not the enemy; Satan is.

Second, if you want to take apart a carnal stronghold and build the foundation for a divine one, you must go after God. Think vertically, not horizontally. Go after God by personally becoming a Presence seeker: worship him, set your heart and mind on him, get caught up in him, and invite his Presence to come down. Not only will you see better results with less collateral damage, but you yourself will be preserved and insulated in his company. If you don't remember anything else written in this book, remember that. His Presence is not just powerful; it is sufficient. Pursue it.

His Presence is not just powerful; it is sufficient. Pursue it.

Tabernacle Worship Model

In The Presence Based Church we talked about a model for worship established by the series of three tabernacles in the Old Testament—the tabernacle of Moses, the tabernacle of David, and the temple of Solomon. While each of the three shared the honor of hosting the Ark of the Covenant and therefore being God's earthly dwelling place, each was distinctive in its style and worship protocol.

The tabernacle that Moses built was characterized by

waiting. The first generation of Levites appointed to attend to the Presence, when they weren't maintaining the holy temple trappings such as fire on the altar, sacrifices or incense, spent most of their time waiting in silence before the Lord. There was no script, no hymnal, no order of worship and no sermon. In fact, there were no chairs. The Levites reverently stood, knelt or laid prostrate in front of the Ark.

When David later relocated the tabernacle, he introduced musical praise as a key component of worship. David wrote hundreds of songs, many of them recorded in the book of Psalms, for the Levites to sing to the Lord, and he gave them instruments to play. David appointed many to be full time musicians, worshiping the Lord around the clock in song.

Finally, David's son Solomon built the permanent temple and consecrated it as a place of prayer. He dedicated the temple, saying, "Now, my God, may your eyes be open and your ears attentive to the prayers offered in this place" (2 Chronicles 6:40). And with that, the pattern of tabernacle worship was complete.

This Old Testament model for attending to the Presence is still proper protocol today. The important thing to note is that worship was a combination of all three—waiting, praise and prayer, in that order. When we use the term "worship" today, we are usually referring to praising God with music and song, however, a broader understanding of worship encompasses so much more.

In the remainder of this chapter, I want to offer you a job description for a modern day Levite and hopefully convince you that simply by becoming a lifestyle worshiper, you can help win the stronghold battle in your church. In the next chapter, we will talk about specifically crafted prayer, and how it works to "take every thought captive" and rewrite belief scripts. Between the two—lifestyle worship and crafted prayer—you have the tools to establish a pattern of God's Presence in your church.

Worship and Strongholds

Back in the first chapter I explained that worship is the primary key to being a Presence based church, and to the establishment of divine strongholds. I suggested three reasons why this is true: 1) worship is the necessary protocol for hosting the Presence of God; 2) it sharpens our revelation of Jesus; and 3) it firmly establishes him as the Most High in our thinking. Let me explain a little further what this means in terms of strongholds.

When I hear Christians talking about "enjoying the Presence of God," or how "the Presence of God was so sweet," it always makes me wonder if we, as the church today, are truly experiencing his Presence, or if we are only experiencing some facsimile of it. In the Bible, his Presence never seemed to be characterized as sweet, and the people who experienced it always fell down trembling. I don't think they would have described it as enjoyable. Glorious maybe. Or amazing. But not necessarily enjoyable.

The Presence of God was awe-inspiring; powerful beyond compare; a force like no other. For example, in 1 Samuel 5, after capturing the Ark of the Covenant, the Philistines placed it in a tent next to their idol-god, Dagon. The next morning, their beloved idol was on the ground, face down, in front of the Ark. They put Dagon back in his place, but the following morning, he was again found on the ground before the Ark, this time with his head and hands broken off (v 1-4).

In his Presence, evil is exposed. Lies are uncovered. The enemy flees.

The Presence is so powerful and so holy that idols can not stand anywhere near. In his Presence, evil is exposed. Lies are uncovered. The enemy flees. This is what happens when we welcome his Presence through worship—we don't have to fight because the very authority of God's proximity is enough to reduce strongholds to rubble. Worship is our best weapon against carnal belief systems and controlling mindsets.

Other stories in the Bible support the idea that praise and worship are effective in battle. Remember the battle of Jericho?

Then the Lord said to Joshua, "See, I have delivered Jericho into your hands, along with its king and its fighting men. March around the city once with all the armed men. Do this for six days. Have seven priests carry trumpets of rams' horns in front of the ark. On the seventh day, march around the city seven times, with the priests blowing the trumpets. When you hear them sound a long blast on the trumpets, have all the people give a loud shout; then the wall of the city will collapse and the people will go up, every man straight in" (Joshua 6:2-5).

For seven days, Joshua's army did as God had commanded them, marching around the city with the Ark, priests and musicians leading the procession. On the seventh day, it happened just as he promised, and the walls of the stronghold crumbled to the ground, giving Joshua the city. With his Presence and the worship team going before, the battle was already won.

Another biblical military leader who sought the Lord was Jehoshaphat, a man who we know was far from perfect. Jehoshaphat was just like you and me—a shining example of human weakness and inconsistency. As the king, he did many things that were right in the eyes of the Lord, yet he failed to remove many of the high places in Judah. He also made several alliances with evil leaders rather than trusting in God for protection. However, he did not allow his imperfection or sin to keep him from understanding the importance of worship, even in difficult times.

When faced with war against the Moabites and Ammonites, Jehoshaphat knew he was outnumbered. So he brought the nation together in front of the temple and he cried out to God:

O Lord, God of our fathers, are you not the God who is in heaven? You rule over all the kingdoms of the nations. Power and might are in your hand, and no one can withstand you. O our God, did you not drive out the inhabitants of this land before your people Israel and give it forever to the descendants of Abraham your friend? They have lived in it and have built in it a sanctuary for your Name, saying, "If calamity comes upon us, whether the sword of judgment, or plague or famine, we will stand in your presence before this temple that bears your Name and will cry out to you in our distress, and you will hear us and save us."

But now here are men from Ammon, Moab and Mount Seir, whose territory you would not allow Israel to invade when they came from Egypt; so they turned away from them and did not destroy them. See how they are repaying us by coming to drive us out of the possession you gave us as an inheritance. O our God, will you not judge them? For we have no power to face this vast army that is attacking us. We do not know what to do, but our eyes are upon you (2 Chronicles 20:6-12).

When Jehoshaphat finished praying, all the men, women and children of Judah stood before the Lord and waited. God likes it when we wait on him, and he answered Jehoshaphat's prayer quickly. The Lord spoke to the people through a prophet, saying, "Do not be afraid or discouraged because of this vast army. For the battle is not yours, but God's. You will not have to fight this battle. Take up your positions; stand firm and see the deliverance the Lord will give you, O Judah and Jerusalem" (v 15, 17).

Upon hearing the word of the Lord, Jehoshaphat responded:

Jehoshaphat bowed with his face to the ground, and all the people of Judah and Jerusalem fell down in worship before the Lord. Then some Levites from the Kohathites and Korahites stood up and praised the Lord, the God of Israel, with very loud voice.

Early in the morning they left for the Desert of Tekoa. As

they set out, Jehoshaphat stood and said, "Listen to me, Judah and people of Jerusalem! Have faith in the Lord your God and you will be upheld; have faith in his prophets and you will be successful." After consulting the people, Jehoshaphat appointed men to sing to the Lord and to praise him for the splendor of his holiness as they went out at the head of the army, saying: "Give thanks to the Lord, for his love endures forever."

As they began to sing and praise, the Lord set ambushes against the men of Ammon and Moab and Mount Seir who were invading Judah, and they were defeated (v 18-22).

Jehoshaphat was not perfect but he knew who he was. He had a hard time saying no to the wrong people, but he knew how to say yes to God. By putting worship in the lead, he invited the favor zone of God to surround his army, and the enemy came unraveled.

Worship is the proper protocol for inviting the Presence of God. And where his Presence inhabits, idols fall, strongholds are broken and the enemy is driven out. But worship is not just about demolition. In addition to being our most powerful weapon against carnal strongholds, worship is also a key to building divine strongholds by sharpening our revelation of Jesus, and keeping him in our focus as the Most High in our thinking.

Our goal is to establish our church as a place where God is at home—a place where he feels so welcomed and comfortable that he will reside. Because I travel a lot, I have a deep appreciation for what it means to feel "at home." When I return from a trip, I like to put on my blue jeans and sandals and head out to my back porch, coffee cup in hand, and hang out with my labs. I love to watch them chase the squirrels and play with each other; they are always so excited to see me (whether I've been gone three days or three hours). I love it when Doogie, the rescued, slightly neurotic chocolate mix, comes and sheepishly wraps his body around my legs, because I know he won't go near anyone else when I'm gone. I love it when my mellow old black one, Bear, greets me with all the enthusiasm of a puppy before finding a spot nearby to stretch out and take a nap. And I love it when Samson, the yellow one whose world I am, finally settles down enough to climb up on the bench next to me, playfully frisk me with his lion paws, and lay his big happy head across my lap. My dogs are a great welcoming committee, and there on the back porch, I feel at peace. I am home.

God is attracted to our worship and adoration, whether we are soulful and melancholy or joyful and exuberant. Our expressed love and devotion to him pleases him and makes him smile at us. We are his delight, and he delights in our praise. It is our sincere, unashamed worship—not our good deeds or biblical knowledge or impressive buildings—that makes him feel most at home. When we worship, he draws near. When we continually worship, he moves in to dwell.

Praise enlarges God in our minds. It places him at the center of our lives. It clarifies our picture of Jesus, ever sharpening his image as the high place in our thinking. The more we worship, the more God is able to reveal to us, in carefully measured increments, the glory of his Son. He becomes a holy fixation in our minds. This is how praise helps us take every thought captive, and put on the mind of Christ.

Today, God is seeking worshipers (John 4:23). He is not seeking studiers or preachers or micro managers. He is not looking for people whose beliefs are theologically perfect nor those whose tithing records are spotless. He wants worshipers—faithful, devoted, authentic worshipers who will worship him in spirit and in truth. He is searching the earth for a new order of Levites, those called and consecrated by the Holy Spirit, to attend to his Presence not just for 20 minutes on Sunday morning, but day after day and week after week, and not just because there is a problem or a need, but because he is so worthy. When we worship, everything else in life will fall into place. Worship is first, last and eternal.

Worship is not defined by what happens on Sunday morning. You can't really go to church once a week, sing two or three songs, listen to a sermon, and call yourself a worshiper any more than you can go to a gym once a week and lift weights for 15 minutes and call yourself a body builder.

Good church is wonderful. For 28 years as a pastor, I loved the challenge of making every weekend service a unique opportunity for my congregation to personally experience as much of the Presence of God as possible while they were in the building. But I learned over the years that no matter what we did, the service "experience" we could offer would always be limited by the extent to which the people were interacting with and encountering God throughout the week in their daily lives.

I started to see that the people themselves were the vessels of worship, and that our worship was not something we did at church, but rather something we brought.

I started to see that the people themselves were the vessels of worship, and that our worship was not something we did at church, but rather something we brought. Some came to church completely empty, while others came overflowing. Then together we poured ourselves out before the Lord in a collective worship offering. What wasn't already there couldn't be fabricated with mood lighting or great music or drama or slideshows.

Unfortunately many churches have bought into the idea that their job is to manufacture worship and then offer it to the masses on Sunday morning. And they've sold that idea lock, stock and barrel to churchgoers who are eager to shed any personal responsibility for their own worship life. But true worship can't be engineered because it is not a production but a giving of oneself, an individual offering of love and devotion. William Temple described it eloquently:

> Praise is the submission of all our nature to God. It is the quickening of conscience by His holiness; the nourishment of mind with His truth; the purifying of imagination by His beauty; the opening of the heart to his love; the surrender of will to his purpose—and all this gathered up in adoration, the most selfless emotion of which our nature is capable and therefore the chief remedy for that self-centeredness which was our original sin and the source of all actual sin.[1]

LIFESTYLE WORSHIP

If you want to see God's Presence drive out carnal strongholds and establish a pattern of kingdom activity in your church, raise up Levites that will become an army of personal, lifestyle worshipers throughout the week. Whether you are a pastor or a church member, start by becoming one yourself, and then ask the Holy Spirit to lead you to others who will answer the same call. Read through the Bible passages about the Levites and then wait on God to show you how you can incorporate worship into your own life at every level. Following are 12 guidelines to get you started.

1. Get help from the Holy Spirit.

I love worship leaders. Passionate lovers of God, they are some of my favorite people in the world. I have worked with some of the best who could lead you right to the very steps of the throne if you were willing to follow, and I love the gifts and talents they bring to the church. But you don't need one to worship.

You can worship God at home, in your car, at your workplace or anywhere else without a paid professional to set the mood and provide music because you have heaven's lead worshiper living inside of you. The Holy Spirit is the lover of Jesus Christ and to be filled with him is to love Jesus as he does. He is your helper in prayer and worship, and he is highly qualified because he's worked very closely with the Father for a long time!

The Holy Spirit can help you in a number of ways: He can pull back the curtain to reveal sightings of the Son that will leave you in awe of his beauty and glory. He will highlight for you promises and truths in scripture that you can offer back to God in praise. He can interrupt your day at unusual moments with a reminder of God's faithfulness in your life. And he can give you creative ideas in worship that are not locked into a script or pattern. The Holy Spirit is a worship expert, and he will be your very own personal worship trainer if you let him.

In consumer based settings where carnal belief systems are in control, worship is planned and predictable. It may follow an order of worship (or order to worship) that is printed in the bulletin and distributed to each person so that everyone knows when to sit, when to stand, when to sing and when to shake hands. Or it may just follow the same pattern week after week. Consumer based churches like familiarity because it affords a sense of control. And if everything in the worship service is controlled, then there is no risk of anything happening that might be uncomfortable or inconvenient.

Private worship allows God to be God on his terms. The Spirit leads the way and each experience is different from the last.

This kind of worship may pay tribute to God, but often it is more of a token or routine than a genuine, passionate outpouring of adoration. It may invite you to acknowledge God but will rarely draw you into his Presence for a "never to be the same again" encounter. Private worship, on the other hand, allows God to be God on his terms. The Spirit leads the way and each experience is different from the last.

Worship is not about a place but the person of Jesus. With the help of the Holy Spirit, you can become a worship offering and expect to see the results of his Presence in and through your life. The apostle Paul encourages us, "be filled with the Spirit. Speak to one another with psalms, hymns and spiritual songs. Sing and make music in your heart to the Lord, always giving thanks to God the Father for everything, in the name of our Lord Jesus Christ" (Ephesians 5:18-20).

2. Get a revelation.

When Jesus asked his disciple Peter "Who do you say I am?" Peter correctly replied, "You are the Christ, the Son of the living God." Then Jesus commended him, explaining, "Blessed are you, Simon son of Jonah, for this was not revealed to you by man, but by my Father in heaven. And I tell you that you are Peter, and on this rock I will build my church..." (Matthew 16:15-18).

Peter was perhaps the first person to really see who Jesus was, and Jesus took the opportunity to make an important point: that the revelation of his true identity can only be attained one way—it must be given by the Father. He adds that this revelation of his glory is so important that it is the foundation upon which he will build his Church. You can learn a lot of information by reading books, studying scripture and listening to teachers talk about Jesus. But to see him clearly, even encounter him personally, as Savior, God Incarnate, Emmanuel, requires God to reveal the glorified Jesus to you through the Holy Spirit.

Paul recognized the same truth, telling the Galatians, "I want you to know, brothers, that the gospel I preached is not something that man made up. I did not receive it from any man, nor was I taught it; rather, I received it by revelation from Jesus Christ" (Galatians 1:11-12). As offspring of Adam and Eve, made from the dust of the earth, we don't have the ability to comprehend or see into the spiritual realm without the help of the Holy Spirit. We can learn facts, but to know the things of God, we need revelation.

The revelation of Jesus is the fuel for genuine worship. The more clearly you are able to see him, the more compelled you will be to praise him. We know from John's description on the Isle of Patmos that he is more radiant than the sun, more beautiful than anything we have ever seen, more breathtaking than the greatest spectacle on earth. When John saw a glimpse of him, the sight was so overwhelming that he "fell at his feet as though dead." He later wrote what he remembered, "In his right hand he held seven stars, and out of his mouth came a sharp double-edged sword. His face was like the sun shining in all its brilliance" (Revelation 1:16-17). Wow!

The truth is that none of us can handle any more than small increments of the savior's image. He is too much for us to take in. But as you wait on the Lord, search the truth of his Word, and press into his heart in worship and prayer, he will reveal bits and pieces of the picture, as much as you can digest. With each fresh sighting, you will fall more in love, and yearn to go deeper and see clearer.

3. Get informed.

You can not do what you do not know. It's not terribly profound, but true. If you want to be a worshiper of God, take the time to learn about your worship heritage. Read back through the history of Israel to answer one question: what part did worship play?

In *The Message*, Eugene Peterson introduces the Chronicles as "a witness to the essential and primary place of accurate worship in human life." In the assessment of what defined Israel's identity, he asserts:

> Right and faithful worship turns out to be what counts most of all. The people of God are not primarily a political entity or a military force or an economic power; they are a holy congregation diligent in worship. To lose touch with the Davidic (and Moses-based) life of worship is to disintegrate

as a holy people. To be seduced by the popular pagan worship of the surrounding culture is to be obliterated as a holy people.[2]

The Ark of the Covenant, the tabernacle, the priests and Levites wholly dedicated to the worship of the Lord—these are the things that set the Israelites apart from other nations. They were a people of worship because that is what God chose them to be. When Moses led them out of Egypt, God told them, "Now if you obey me fully and keep my covenant, then out of all nations you will be my treasured possession. Although the whole earth is mine, you will be for me a kingdom of priests and a holy nation" (Exodus 19:5-6). And what did he want in return? He wanted their undivided devotion: "You shall have no other gods before me" (Exodus 20:3).

In addition to studying your own worship heritage, and the role of worship in the Old Testament, get informed about the current worship movement that is sweeping through churches and nations alike. Build a worship library. Here are some of my favorites from my own personal collection, a few old classics and a few new ones: *Worship God* by Ernest Gentile; *Worship His Majesty* by Jack Hayford; *Let Us Praise* and *Let Us Worship* by Judson Cornwall; *The Hallelujah Factor* by Jack Taylor; *The Heart of Worship*, *FaceDown*, and *The Unquenchable Worshipper* by Matt Redman; *The Air I Breathe* by Louie Giglio; and *Heights of Delight* and *Rivers of Delight* by Dick Eastman.

I have always found it especially inspiring to listen to worshipers in a different language. God is so big, and our world tends to be so small.

There are so many good resources—books on worship, worship collections, worship conferences, even websites devoted to worship. Jump in the stream. Learn about what's out there. Discover what God is doing in other parts of the world. I have always found it especially inspiring to listen to worshipers in a different language. God is so big, and our world tends to be so small.

The church today is worship deprived and therefore Presence deficient. When we bought into the lie, somewhere along the way, that sitting through a weekly service constituted adequate worship, we veered so far away from what God intended that the church as an institution may never find its way back. But you can. And with you, a remnant of Levites in your local church congregation can. With the help of the Holy Spirit and a hunger for the revelation of Jesus, you can rediscover the lifestyle worship that set the Israelites apart.

4. Get musical.

Even if you never turn on a radio, you hear music every day. It is all around us, piped into the grocery store or the mall while we're shopping, playing in the background at the dentist office while we're having our teeth cleaned, ringing out from cell phones like a disjointed symphony while we stand in line at Starbucks, blaring from loudspeakers at sporting events. We hear it everywhere, whether we want to or not: in an elevator, on the phone, from the car in the next lane or house next door, on TV, on the computer, and in restaurants. Music—not always of our choosing—is the soundtrack of our lives.

We love music because it touches us emotionally and expresses for us things we don't know how to express ourselves. Music ties us to people and places, events and circumstances. It is somehow deeply connected to our memory. How many times have you heard a song that instantly transported you back to a specific time or place? And why is it that we have a hard time remembering the name of a person we met last week, but we can sing along verbatim with a song we haven't heard in 20 years? Our relationship with music, and the way it tattoos us with feelings and impressions, is special. It shapes our lives, while at the same time preserving them in a chronological medley.

Because music is such a powerful force in our lives, I don't think you can overestimate the importance of the role music has played in the history and formation of the church, and that it plays now in our identity as Christians and in our own private worship. Key figures in the birth and explosion of Protestant hymns, Martin Luther (early 1500s), Isaac Watts (late 1600s) and the Wesley brothers, John and Charles (early 1700s), laid the foundation for hymns as we know them, and many of the words they wrote are still a huge part of church culture.

Each of these musicians and theologians, in their own way, helped to establish hymns as the worship language of the masses through their prolific writing and their progressive ideas that hymns should not only reinforce scriptural teaching, but should also stir the passions and emotions of the congregation toward God. Their songs, which many today have shelved in lieu of "contemporary" worship music, were actually very contemporary in their day. The hundreds of hymns written by Charles Wesley were very influential in the worldwide surge of Methodism as droves of people left the more established, traditional churches for the passion and fervor of the early Methodist meetings. The people loved to worship! And they were drawn to these rousing declarations of faith, many set to familiar bar tunes, which were easier to sing and understand than earlier generations of Latin verses and chants.[3]

What I find most fascinating is that when hymnals began flooding the church landscape thanks to the advent of mass printing technology, they were distributed to every family or individual and kept at home, just like the Bible. The hymnals were not just used at church—they were a part of the Christians' every day worship lives.

Not long ago when I was speaking at a church in Alliance, Nebraska, a man came up to me during the lunch break and said he had something to give me. I had been talking about this very topic of praise and worship, and the influence of music and hymns in the church. He handed me a tiny "pocket" hymnal, about the size of a deck of cards only twice as thick. Published in 1849, the pages were yellowed and the cover looked like it might fall off if I opened it too wide. It was one of the early Methodist song books that would have been kept in a man's breast pocket or at home right by the family Bible for daily use. I was blown away that the man said he wanted me to keep it. It is a treasured possession.

That pocket hymnal is a reminder that without mp3 players and CDs and stereo systems and recording artists, music had to be made, not just absorbed. The people sang and worshiped often in their private lives, so that when they did come together corporately, God's Presence attended in powerful ways.

The fact that so many of those early hymns have withstood centuries of time speaks to their significance. I love the wide selection of contemporary worship music that is available today; in fact, I'm a junkie. But there is something mightily compelling in the refrain of "When I Survey the Wondrous Cross" or "O For a Thousand Tongues to Sing" bellowing from the pipes of a grand organ accompanied by a congregation that has sung the words so many times they don't need the book. It stirs the spirit. Worship has evolved just as one would expect, but music's ability to reach deep into the human soul and connect us with God in a unique way is the constant.

Worship has evolved just as one would expect, but music's ability to reach deep into the human soul and connect us with God in a unique way is the constant.

If you want to become a Levite, a true worshiper of God, incorporate music into your personal worship life. We have been taught, those of us who have been walking long in the Christian faith, to read our Bible and to pray every day, but few of us have ever been taught to worship personally. It's a tragic omission. Explore the huge variety of worship music available today and rediscover the power of singing to God in your home or in your car. Make worship music a part of your life and I can almost guarantee that you will experience church at a whole different level.

The apostle Paul underscores the importance of personal praise for every follower of Christ, "Speak to one another with psalms, hymns and spiritual songs. Sing and make music in your heart to the Lord" (Ephesians 5:19). Furthermore, the longest book in the Bible is a collection of songs that were written to be set to music and sung to God in praise. The Psalmist writes, "Praise the Lord. How good it is to sing praises to our God, how pleasant and fitting to praise him! Sing to the Lord with thanksgiving; make music to our God on the harp (Psalm 147:1, 7). The Psalms are filled with references to music and instruments to be used in worship. As we have already seen, praise isn't the only component to worship, but it is a very important one.

Some of my favorite worship songs are what I would consider prayers set to music—songs we sing to God instead of about him. I love worship music that expresses our love to him and that mentions his wonderful name: Jesus. I also love simple choruses that can be remembered easily and sung over and over because I think the repetition cuts mental worship grooves.

Another important point to make about getting musical is that while listening to worship music is wonderful and has its place in personal meditation, actually singing is significant too. Listening to music and actively singing or engaging in the music are different activities that stimulate different parts of the brain. I will talk more about the truth behind this in the next few pages as we look at "getting physical" and "getting in the groove," but actively participating in praise and worship is definitely more powerful than just being a spectator.

5. Get physical.

I love football. Living in the Houston area, I've really enjoyed watching the Houston Texans build a team over the past several years. I say I've enjoyed it—I suppose that's not entirely true because at times it has been painful and frustrating to watch them take a few steps forward only to go reeling back into seemingly the early stages of their infancy. But I love it just the same. Fortunately we have another team in Texas and having lived here all my life, I have Dallas Cowboy affinity too. The Tom Landry-Roger Staubach era made me a lifelong lover of the blue and silver.

I've been to a couple of the Texan games here in the past few years, my first time ever to see professional football in person. I never would have imagined how much fun it is to go see a football game! It's amazing how tens of thousands of strangers can come together in one place and rally around one single desire—to see their team win. The tailgaters outside of the stadium before kickoff remind me of the world's largest family reunion. It's hard to imagine, walking through the parking lot filled with tents and portable grills, that none of those people eating barbecue and drinking beer actually knew each other 3 hours earlier. The way they laugh and talk and share food and carry on, you would think they were lifelong friends.

And once inside, the crowd is totally unified. When the Texans do something good, they hoot and holler and high five and dance in the most undignified ways. It's so exciting and emotional, and it sort of catches you up until you find yourself hooting and hollering and giving high fives and dancing right along with them! Being a spectator at a Houston Texan football game is anything but passive.

Why is it that we can be so expressive about a sporting event, and yet so reluctant to show even the slightest emotion in church? Why do we insist on making worship so cerebral and, let's just admit it, boring? It's no wonder God's Presence doesn't always attend our worship; when he looks down from heaven on our Sunday morning exercises, as we file in, go through the motions, and then file out to lunch, he must wonder why we like football better than him.

For the Levites and David and other worshipers in the Bible, the practice of praising God was very physical:

> Clap your hands, all you nations; shout to God with cries of joy (Psalm 47:1).

> Sing to him a new song; play skillfully, and shout for joy (Psalm 33:3).

> Shout for joy to the Lord, all the earth, burst into jubilant song with music (Psalm 98:4).

> Come, let us bow down in worship, let us kneel before the Lord our Maker (Psalm 95:6).

> Lift up your hands in the sanctuary and praise the Lord (Psalm 134:2).

Getting physical in worship goes beyond singing. The English biblical word praise is actually translated from several different Hebrew words which help us define various facets of worship from extending the hands (yadah) to bowing (barak). In his book *Worship God*, Ernest Gentile offers nine different expressions of praise and worship based on these Hebrew words and his study of David. He breaks them down into three categories:

> Our Voice: speaking, shouting, singing

> Our Posture: bowing (kneeling, lying), dancing, standing

> Our Hands: playing instruments, clapping, lifting hands[4]

Just as important as exploring a variety of worship music is exploring the range of physical worship expressions. Depending on your church background, you may be very comfortable shouting, dancing or clapping your hands in worship, or you may not. For those raised in very traditional churches, such displays of emotion often feel awkward, intimidating or embarrassing. But for that group I would challenge you to be bold. Take a risk. Push yourself to the edge of your own comfort zone by picking one expression of worship that is not part of your experience and trying it. You don't have to make a grand exhibition at church; simply incorporate something new and thought-provoking into your own personal worship time at home.

When no one else is around, lift your hands as an act of surrender and say out loud, "Lord I submit my will and my life to you." Raising your hands and speaking the words audibly impresses your mind in a way that simply thinking those thoughts can not. Or you might try turning your palms up as if you are about to accept a gift when you are asking the Lord for special requests. Physically positioning your body to receive can bolster your faith in prayer. You could even try bowing, kneeling or dancing during your personal worship time just as a gesture to God that you are willing to lay down your personal pride and express emotion toward him. Imagine how much that show of affection would mean to him as your Father!

Sometimes your body just needs to be actively involved in something in order for it to leave permanent impressions in your mind.

Sometimes your body just needs to be actively involved in something in order for it to leave permanent impressions in your mind. For example, talking about a perfect golf swing or watching someone else perform a perfect golf swing may help you improve your own swing a little bit, but not nearly as much or as rapidly as actually going to the driving range and practicing it yourself, over and over. That's because physical motion stimulates a different part of your brain than cognitive activity. You remember experiences differently when movement is involved. Getting physical is a fundamental component of the Levitical lifestyle, and it is important if you want to take your worship life to a new level.

6. Get in a groove.

By now you should understand how important thought patterns and mental grooves are in the stronghold battle. Carnal strongholds are dismantled by taking every toxic thought captive and divine strongholds are established by creating new grooves in line with the mind of Christ. One of the ways you can use worship to aid in this process is to "get in a groove"—in other words, select a specific worship phrase such as a psalm, a praise song or an attribute of God, and meditate on it for a period of time until it sinks deep into your spirit. Repeat it to yourself as you go throughout your day. Whisper it under your breath. Say it or sing it out loud while you take a shower or drive to work. The repetition helps etch the truth into your mind.

I also encourage people to break the sound barrier by making it a habit to pray and worship out loud at least some during personal times with the Lord. This is very important because scripture indicates that our spoken words have both creative and destructive power over and above our thoughts, and can impact our lives and the lives of those around us. Hearing ourselves say something, especially over and over, tends to reinforce our faith in what we are saying. You may recall from Chapter One that confession is one of the key components of stronghold formation.

Consider what the following verses say about the power of our words:

And God said, "Let there be light," and there was light (Genesis 1:3).

I tell you the truth, if anyone says to this mountain, "Go, throw yourself into the sea," and does not doubt in his heart but believes that what he says will happen, it will be done for him (Mark 11:23).

For it is with your heart that you believe and are justified, and it is with your mouth that you confess and are saved (Romans 10:10).

Reckless words pierce like a sword, but the tongue of the wise brings healing (Proverbs 12:18).

The tongue has the power of life and death, and those who love it will eat its fruit (Proverbs 18:21).

Do not let any unwholesome talk come out of your mouths, but only what is helpful for building others up according to their needs, that it may benefit those who listen (Ephesians 4:29).

Notice that our words have the power to tear down or build up, harm or heal. The Proverbs even go so far as to credit our tongues with the power to bring life or death—a sobering thought. No wonder Paul warned the Ephesians to censor what comes out of their mouths.

Also notice God did not think the heavens and earth, plants and animals into being in Genesis; he "said," and the world was fashioned. As his children, formed in his image, we have an expression of that same authority. The extraordinary influence we have in the spoken word is not just coincidental; it is a scriptural promise by God's design. So use your voice to create an atmosphere of praise in your home and around your life. As the Psalmist says, in the morning let him hear your voice (5:3). Extol him at all times, and let his praise be on your lips (34:1). Cry out to him with your mouth, and let his praise be on your tongue (66:17). Get in a groove by speaking into existence that which you want your spirit to believe and act on!

7. Get creative.

If there is one thing that can be said about worship in most American churches, it is that it is predictable. At 9:00 a.m. on Sunday morning the gates of heaven are stormed with 20 minutes of perfunctory praise. At 11:00 a.m. another 20 minutes goes up. By noon all the cafeterias are full and the worship spigot all but shuts off for a week.

As I've said before, I'm not against church. I love church. But if worship is supposed to be a love expression toward God, shouldn't it be a little more, well, expressive? Shouldn't our relationship with the bridegroom have at least some elements of spontaneity and excitement, maybe even passion?

If worship is supposed to be a love expression toward God, shouldn't it be a little more, well, expressive?

When I am in an airport and I see troops returning from overseas duty, I love to watch that moment of reunion when they greet their spouse or children or loved ones. Sometimes the family has balloons or gifts in hand. I've seen them holding "Welcome Home" signs obviously made by children barely old enough to understand why Mommy or Daddy has been away. And when they step out of the jetway and catch sight of each other, they don't walk up, shake hands and recite a creed of devotion. It's usually an instant release of all kinds of emotion. Often, there are no words spoken. They embrace, kiss, cry, laugh, and embrace again. It's almost a holy occasion and I always feel a little undeserving but blessed for being an accidental part of it.

God created us with an enormous capacity to feel and love. We are highly emotional beings, and worshiping God should be the supreme romance of all from the moment we first encounter him to the day we stand at the throne. Romance implies playfulness, anticipation, empathy, interaction, desire and creativity. Good romance is full of wonderful surprises and doing things out of the ordinary just to delight in our beloved and see a smile on his or her face. Yet many of us simply don't experience that kind of passion or romance in our relationship with the One who created us and loves us the most.

As you seek to become a lifestyle worshiper, ask the Holy Spirit to release in you feelings and emotions in worship that will lead to creative love expressions. Ask him for fresh ideas and new

inspirations for ways and times to worship. Ours is a love relationship with God, and it takes some effort and commitment on
our part to keep it alive and growing.

Be willing to be creative. As we just mentioned, explore
some new styles of worship music. Experiment with some different worship postures. Consider various times and places where
you can worship. Take a walk outside and focus your attention on
unique things of beauty that God has created in the natural world
for us to enjoy. Or go to your church during the week and spend
a few minutes quietly kneeling at the empty altar. You could even
go to a different church, one that is not like yours, and just thank
God for the freedom we have to worship and the diversity of the
body of Christ. Put flowers on the altar just for him. Write him a
love note. Go in your closet and see what it feels like to shout to
the Lord! Sing a great hymn or just read the words out loud as a
prayer. Whatever you do, be determined to care more about what
he thinks than what anyone else thinks, especially yourself.

Being creative in worship doesn't have to mean big plans or
grand ideas. Little things—like stopping in the middle of a busy
day to tell God how much you love him, or using those times
in the middle of the night when you find yourself awake to just
thank him for all the ways in which he has provided for you—
these can be sweet moments of affection that keep you in tune
to God's heart. You might be standing at the kitchen sink doing
dishes, and just stop briefly to lift your hands and say, "Lord I love
you. Thank you for washing me clean!"

You have the privilege of worshiping the God of the universe. Allow your imagination to help you honor him in a manner that compliments his grandeur.

8. Get thankful.

I saw a church promotional piece at Christmas time with the
invitation "Come celebrate our new building this Christmas!"

Almost immediately I had to repent for the barrage of judgmental thoughts bouncing around in my head. Celebrate a building?

In carnal, people-based strongholds, we celebrate a lot of things: new buildings, awards, accolades and accomplishments. But I fear that so much of what we are truly thankful for is directed at each other. We are grateful for what the institution did for us, or what a group of donors gave to us. We are so appreciative of endowments and gifts and contributions of people. Gratitude like that may be fitting at times, but it does not necessarily turn our focus to the Savior or inspire us to worship him. We can stay so busy appreciating and praising the works of people that we don't develop a heart of gratitude toward God first and foremost.

If we did nothing else throughout our lifetime for God except to stand and thank him every day for the gift of salvation and his great sacrifice which bought it, then we would have fulfilled our most noble calling

If we did nothing else throughout our lifetime for God except to stand and thank him every day for the gift of salvation and his great sacrifice which bought it, then we would have fulfilled our most noble calling. He gave us life. And then because he loved us so much, he offered us the gift of eternal life with him in heaven as adopted sons and daughters. This is where thankfulness starts. It starts with the question David asked, "O Lord, what is man that you care for him, the son of man that you think of him? (Psalm 144:3)—the realization that he is omnipotent and holy and we are like blades of grass that are here one day and withered and gone the next. Yet even still, we are so precious to him that he has the very hairs on our heads numbered!

The Bible says we are to "enter his gates with thanksgiving" (Psalm 100:4), so we should start off our worship time by expressing our gratitude to God. David recorded several "thank you" lists during his lifetime in the Psalms. In fact, the first lit-urgy he wrote for the Levites was a Psalm of thanks which they were to offer to God every day. You can read it in 1 Chronicles 16:7-36. Over and over you see a common refrain in David's heart, "Give thanks to the Lord, for he is good; his love endures forever" (Psalm 106:1). Even Jesus, throughout the gospels, regularly gave thanks to God because it was always in his mind to direct atten-tion to the Father.

The Lord is worthy of our heartfelt gratitude every day. Giv-ing thanks to him is a tremendous source of humility, and it puts God in his proper place in the minds of men as the Most High. Keep a journal to remember the deeds of God in your life. Make a list of the various names of God to keep in your Bible and thank him each day for a unique part of his character. Establishing a habit of thankful praise is the perfect antidote to pride and self-sufficiency. How good it is to be reminded of who our God is in the face of carnal strongholds!

9. Get determined.

If you are facing carnal strongholds, praising God may not be an easy thing to do. When you feel surrounded by people who are angry, bitter, disapproving, prideful, jealous, seditious, judgmen-tal, self-righteous or pessimistic (just to name a few), you may not feel like you have much to sing about. That is when worship be-comes an act of will, or as the writer of Hebrews describes it, a "sacrifice of praise" (Hebrews 13:15).

The Levites came to the tabernacle every day to worship the Lord and attend to his Presence. It was their duty, their respon-sibility as the appointed tribe. That is not to say that at times, they must have been the envy of all the other Israelites because of their closeness to Jehovah. But there must have been days when no fire came down from heaven, no miraculous signs appeared, the tabernacle seemed lifeless, and no one even said "thank you." There were probably times when even the Levites felt discouraged or uninspired; maybe even grumpy. However on those days, they worshiped just the same. They worshiped every day and every night because they were Levites. That was their job. And he was worthy. Period.

One of my favorite passages of scripture is Isaiah 61:1-3:

The Spirit of the Sovereign Lord is on me, because the Lord has anointed me to preach good news to the poor. He has sent me to bind up the brokenhearted, to proclaim freedom for the captives and release from darkness for the prisoners, to proclaim the year of the Lord's favor and the day of vengeance of our God, to comfort all who mourn, and provide for those who grieve in Zion—to bestow on them a crown of beauty instead of ashes, the oil of gladness instead of mourning, and a garment of praise instead of a spirit of despair. They will be called oaks of righteousness, a planting of the Lord for the display of his splendor.

I love this passage because it refers to praise as a "garment," or something you put on. You may go into your closet in the mornings and think to yourself, "I am so tired of these clothes; I am sick of wearing the same things again and again." Yet you still put something on every day, regardless of how you feel. The garment of praise can be similar—you put on the pants of thanksgiving, pull over your head a mantle of song, and slide your feet into dancing shoes so that you are clothed with a merry spirit!

This is how we worship in the face of difficult circumstances, bad reports and contrary people. When you don't feel like putting on the garment of praise, you tell yourself just like David did, "Praise the Lord, O my soul; all my inmost being, praise his holy name" (Psalm 103:1). Sometimes you may need to talk to yourself in order to overcome your feelings.

I often hear someone suggest that if we just praise God in the midst of hard times, he will work everything out. And in some cases, this may happen. But worship is not a magic lamp that we rub in order to make God like us so he will act on our behalf. Worship is for him; for his pleasure. So much in the consumer based church is for our benefit—it almost seems at times that we think God exists to serve us and our feelings and so we expect him to come through. But the opposite is true. We exist to bring pleasure to our heavenly Father, and to offer him all praise, honor and glory that is due his name! We worship because of who he is, not how we feel.

One of the greatest examples of a life determined to praise him was Fanny Crosby. Born in 1820, Fanny contracted an illness as an infant while the family doctor was away. A man posing as a doctor offered to treat Fanny, but the hot mustard poultices he prescribed for her eyes left her completely blind, even though the illness itself eventually subsided. When the "doctor's" identity was discovered, he disappeared.[5]

Despite enduring such a cruel twist of fate, Fanny never became embittered, but rather over the next 95 years wrote over 9,000 hymns, many of which are still sung today. One of my favorites is, "Praise Him! Praise Him! Tell of his excellent greatness; Praise Him! Praise Him! Ever in joyful song!"

About her blindness, she said:

It seemed intended by the blessed providence of God that I should be blind all my life, and I thank him for the dispensation. If perfect earthly sight were offered me tomorrow I would not accept it. I might not have sung hymns to the praise of God if I had been distracted by the beautiful and interesting things about me.

What an amazing legacy of determination and worship.[6]

10. Get together.

It is fairly common knowledge that most beneficial disciplines in life are easier attained with the support of like-minded, like-hearted friends who will make the journey with you and encourage you along the way. Whether you are talking about losing weight, learning a new skill or quitting a bad habit, as humans we crave the support and camaraderie that comes from having a network of allies on our side. No one wants to fight alone.

Therefore, in your quest to become a lifestyle worshiper, find others who will worship with you and hold you accountable. If at first you feel alone and you don't know of other Levites that might be lurking in your church, ask God to intervene and lead you to them. I believe he will. I have taught in many, many churches where it seemed that this message fell on deaf ears. But then, at the end of the day, one by one they would come to me with tears in their eyes. I knew right away, "This is a Levite!"

They are out there, yearning for someone to call them out of the shadows and release them to worship as a ministry. They don't want to work in the nursery; they don't want to volunteer at a mission. They want to be like Anna, who "never left the temple but worshiped night and day, fasting and praying" (Luke 2:36-37).

[Anna] never left the temple but worshiped night and day, fasting and praying.

Getting together does not mean that you necessarily have to be physically in the same place. When I talk about corporate worship, I believe that if you are singing a song to the Lord in your house, and another Levite is worshiping in his car, and another is waiting quietly on him at the church altar, and still others are offering praise phrases on their lunch break or while waiting in line at the bank, then together you are creating an atmosphere of worship within your church. All that worship adds up. Whether you are together in one room or apart, you are a worship community that is welcoming the Presence of God to come and take over. Individually your efforts may not feel significant, but collectively they are changing the spiritual climate in your congregation, making it hard for carnal strongholds to survive.

In 1727 one of the most famous prayer meetings in history was initiated by a young man named Nicholas Zinzendorf in a small German village called Herrnhut. What happened at Herrnhut was significant because not only did this small but passionate revival mark the beginning of the Moravian movement and the Protestant World Mission Movement, but it lasted an astounding 100 years!

For 100 years, the people of the village, formed into prayer choirs or teams, prayed around the clock. The people prayed in relays throughout the week, then on Sundays would join together in corporate prayer and worship from five in the morning until nine at night. Each week culminated with the men marching around the village singing one final song of praise. I love the idea of people praying and worshiping individually and then coming together to wrap it up with a joyful team effort.

When you can get together for corporate worship, do it. Organize an eight hour prayer and worship vigil during the day in which people sign up for an hour time slot to come to the church and worship. Arrange for live or recorded music, as well as times of silence and meditation. Make allowances for different worship styles and personalities. Or you might make it a habit to meet early before weekend services for a time of "pre-worship," simply inviting God to be blessed by everything that goes on and to wave his hand over your church. However you do it, getting together will make a Presence difference and move you closer to establishing divine strongholds.

11. Get expectant.

One of the main characteristics of a divine stronghold is divine displays. Where his Presence dwells, God manifests himself in all sorts of ways to heal, set free, touch, take over, speak, save, renew, deliver, bless and change. This is quite a contrast to the people based church, which is more likely to experience replays—man-made reruns of the same things that happened last week and the week before.

As I said earlier, expecting something to happen is different than wanting it to happen or even believing that it can happen. When you expect something, you prepare for it. Down here close to the Gulf of Mexico, hurricane tracking is a big deal; for some people it's a hobby. They pick up hurricane tracking guides, put out every year by local weather stations, at the beginning of the storm season and watch the paths and patterns of tropical systems that threaten the Gulf coast. Few people start buying plywood and generators, however, until the weather man says one is headed this way. When a storm is forecast to make landfall somewhere close to us, people start preparing. The closer it gets, the more feverish the preparations become. True expectancy produces action.

Often when we worship, we don't seem to expect much to happen because we don't invest anything in preparing for God's Presence to come. We receive little because we give little of ourselves to God, and therefore expect little in return.

Worship is the language of the amazing love relationship we have with the God of the universe. So when you praise him, do so with eager anticipation of all that he intends to do. God wants to accomplish things in and through your church; he created it for a purpose and destiny, and he wants nothing more than to see all of it fulfilled for his glory. As you invite him to take dominion and control, expect him to move. You are likely to discover that he will catch you up and astound you with blessings and revelations you never dreamed of. He is a ruler and king, but he has a pocket full of gifts and miracles beyond what we can imagination.

12. Get inspired to serve.

Our personal worship is, at the core, an offering to God. As we have said, it is a giving of ourselves to him. It is also an act of service, just as the Levites served in the tabernacle and tended to all of the daily responsibilities of worship. It is fitting, then, that one of the words for worship in the Old Testament also means "to serve." We serve that which we worship, and worship that which we serve. The two actions result from the same motivation—love.

> *We serve that which we worship, and worship that which we serve.*

This explains why churches that regularly enjoy good, authentic worship also tend to be churches that are very effective in serving the needs of their communities. Serving God by serving others is a natural outgrowth of lifestyle worship because when we give ourselves to God in worship, he in turn gives us his heart and we want to pay his love forward to others. This isn't the kind of serving that invests and then expects a return and recognition, but the kind of service that divests, taking no ownership in the outcome and expecting nothing in return except for the privilege of loving and worshiping God.

Author and theologian Oswald Chambers called this kind of worship offering *My Utmost for His Highest*. In his timeless devotional book by that title, he writes, "If we are devoted to the cause of humanity, we shall soon be crushed and broken-hearted, for we shall often meet with more ingratitude from men than we would from a dog; but if our motive is love to God, no ingratitude can hinder us from serving our fellow men."[7]

Plowing the Soil

Back in the days when I was working all kinds of jobs in order to support my pastoral habit, I used to operate a bull dozer clearing land. After the land was cleared initially, we would go over it again with a Rome plow, a deep-bladed disc that churned the soil 10-12 inches down. Then the land would be plowed yet again with a more shallow blade. Without this preparation process, the seed would never have taken root in the hard, rocky Texas soil. Each step was important in getting the ground ready to produce a new, healthy crop.

Worship is like a Rome plow that digs deep into the hardened thinking of mental fortresses created by cognitive closure. It loosens and stirs up the soil of our minds, making us ready to receive the seeds for new attitudes and ways of thinking. When our hearts have been prepared in worship, strategic prayer can then plant kingdom seed that will reap attributes of the mind of Christ.

*You are enthroned as the Holy One! Hallelujah!
This is our prayer: less of us; more of you. As we
worship you and seek you in prayer, we want to
decrease so that you can increase. Shine Jesus shine!
(Psalm 22:3; John 3:30)*

9

CRAFTED PRAYER

While I believe that GPS navigational systems like my tomtom are pretty much the most fascinating and useful inventions in the past decade, I have a friend who learned the hard way that it can be risky to rely on one. She started out on a road trip with her daughter—they were expecting to drive about six hours or more to their destination. She had fed Tom the name of the town (I think she actually listens to Tim's voice, the "James Bond" sounding character with a handsome British accent), loaded the car with travel snacks, and they were on their way.

They laughed and talked and listened to music, all the while following the happy green arrow on the screen and Tim's reassuring instructions. They stopped for lunch and drove some more. At some point in the afternoon, thinking that they must be getting close to their destination, my friend noticed that her tomtom indicated they still had almost 200 miles to go. "That can't be right," she said out loud.

She pulled over and dug a travel atlas out of the back of her car. After a little research, she discovered that the tomtom was as reliable as ever—she had just entered the wrong city name into it before they left home. They had basically been driving for several hours to the wrong side of Pennsylvania.

Even when you think you know where you're headed, it's always a good idea to periodically look up and read a road sign. Check the map. Even with good directions it's easy to make one wrong turn that can change your course dramatically.

In the consumer based church, we can get so busy making things happen, following along with the group, that no one really ever stops to read a road sign. No one wants to pause long enough to ask the questions, "Are we headed in the direction we set out to go? Are we getting closer to our destination? Are we even aiming at the right goal?"

Where carnal strongholds are in full force, the corporate mindset has run so far off the track toward false high places and idols that it is lost. And not only is it lost, but it is oblivious to its own lostness. That is a bad place to be. To satisfy its own desires, it has established belief systems that have the form of righteousness but are void of any real godly influence. Sadly, the people on board keep right on feeding the engine because, despite all their intellectual analysis and church growth theory, they have no idea that somewhere back there, they veered off course. Read Paul's description of such a church:

> For those who are according to the flesh and are controlled by its unholy desires set their minds on and pursue those things which gratify the flesh, but those who are according to the Spirit and are controlled by the desires of the Spirit set their minds on and seek those things which gratify the [Holy] Spirit. Now the mind of the flesh [which is sense and reason without the Holy Spirit] is death [death that comprises all the miseries arising from sin, both here and hereafter]. But the mind of the [Holy] Spirit is life and [soul] peace [both now and forever]. [That is] because the mind of the flesh [with its carnal thoughts and purposes] is hostile

to God, for it does not submit itself to God's Law; indeed it cannot (Romans 8:5-7, *Amplified Version*).

As I have said already, you don't want to confront carnal strongholds head on, and Paul's portrayal here helps you understand why. He explains that the mind of the flesh leads to death (spiritual death) and can not submit itself to God's law, or scriptural truth. So if you fight as the world fights, with arguments, discussions, campaigns, slander and debates, you will not win even with scriptural truth on your side, because the stronghold is blinded to anything other than its own created rule:

> For though we live in the world, we do not wage war as the world does. The weapons we fight with are not the weapons of the world. On the contrary, they have divine power to demolish strongholds. We demolish every argument and pretension that sets itself up against the knowledge of God, and we take captive every thought to make it obedient to Christ (2 Corinthians 10:3-5).

So we fight with the weapons of worship and prayer. Minds can not change minds. Only God can break through the deception to bring about transformation. Therefore the only hope we have to demolish strongholds is to invite him to come—his Presence, along with strategic prayer, is the divine power we have to demolish strongholds. If we experience his Presence enough over a prolonged period of time, the grip of the carnal belief systems can be weakened and we can experience freedom and a new way of thinking.

Jesus paid for that new way of thinking on the cross; the crown of thorns gave us access to a renewed mind in Christ.

Jesus paid for that new way of thinking on the cross; the crown of thorns gave us access to a renewed mind in Christ.

Paul is a good example of someone whose mindset was radically changed as a result of experiencing God. Before he was converted on the road to Damascus, Saul (his former name) was a hater of Christians who did everything he could to discredit their message and make life miserable for those who proclaimed it. He harassed the early disciples, going from town to town throwing as many in jail as he could. He was even involved in the stoning death of one of the twelve, Stephen. Paul had a mind that was imprisoned by carnal belief systems, and no amount of persuading was going to change it. In fact, the Christians were so afraid of him that they would have been terrified to try.

But then he encountered the unmistakable, inescapable Presence of God. The meeting was so dramatic that it changed Saul instantly, and God even gave him a new name as a symbol of his new identity. The mental make-over was so complete, that from that moment on, Paul became the most outspoken voice of the early church and activist for Jesus' message of grace and salvation. He planted new churches everywhere he preached, and then wrote half of the New Testament, just to top it off. Real life encounters with the Presence change people.

Think About Such Things

We have talked about how worship invites his Presence, sharpens our revelation of Jesus, and establishes him as the Most High in our thinking. As his Presence draws closer and begins to wave over us, carnal strongholds and high places are weakened and eventually crack, crumble and fall. And as we see Jesus more and more clearly, he becomes the high place—where we go for affirmation and help. He takes his rightful place on the central throne in our lives.

Worship also washes our minds clean to clear a path for new ways of thinking. As carnal strongholds weaken, we have freedom to make new choices and establish new patterns. Worship sheds the light of heaven's perspective on carnal belief systems, exposing them as flawed and sinful. In the atmosphere of praise, we are primed to adopt new ideas and attitudes which reflect the mind of Christ.

We know from scripture that God will not renew our minds for us; rather we have to become active participants in the process by working to take every one of our thoughts captive and bring them under submission to Jesus. We can't, however, accomplish this under our own power! We need the help of the Holy Spirit. As we step out in faith and commit to making changes, he supernaturally multiplies our efforts and becomes our partner. He is our advocate before the Father.

As you read through the following scriptures, notice how often we are instructed about the importance of what we think about. Also notice that in every case, the responsibility for renewing or directing our thought life is placed on us:

Finally, brothers, whatever is true, whatever is noble, whatever is right, whatever is pure, whatever is lovely, whatever is admirable—if anything is excellent or praiseworthy—think about such things (Philippians 4:8).

Seek the Lord while he may be found; call on him while he is near. Let the wicked forsake his way and the evil man his thoughts. Let him turn to the Lord, and he will have mercy on him, and to our God, for he will freely pardon. "For my thoughts are not your thoughts, neither are your ways my ways," declares the Lord (Isaiah 55:6-8).

Since, then, you have been raised with Christ, set your hearts on things above, where Christ is seated at the right hand of God. Set your minds on things above, not on earthly things. For you died, and your life is now hidden with Christ in God (Colossians 3:1-3).

But now you must rid yourselves of all such things as these: anger, rage, malice, slander, and filthy language from your lips. Do not lie to each other (speak things that are not true and not in agreement with God's perspective), since you have taken off your old self with its practices and have put on the new self, which is being renewed in knowledge in the image of its Creator (Colossians 3:8-10, parentheses mine).

Do not conform any longer to the pattern of this world, but be transformed by the renewing of your mind. Then you will be able to test and approve what God's will is—his good, pleasing and perfect will. (Romans 12:2).

Let this mind be in you which was also in Christ Jesus... (Philippians 2:5, *New King James Version*).

So how do we go about renewing our minds and bringing our thoughts into submission to Christ? We cut new grooves. We make the deliberate choice to start driving the truck down a different path. When the old way seems to beckon us back, we hold firm on the wheel, following tight the path marked out for us by the Holy Spirit. It won't be easy at first. The way will seem rough and unfamiliar. But if we persevere, we will carve out a new pattern that will replace the toxic one.

Our ultimate goal, as it is in every area of life, is Christlikeness. We want to have a mind that leads us to think and live as Jesus did. If you look down the list of divine strongholds, you will see that Jesus' life was a shining example of all of them. He lived and walked in passion, humility, honor, unity, grace and faith. In fact that is all a divine stronghold really is—a characteristic of God's nature being fully realized in your church "as it is in heaven" (Matthew 6:10).

Crafted Scripture Prayer

As old, carnal ways of thinking begin to weaken in his Presence, we must replace those thought patterns with new ones to keep from falling back into the well-worn grooves. We must cut new grooves in our minds, and we can do this through specifically targeted, consistent prayer.

We always want to remember that the Bible is our prayer language. In every circumstance, prayer is most effective when it is wrapped around the core of God's written word. Praying scripture based prayer ensures that we are parking on the promises of God instead of the problems, and asking in line with biblical truths and kingdom purposes. For these reasons, I have always found simple, focused prayers based on one or two specific verses to be very helpful prayer tools. We have written several sets of these topical prayers called *Keys to the Kingdom*.

There are times, however, when longer, more involved prayers may be appropriate. There are times when we don't even know how to pray. There are times, such as in dealing with personal or coporate strongholds, when our prayers need to be formed and fashioned in the crucible of our own fellowship with God.

At such times, we can come before him seeking, waiting, listening, and he will show us how to pray. If we are willing to take time and invest of ourselves in the process, the Holy Spirit will be the very author of our prayers. We don't have to wonder whether or not our prayers will be answered, because if we will ask him, God will tell us what he wants to accomplish in a situation, and then we can pray it to completion. When we take time to write a prayer in this manner, just as we might devote ourselves to penning an important letter, we can then live out of that prayer for weeks, months, even years. In a church setting, we can print it, distribute it, and stand in agreement on it.

Writing topical, scriptural prayers to be prayed regularly is not a new idea. *The Book of Common Prayer*, first published in 1547, was written by a group of clergy and laypeople as a liturgical guide for the Episcopal Church. It contains, in addition to daily readings and sacraments, hundreds of written prayers on a variety of subjects—for rain, for a person under affliction, for social justice, for prisoners, for a sick child. *The Book of Common Prayer* is still used in the Anglican tradition today, meaning that those prayers written ages ago have been prayed by Christians all over world throughout centuries. It's an amazing thought. What strikes me about the work is that none of the original writers are named. No one took credit.

Graham Cooke, in his book *Crafted Prayer,* coined that term for this ancient method of prayer, and I like it.[1] It emphasizes the *process* of constructing a prayer born from the heart of God and co-created with the Spirit. It denotes an artistic process which produces an original work. As a church, we can craft "uncommon" prayers that can become a personal creed—a declaration of what we desire, believe and expect in faith for God to do in our lives. As we craft prayers, we claim where we want to be, and create a new script that enables us to speak the desired kingdom fruit into our church until it is fulfilled.

When well-built, crafted prayers become a personal creed—a declaration of what we desire, believe and expect in faith for God to do in our lives.

Some churches I have known have actually crafted a visionary prayer that functioned much like a mission statement. In fact, most church mission statements could be turned into prayers, meaning that instead of just hanging on the wall or being printed in the bulletin for people to read, they could actually be offered back to God consistently across the life of the church. Such a crafted prayer would reflect and affirm God's purposes for the congregation.

Simply put, crafted scripture prayers are based on two things: 1) what God tells you to pray about a given situation; and 2) scripture. Good crafted prayers take time to write because they are well thought out and reflect both elements of the past and vision of the future. They require times of hearing God. Additionally, they may evolve over time, as progress is made or the vision becomes clearer.

Let's assume for a moment that you have a small group of people who have decided they want to intercede on behalf of your church. Their goal is to tear down a carnal stronghold and invite God's Presence to establish new thought patterns in the form of divine strongholds. You all decide to meet together to formulate a prayer plan. The process for constructing a crafted scripture prayer with your group might go something like this:

- Worship together for 30 minutes.

- In prayer, ask God to speak to each individual about how he wants you to pray. Ask questions like, "What do you want to teach us through this situation? How should we pray? What do you want to do in and through this situation? How do you want us to change and grow?

- Then ask each person to quietly spend 15 or 20 minutes waiting on God, listening for his voice. Ask them to jot down any specific words, phrases or scriptures that they sense he is speaking.

- Come back together as a group, and compile a list of all the words and scriptures. Each time a duplicate comes up, put a check mark beside it.

- Ask each person to again go quietly before the Lord to wait and listen for another 15-20 minutes. Ask them to write down single prayer sentences utilizing the list, focusing on any items that appear more than once. Use wording from scripture where possible.

- Come back together as a group and craft a prayer using the sentences. Write out the final prayer and distribute it to the group.

- Commit to pray the prayer daily until God fulfills what he said he will do!

As you can see, composing crafted scripture prayers requires an investment of time. You might create such a prayer in one two-hour meeting, or your group might need to soak longer, spending more time waiting and listening before the Lord. This is really important to the outcome, so that we are ultimately asking God what he wants us to pray, and then we are praying that until we see results.

Praying in this manner is so exciting because since we have spent time hearing God's heart on the matter, and since we have sought out what the Bible says about it, we are truly praying the answer from the very beginning. If we get discouraged or feel old habits creeping into our thinking, we pull out the crafted scripture prayer and speak it again and again, renewing our minds in the process. This is how we take thoughts captive, by taking the time to sculpt new ones and then meditating on them until they become a part of our belief system. Since our prayer came from God's heart and his word, we know that we are putting on the mind of Christ, and we can rest in the assurance that if we persevere, we will see new attitudes and thought patterns form.

We looked in the last chapter at how powerful our words are. We have the authority, with our words, to change the spiritual climate around us, and speak scriptural promises into existence. What we speak has great influence both over us and over those around us. At the same time, the Bible assures us that the word of God is our most powerful weapon, and when we pray it back to him, it is not just empty words, but the sword of the Spirit in action:

> Take the helmet of salvation and the sword of the Spirit, which is the word of God. And pray in the Spirit on all occasions with all kinds of prayers and requests. With this in mind, be alert and always keep on praying for all the saints (Ephesians 6:17-18).

> As the heavens are higher than the earth, so are my ways higher than your ways and my thoughts than your thoughts. As the rain and the snow come down from heaven, and do not return to it without watering the earth and making it bud and flourish, so that it yields seed for the sower and bread for the eater, so is my word that goes out from my mouth: It will not return to me empty, but will accomplish what I desire and achieve the purpose for which I sent it (Isaiah 55:9-11).

In this first familiar passage, Paul exhorts the Christians at Ephesus to take up this sword by praying "all kinds of prayers" on "all occasions." In another letter, he urges us to "pray continually" (1 Thessalonians 5:17). In the passage in Isaiah 55, God promises us that his word will always accomplish the purpose for which he gave it. When we base our prayers on scripture, we have good reason to be confident that God will hear and respond, upholding his promises and fulfilling his plans.

The power of our words combined with the supremacy of scripture gives us greater command in the earth than we realize. I often think that if we really understood how powerful our prayers can be, that we would do nothing else all day except pray! We would pray about everything all the time if only we could see the effects our prayers have in the spiritual realm. By choosing to speak the word of God persistently, intentionally and boldly into situations in our lives and in our church, we can see the Presence of God drive out evil and establish a pattern of his activity.

Another benefit of corporate, crafted prayer comes from one of the most basic prayer principles—the power of agreement. When people pray together—and when I say together I mean with like heart and mind, claiming the same scriptures over a common theme, but not necessarily physically in the same place—something in the economy of God says that those prayers become exponentially more effective.

The power of agreement in utilizing crafted prayer in an atmosphere of worship can invite God to be fully God on the scene and change our perspective to match his.

> *And pray in the Spirit on all occasions with all kinds of prayers and requests.*
> *Ephesians 6:18*

PRAYER ARSENAL

When Paul said we were to pray "with all kinds of prayers and requests" (Ephesians 6:18), it is important to note that he seemed to understand that not all prayer is alike. Different situations call for different types of prayer. The effectiveness of crafted prayer lies in hitting the bull's eye—aiming prayer at the heart of issues God is revealing to you.

Following is a look at six different kinds of prayers that can target the carnal strongholds, each one inviting God to renew a specific thought pattern and establish some aspect of the mind of Christ in us. With each kind of prayer I offer a few examples of short scripture prayers that you can use as starters for your own crafted prayers. I believe God will give us what we earnestly seek in prayer, especially when we are desiring to be conformed to the image of his Son.

Prayers of Seeking - From Religion to Passion

Jesus' life was a divine stronghold of passion. He lived with a purpose; he lived with joy; he understood the emotions of the Father. The movie that shook the Christian community several years ago called *The Passion of the Christ* was aptly named because his entire life—not just the crucifixion—reflected God's passionate heart towards us, his creation. It was Christ's passion to be born, it was his passion to live as a man, it was his passion to heal and minister to the lost and hurting, and it was his passion to die so that we might be reconciled to the Father.

Obviously, Jesus' relationship with the Father was unique—they were one and yet separate, different and yet the same. Jesus did not have to seek God to know him because he had been with him since before time began. Yet for us to have intimacy with the Father, we must seek him. If we truly want to put on the mind of Christ, we must seek the Father's face and not just his hand. We must seek to know him and his abiding Presence.

We need to push away the distractions, clear our minds, and resolutely hunger for the Presence of God. We must choose to do those things that create a vacuum for him to invade. We can craft scripture prayers around the theme of seeking God to introduce new ideas and thought patterns that will counteract the legalistic spirit of religion.

The effect of this kind of prayer on religious mindsets is that God becomes real. When we seek him he is revealed as high and majestic. If we have made a god in our image, the correction is quickly made when the real God shows up and we discover that we are made in his image. To seek God is to experience him, and his Presence puts the humanistic spirit in the right perspective. We begin to do things not by our might but by his Spirit. Where religious mindsets safeguard the traditions of the institution, the corporate mind of Christ yearns to see the new thing God is doing.

Therefore, we take on the corporate mind of Christ as we seek more of God together. We don't seek his hand, but his countenance. This is Presence based theology; we say to ourselves, "Go after God" and we call out other Levites, if there are any, to seek his face together.

- Holy Father, I love and adore you. I confess that I seek your hand more than your face. In times of trouble you have been there for me, and in so many ways you have blessed me beyond measure. Thank you! Now with passion, may I look to your face and seek you for who you are, not just for what you give. Selah (Psalm 27:8).

- One thing I ask of the Lord, this is what I seek: that I may dwell in the house of the Lord all the days of my life, to gaze upon the beauty of the Lord, and to seek him in his temple. Lord, capture my gaze with the beauty of your countenance. Make me so enamored with you that I look to no other! Yes and so be it (Psalm 27:4).

- Lord, your voice is powerful and majestic. With a listening ear, I await your words. Teach me to be silent before you. Let me seek your face and hear what you have to tell me. I will ascribe to you the glory due your name, and I worship you in the splendor of your holiness. Amen (Psalm 29).

Prayers of Surrender – From Pride to Humility

Jesus' life was a divine stronghold of humility. Everything he was and did, from the circumstances of his birth to his undeserved death, revealed the highest form of humility in the very heart of God. That Jesus would display such humility is even more poignant a fact because he certainly didn't have to. With each insult and accusation, at each strike of the scourge, he could have called on legions of angels to set the record straight. But he did not. He chose to endure because he was completely surrendered to the Father's plan.

Even at a young age, Jesus was yielded to his eternal purpose. At age 12 his parents found him in the temple, amazing the people with his teaching (Luke 2:41-52). When he walked through the streets, crowded in on every side, he felt one woman's touch on the hem of his clothes because he sensed healing power flowing through his body (Mark 5:30). And have you ever noticed that despite constantly being sought out and interrupted, Jesus never seemed upset or frustrated by unexpected circumstances or intrusions? He simply used every opportunity to glorify his Father and further his plan because his time and life were directed by heaven's perspective (Luke 19:1-10). Without resistance he yielded to the work of the Spirit.

The one time we know Jesus experienced intense struggle between his own human desire and submission to his Father's will was in the Garden of Gethsemane. The Bible tells us that he bore every temptation and every sin, and I believe those moments of anguish before his arrest testify to that. Yet even then, he yielded his mind so that by his wounds, the curse of insanity could be broken. As a result, the power and inevitability of crazy thinking ended at Calvary.

The only way to demolish a stronghold of pride is to circle it with the Presence. Like Jericho, corporate pride is an impregnable fortress. Only the divine power of God can penetrate a mindset that has been in place for a long time. Trying to argue someone out of a mental fortress is like trying to climb a mountain without a rope; it's just hard to get anywhere.

...the power and inevitability of crazy thinking ended at Calvary.

The idolatry of pride in our own abilities and accomplishments is so tempting to the human spirit. We are self-reliant and entrepreneurial, and we love to admire a job well done. In order to have the mind of Christ that is clothed in humility, we need to surrender our own will every day. Therefore, to come against pride we craft prayers of surrender that train our minds to think like Jesus, yielded in every way to God's heavenly perspective. We come down off of our high horse, prostrate ourselves before him and give up the reins. We abandon our own mental citadels and unconditionally surrender to his way of thinking.

- You, oh Lord, are the Most High God. We bow before you and pray that we can take every thought captive to obey Jesus Christ. We confess that we have high places of pride in our lives, and we ask that in your Presence, they be demolished. Amen (Psalm 83:18, 95:6; 2 Corinthians 10:5).

- In your name, Jesus, right now I lift my hands to you in praise and surrender. I do this in behalf of the many who do not bow before you. With mercy, cleanse us all of arrogance and presumptuous thinking. Now bless the Lord, oh my soul (Psalm 19:13, 63:4).

- May we embrace the rest of your Presence, and cease striving to protect an image or reputation. Heal hurts caused by clashes of egos and wars over things that don't really matter. May we simply give up, let go, and experience yieldedness as a way of life—life in Christ Jesus. Amen (Hebrews 4).

Prayers of Covering – From Sedition to Honor

Jesus' life was a divine stronghold of honor. As we have seen, he honored his Father by taking time to be with him, and by completely surrendering his desires to the higher purposes of his calling. He honored his earthly parents with his love and respect, his twelve closest companions with his friendship, and the religious and government leaders of the day with his complicity—he honored them all. He demonstrated honor to the elderly, women, children, and even sinners by loving them and healing them.

The stronghold of sedition shows dishonor to pastors and church leaders, which in turn dishonors God. It is a language that exposes the faults of another. When we complain and grumble about circumstances within the church or the leaders at the helm, we are not only causing pain to pastoral families, but we are also keeping the church from walking in the favor of God. We are actually helping Satan do his job by holding up one of God's anointed to ridicule, judgment and public humiliation. No matter what the situation, that is just counterproductive in every way to the church's mission!

If we want to reverse the damage and put ourselves back in right standing with God, then we must shut down the thought patterns that drive us to expose others and instead learn what it means to cover our shepherds in prayer; and not just our shepherds, but all other civic and government leaders as well. The Bible is very clear that we are to honor and pray for "kings and all those in authority" (1 Timothy 2:2). As Christians it is our responsibility to honor the offices of leadership by covering them in prayer, even when we may not agree with the people holding the offices.

Covering is an essential part of life, both physically and spiritually. Without covering, one is exposed to all sorts of harm. The first thing that Adam and Eve did after they had sinned in the Garden was to cover themselves with fig leaves because they suddenly realized they were naked and exposed. God in his compassion clothed them with animal skin just as he would later clothe us with salvation and righteousness:

> The Lord God made garments of skin for Adam and his wife and clothed them (Genesis 3:21).

> I delight greatly in the Lord; my soul rejoices in my God. For he has clothed me with garments of salvation and arrayed me in a robe of righteousness, as a bridegroom adorns his head like a priest, and as a bride adorns herself with her jewels (Isaiah 61:10).

When we pray scripture over someone, we are clothing them in the living word of God. We are putting a hedge of protection around their life, shielding them from spiritual darts and attacks of the enemy. To cover our leaders doesn't mean that we believe they are sinless or that we are trying to hide their shortcomings from God (who sees all the dirt anyway); it simply means that we offer them a protective shield of grace behind which to grow into the leaders God has appointed them to be. We pray prayers of covering that will guard their lives from the enemy's assaults so that God can deal with them and work through them within a place of safety.

- Renew the pastors of our city in the Holy Spirit. Let them hope in you and soar on wings like eagles. Quicken them with your Word and refresh their vision. Grant them confidence to stand in strong personal convictions that honor you. Cover the shepherds of your people, and protect their ministries. Thank you Lord (Romans 8:11; 1 John 5:13-14; Acts 5:42).

- Father, in Jesus' name we bind the enemy and his assignments against church leaders. May all plots of the evil one be canceled in your authority. Let every elder, deacon and leader be clothed in the full armor of God, shielded from sedition and gossip. Grant them many opportunities to pray and worship together. Amen (Matthew 10:1; Ephesians 6:10-11).

- Our Father in heaven, you are high and lifted up. Be so in our state government. Let your kingdom come in all areas of our legislature and judicial system. As it is in heaven, may it be throughout our state capital. We worship you for all the ways in which you have blessed this state, and we seek your forgiveness for ways in which we have failed to acknowledge and honor you. Deliver us from evil thoughts, words and actions, and lead us toward righteousness. Be worshiped here in this state, for yours is the glory forever (Matthew 6:9-15).

Prayers of Blessing – From Parochialism to Unity

Jesus' life was a divine stronghold of unity. From his heavenly outlook, he did not see people as rich or poor, slave or free, Jew or Gentile, man or woman, adult or child, farmer or tax collector. He showed little preference for the company he kept based on social status or reputation. Jesus seemed to deal with people on a level that completely transcended earthly categories and labels, concerning himself only with the question, "Who do you say that I am?" And it was this perspective he asked the Father to give us, his body, in his prayer in John 17. Only through complete unity in him will the Father be glorified, and the world see clearly the testimony of his love.

In order for us to achieve the unity Jesus prayed for, we must break the cycle of parochial attitudes and behaviors. We must renew our thinking about the groups, sects and denominations making up Christianity to see them as Jesus does—one body, of one Spirit, all saved and sanctified by the same blood. Our only real concern should be, "Who do you say Jesus is?"

To shatter the stronghold of parochial thinking, we start by crafting scripture prayers of blessing. Following Jesus' example, we cut new mental grooves that look past race, creed and any other label that separates, straight to the heart of others like us who are recipients of grace with little else to boast about. We establish new patterns of speaking blessing and favor over other parts of the body, even those parts that seem different from us.

Jesus lived to bless, not to curse. He came to earth to be a blessing in every way to all who would receive. The act of blessing played a huge role in how biblical history played out, from the appointment of kings to fathers of nations. As a part of every covenant agreement between God and man, blessing was not taken lightly, because a spoken blessing backed by God's authority was not negotiable, retractable or transferable. It was a done deal. Blessings became powerful prophecies that shaped lives, destinies, and legacies.

...blessing was not taken lightly, because a spoken blessing backed by God's authority was not negotiable, retractable or transferable.

The political spirit of parochialism would like to steal the blessing of God and believe that its adherents are the only ones eligible to receive. But God's blessings are open-ended, with no regard for man-made rules and boundaries. His blessings are available to all, and as heirs to the covenant it is our responsibility to extend his blessings to others. So we build prayers that bless, and we speak them over other believers, churches and pastors. Then with gratitude, we meditate on the goodness of God that he did not exclude even us from his covenant promises.

- Lord Jesus, we worship you and thank you for your love and grace. Forgive us for ignoring other churches in our city, for in doing so, we are failing to recognize part of our own body. Have mercy on us for any way in which we have hurt other believers, or repelled non-believers, with our parochial attitudes and isolationism. Make us one (1 Corinthians 11:29-30).

- Lord, you are a covenant-making God. We especially thank you for the New Covenant we have in Jesus. Forgive us for acting like it is with us alone; we humbly confess there is only one covenant, available to all who call upon your name, even those who believe differently than we do. We want to lift up your name, not ours. Give us the mind of Christ to freely share all that you have given us with other churches and those in need. Let our pantry be open. This is our prayer: one identity to glorify Jesus Christ. Always and amen (Exodus 34:10; Matthew 26:28; John 17:10).

- Your are Elohim, our creator. You created and are creating even now; therefore we humble ourselves and ask that you create ways for the body of Christ in our city to worship together. We want your Presence in greater measure, and so we desire to be unified in worship like it is in heaven. Raise up Levites as lifestyle worshipers in every church. Let our pastors call for special times of seeking you, not because of a problem but for you alone. Amen (Genesis 1:1; 2 Chronicles 7:1-3; Revelation 4).

Prayers of Compassion – From Judgment to Grace

Jesus' life was a divine stronghold of grace. He offered his unconditional love to us "while we were still sinners" (Romans 5:8), paying the ultimate price for our salvation. His love is "agape" love—not dependent on our worth, but rather imputing worth to us. At every point of our sin he sees us, covers us, forgives us, and calls us into deeper relationship with him. That is why we sing, "amazing grace, how sweet the sound."

As we saw in our discussion of the grace stronghold, God's

love expressed through us to sinners is called compassion. Therefore it is compassion that we offer in crafted prayer as an antidote to the carnal thought patterns of judgment. It is not our job to judge, nor are we qualified, so we simply extend the love of Jesus by praying for the felt needs of the lost. With compassion, we invite the hurting and disenfranchised to experience God's Presence and we let the Holy Spirit do the rest.

As we craft prayers of compassion, we rewrite our self-righteous scripts and let go of prideful attitudes. We offer acceptance instead of condemnation, kindness instead of censure. The more we pray for the lost, speaking what the Bible says over them, the more our minds can be renewed to think like Jesus, to see the lost as he sees them. And when they encounter unmerited love and grace in the atmosphere of his Presence, they are in a position to be drawn into relationship with Jesus. Prayers of compassion are the summons to salvation.

- We thank you and worship you, Father God, for loving us so much that you sent your Son Jesus to earth not to condemn us, but to save us. Even now we take our thoughts captive to live out of this truth. We pray to see others through your great love for them. Let no condemnation for anyone reside in us. Amen (John 3:16-17).

- Jesus in your name we want to tear down all our high places of self-righteousness. We acknowledge that we are not qualified to judge, and we repent of our tendency to point out the specks in everyone else's eyes when there is a giant log in our own! With your help, we relinquish our desire to control by looking down on others and pronouncing verdicts on their lives. God you are the only judge now and forever (Matthew 7:1-3; 2 Corinthians 10:4-5; James 4:12).

- Lord Jesus, you are our source in all things; grant us laborers to seek and save the lost. Give us each a "most wanted" list of names to pray over—family members, friends, even famous people—that we might see them accept your salvation gift. As you sent Philip to the Ethiopian on the desert road, send people ready to share the Gospel into their lives; intersect them where they work, play and live. Make our "most wanted" ready to hear. May they receive you as savior and rejoice! Amen and soon (Matthew 9:38; Acts 8:26-40).

Prayers of Agreement – From Fear to Faith

Jesus' life was a divine stronghold of faith. He was sure of what he hoped for and certain of what he did not see. He endured discomfort and the frustration of the incomplete because he knew that in time, all things would be completed. He lived looking forward to something better, yet seemed perfectly content in each moment he lived. He never worried or became anxious because he knew that the Father's word was good. Jesus had such trust in his Father's ways that he could fall asleep in a small fishing boat tossed around on a stormy sea, and wake up to command the wind and waves to stop. Faith produces peace of mind.

Where fear has set in as a belief system and has paralyzed a church in a holding pattern of worry and apathy, it is imperative that the grooves of doubt and disbelief be replaced with new thought patterns that lead to faith and hope. This is accomplished by crafting prayers that claim God's promises in agreement with scripture. This is the purpose of all scripture prayer really, to pray the solution—what God says about the situation—rather than focusing on the problem. The Bible has a lot to say, and can speak to just about every need or crisis we might be facing. But our tendency is to meditate on what is wrong, or what might go wrong, or what has gone wrong in the past, rather than focusing on who God is in light of the circumstances.

So we construct prayers of agreement—big, bold prayers that proclaim God's goodness, his nature and his ability in the face of every human dilemma. We speak his word back to him, claiming all that is ours under the covenant. We meditate on prayers that reinforce our trust in God's provision, and our gratitude for all the ways in which he has blessed us over the years. In doing so, we remind ourselves of all we have to be thankful for, and all the reasons we have to believe. God is a God of hope, and if we will choose to agree with him in faith, he will fill our hearts with divine hope for the future.

God is a God of hope, and if we will choose to agree with him in faith, he will fill our hearts with divine hope for the future.

- God of Israel, we welcome you in this place. You are an astounding God who does astounding things. Come and put your power on public display. Let your fire fall! In doing so, burn up carnal thought patterns that control us because we have catered to people for so long. Boldly be God in our church so no one will doubt. We look up and wait for your final settlement. Amen (1 Kings 18:36-39; Psalm 68:1).

- Teach us, heavenly Father, how to live by faith, for it is the title deed to heaven's revelation on earth. By faith, we can speak to the mountains that cause us to doubt and fear, and they will move to make way for your Presence. It pleases you when we come to you, believing that we will receive. Give us divine hope so that we can see as you see. Even so, come now Lord Jesus. Amen (Hebrews 11:1-3; Galatians 2:20; Mark 11:23).

- Father, just as Moses prayed, let our leaders know your ways. May they consistently hear and follow your voice as they worship you. Grant them favor and authority that comes from discerning your heart and being Presence drawn in all matters. Free us from simply repeating the past; do a new thing in our midst! Impart to us a holy faith that creates a divine hope! (Exodus 33:13; Isaiah 43:18-19; Numbers 7:89)

Transcontinental Railroad

On May 10, 1869, the Union Pacific and Central Pacific railroads celebrated the completion of the transcontinental railroad by driving a golden stake into the final segment of track at Promontory Summit, Utah. The idea for the government-funded project, which took seven years to complete, was originally initiated by President Abraham Lincoln during the Civil War. He recognized that the country needed a connection to California where gold had been discovered in 1849 and which had become a state a year later.

Prior to the railroad's completion, the trip from New York to San Francisco was so long and dangerous that many people actually opted to make the journey by sea, around the tip of South America. By land, it took an arduous four to six months. The railroad did nothing less than revolutionize the American economy, reducing the trip down to a mere 6 days. Goods and people could now easily reach the west.[2]

I am encouraging you to lay down tracks of crafted scripture prayer and lifestyle worship so that the Presence of God can travel through your church. He makes all the difference! When we lay prayer and worship side by side, we invite him to rush in. We give him access to every part to change, heal and inhabit. Where issues of control exist, His Presence brings resolution. A renewed passion for seeking and worshiping God will do nothing less than overhaul entrenched corporate mindsets and revolutionize your church.

When you are waging war against a stronghold, you are endeavoring to create a space of time for the person to come to himself or herself. However, there is no guarantee that if that time is created, the person will come to his or her senses. People must make choices by their own free will, and repent of their errant thinking in order to become free.[1]
—John Paul Jackson

10

A Tale of Two Cities

I travel somewhere in the United States pretty much every weekend teaching and doing seminars. I don't fill up stadiums or arenas; I speak mostly in local churches or at regional conferences. Sometimes I travel to big cities, but more often it seems I find myself in places like Chautauqua, New York, Melvin, Illinois or Farmville, Virginia where America lives, works and goes to church. It has given me a great fascination with and love for the small towns that cover the map and how they can be so much alike, and yet at the same time, so different.

When I go somewhere, I like to learn as much as I can about the area before I get up to teach. It's partly a defensive strategy, so that I don't say something embarrassing. But it also helps me relate better to the people, which makes me a better speaker. So I tend to be fairly observant, and I ask a lot of questions. For example, I can often get a pretty reliable idea of what size town I'm in by going into a local diner and asking a simple question, "Is there a Starbucks here?"

"A what?"

"A Starbucks, you know, where I could get some coffee."

"We serve coffee here."

"Actually I was looking for specialty coffee."

"Ours is a dark roast; it's really good. Can I get you some?"

"Thank you. That will be perfect."

Interpretation: The automatic cappuccino machine at the convenience store where I bought water is the closest I'll come to a latte that weekend. The nearest hospital is at least 40 miles away. And if I forgot to pack something, I can buy it at the Dollar General or do without. Towns like that are the heart and soul of our country.

Stepping into a different foyer every weekend, I tend to notice things about churches too. Patterns emerge. Trends become clear. It is more than two decade's worth of these experiences and observations that led me to the conclusion that strongholds are not only real, they operate on some level, for better or worse, in every church.

I know of no other way to bring this book to a conclusion except to give you an idea of how I personally experience these strongholds week after week. I'm not always in a church long enough to analyze the strongholds or completely understand them, but I know they're there. They are unmistakable. So come with me.

CITY #1

I pushed open the double glass doors to the breezeway between the main sanctuary and the educational wing. A little red sign stuck in the flower bed beside the door announced "Office." As I intuitively picked out the correct door, I thought of Forrest Gump and his box of chocolates—I never really know what I'm about to bite into.

Sitting behind a small desk in a cluttered little space filled with a copy machine, a computer, choir robes and dusty hymnals was a round, interesting looking lady who could have passed for Aunt Bee. "Hi, my name is Terry Teykl and I've just flown in from Houston to do a Prayer Encounter here at your church tomorrow."

"Prayer what?" she retorted.

"A Prayer Encounter...a seminar...." She was shuffling papers on the desk and I could see that she really didn't want to know much more.

"No one told me anything about a meeting here tomorrow." It was late on a Friday afternoon and I was tired. She was formidable, and it was pretty apparent that this conversation wasn't going anywhere. So I decided to try a more direct approach.

"Is your pastor here?

"No, he's already gone home."

"Well, if you don't mind, I might just take a look around the church My staff will be along a bit later to set up. I think someone is supposed to be meeting them. Is there anyone here who might know where the seminar will be, and where I might find tables for our resources?

She drew herself up to her full height of no more than five feet, four inches and took a big breath as if the answer was going to come at great cost, "Like I said, I don't know anything about a prayer meeting tomorrow, but you can look around if you want to. You'll need to talk to the janitor or the choir director about setting anything up though. They know what is going on around here."

That answered the all important question of "Who's in charge?" The secretary was merely the gate keeper, strategically placed and loyal to those who could hire her or start the chatter that would get her fired. I smiled to myself as I left her office . My staff was going to have their work cut out for them.

The church sat nestled between the green lawns of once lovely two story homes. Their traditional architecture and majestic trees spoke of a time when families walked to church together for Sunday afternoon socials. But the sidewalks were cracked now, and the original owners of the grand homes were long gone. The church's new neighbors couldn't afford to keep the homes in their original columned glory.

Most of the people living there now were two income families with kids that skateboarded up and down the deteriorating streets. Those kids and their skateboards were a never-ending thorn in the side of the church members. In spite of the downturn in the neighborhood, the church stood well-preserved, yet virtually ignored by its neighbors.

A little while later, my staff arrived at the appointed time and the janitor was there to meet them. His weighty key ring showed that he could open and probably close any door in the church. He led the two women down the hall to a locked closet room that housed church tables.

Jini reached in with a smile and started to remove a new table from the rack. "Thank you so much, these will be perfect."

"Not those! Those are our new tables and we can't have them drug around and scuffed up. We take care of our stuff around here. That is why everything looks like new."

He went on and on and on relating the long history of the doctors and the lawyers and the prominent business men who had lived, died and left their fortunes to First Church. He had been the janitor and key keeper for 42 years, during which time he had seen to it that all the fine things that the church owned were kept in perfect order. Finally he pointed a bony finger at two rickety old tables with scuffed up tops that must have been used in Sunday school when he attended, "You'll need to use these two."

What Jini was thinking and what she said were two different

things. She didn't bother to explain that she actually needed three tables. She would make do.

Since I was housed at a bed and breakfast not far from the church, I decided to take my evening jog and go by to see how things were going. The church was dark except for one light in the foyer. I could see them inside pushing and pulling boxes around the dimly lit hall. I stepped from the dark corridor and they both let out a shrill screech. "Don't jump out of the dark like that! You scared us to death."

"Why don't you turn on more light?" It seemed to be a logical question but they both started laughing.

"That would be because the switch plates are covered and locked. This is the only light the janitor left on."

After a good laugh I offered to help by pulling over another table. I noticed they both had smug looks on their faces as they watched me saunter over to a perfectly good table outside the sanctuary door. I hoisted it up and started to walk away with the table in tow, but was immediately jerked to a sudden halt. The women started laughing again. I looked down to see a substantial chain attached to one leg. Yep, no one was moving that table without permission. It was chained to the floor.

Yep, no one was moving that table without permission. It was chained to the floor.

The picture that greeted me the next morning as I made my way to the church could have been a post card. The trees were on autumn fire. Reds and golds framed the steeple against a beautiful azure sky. "Are you Dr. Teykl?" a voice behind me asked as I got out of my car.

I turned to see two ladies, both dressed as if for Sunday morning, and both carrying containers of cookies and tiny sandwiches and other goodies that I presumed I would see again later in the day. "Yes, I am." I instinctively relieved them of part of their load as I walked with them up the sidewalk.

They quickly introduced themselves and informed me they were both on the hospitality committee. In the same breath, one of them chirped, "We missed you last night."

I had been invited to a dinner with several of the pillar families in the church, but had apologetically declined. I was exhausted from the flight—it was delayed an hour—and then had driven two hours from the airport to the small town. By the time I had checked on my staff and settled into my room, I knew I needed some quiet time to gather my thoughts and prepare myself to teach. Her comment was not the kind of "we missed you" that makes you feel good inside; it was the kind that makes you feel guilty, like you let down your mother. I apologized again, but could tell the damage was done. I had already offended several people and I hadn't even stood up to speak yet.

"Thank you," they both said as they took the Tupperware I was still holding and headed off to the kitchen.

I stepped into the foyer and met a young handsome pastor with a strong handshake and warm smile. I could see in his face the refreshing optimism of youth. He hadn't been pastoring long enough yet to have lost his enthusiastic demeanor to the steely look of determination or sullen look of resignation that pastors so often acquire after years of going round and round with boards and committees and angry parishioners. I wanted to tell him to run, to escape at all cost the bevy of strongholds that would inevitably strangle the life out of his ministry.

Instead I greeted him. "Good morning, pastor. I've been praying for your church. I believe that the Holy Spirit is going to show up today and give them everything they can handle." I was still shaking his hand when a sound blasted from the sanctuary, causing the hair to stand up on the back of my neck.

He evidently saw me jump because he quickly explained that the organist was practicing. "He has some wonderful selections for your day with us." He dropped his eyes and his smile faded.

As he led me toward his office where I could hear, I mean, prepare, he began to relate a familiar story. "I've been working the neighborhood, you know, trying to meet some of the young families that live here. Most of them have teen-aged kids—kids with too much time on their hands. I really wanted to reach out to them and give them a place to come in the afternoons. So many of the families don't go to church anywhere. I know because I see them working in the yard or washing cars on Sunday mornings.

"I was making some headway, too. We were seeing several new families each week and our children's and youth programs were starting to grow a little bit. I thought it would be wonderful to begin incorporating some contemporary music, maybe introduce the idea of adding another, more laid back service. I even thought some of the long-time members seemed excited about the new direction."

By this time in his story, I pretty much knew what was coming. A small group of the "old guard," led by the organist, had risen up like a posse of well-trained guerillas emerging from the jungle. "There has never been anything played in this sanctuary but sacred music in the classical vein, and as long as we're here, that's how it will be. This is our church and we're not interested in anyone coming along trying to change things."

The religious mindsets and judgmental attitudes, fueled by years of prideful thinking and fearful apathy, had circled the wagons...

Then, just to ensure they wouldn't be out maneuvered by the new pastor, they had immediately started a chain discussion, which is sort of like a prayer chain, but instead of prayer concerns they passed along "pastor concerns." Jake the organist called Mabel. Then Mabel called Dottie. Dottie told her husband Howard, and Howard saw to it that Henry who works at the same bank got the scoop.

Henry told Lois and so on. Before the pastor knew he was in a battle, he had been taken prisoner. It was over before he realized what had hit him.

The young families had all but stopped coming. Talk of contemporary music and new service formats had died down. The religious mindsets and judgmental attitudes, fueled by years of prideful thinking and fearful apathy, had circled the wagons around the threat of change and efficiently secured the status quo. Cognitive closure had locked out the perils of passion and hope. Everything was under control.

The pastor just looked at me as if he expected me to say something profound. I put my hand on his shoulder and prayed for him and the day ahead. I knew why I was there.

City #2

I sat on the plane looking over my notes, thinking about what I was going to say the next day. I never know what I'm going to walk into, but I had reason to be hopeful about this particular event. My conference coordinator had told me that 15 or 20 pastors from the surrounding area were expected to attend, each bringing a group of people from their respective churches. The host pastor had personally invited every pastor within about an hour's drive, and even offered to pay their way to the conference. Not just any pastor can pull that off and make it work, so I knew he was a convener—someone respected by his peers and a leader in city-wide unity. I like events that bring together a variety of churches; they have an energy about them that is just missing in single church events. They're also fun, because we can laugh at each other. Something special just always happens when pastors in a given area can build relationships and get on the same page. It's powerful and life-giving.

I also knew that quite a bit of prayer had gone into the preparation. Apparently they had been praying for this event for weeks prior to my arrival, with designated prayer and worship services being held at different churches throughout the community. The prayer effort was culminating in a 48 hour, round-the-clock vigil that would continue throughout the following day as I taught. I'll be the first to admit that I'm a much better speaker when the Holy Spirit shows up!

I swiped the key in the hotel door and walked in. I groped in the dark for the bed, dropped my luggage, and pulled open the curtains. The evening sun poured into the room which was new and clean. On the desk sat a large welcome basket with a note attached: "Terry, we are so glad you're here! We've been praying for you and for this day for a long time. If there is anything you need, please call." The note was signed by the prayer coordinator of the church; I knew she had been largely responsible for organizing details of the event.

I started to turn and organize my things, but I noticed a handmade looking book tucked inside the basket. It piqued my curiosity, so I untied the crisp wrapping and pulled it out. It was a journal, one of those books full of blank pages you can write in. On the cover was the scripture, "How beautiful on the mountains are the feet of those who bring good news, who proclaim peace, who bring good tidings, who proclaim salvation, who say to Zion, 'Your God reigns!'" (Isaiah 52:7).

A strange warmth ran through me as I opened to the first page. On it was a handwritten note from the prayer coordinator. She basically told me again how they had been praying for me and for the weekend, and how excited they were the day was almost here. They had written down some of their prayers and thoughts in the book to encourage me and bless me.

As I turned page after page, reading prayers for me, my family, my ministry, notes of gratitude, encouragement, scriptures that God had spoken, I was completely overwhelmed. I could have panicked from the pressure to deliver under the weight of so much expectation, but instead I felt at peace. I sensed the Presence of the Lord and knew that regardless of my own condition, God was going to use me to accomplish his purpose there. It was powerful. As I was tucking the prayer journal into my briefcase, my phone rang.

It was the pastor. "Is your room OK?" he asked.

"It's wonderful. And thank you for the basket." Then remembering I had no resource help that weekend, I said, "I know it's after hours, but it would really be helpful if I could get up to the church to set up book tables. Will there be someone there who can let me in?"

"Oh, several of our volunteers are still up there working, and several intercessors will be there through the night, so you wouldn't have any trouble getting in the building. But there's no need for you go. Your tables have already been set up and you will have six volunteers there tomorrow to help with your resources. They're pretty efficient and you should be in good hands, so if you need anything, you just let them know."

"Wow. Thanks again." I was tired and relieved to discover I could rest in the room and get to bed early.

"Thank you for coming, Terry. I'll see you in the morning."

I awoke in the morning more rested than usual after a night in a hotel bed. When I arrived at the church around 7:45 a.m., more than an hour before we were supposed to start, cars already peppered the parking lot. The church building was attractive, with three different sections marking three different periods of growth. The original sanctuary was not overwhelmingly large, but was a beautiful example of church architecture. Wide, shallow steps led to a massive set of wooden doors that were chiseled with Latin symbols and various

...the steeple that rose high above the tree lined streets struck me as a beacon of hope in the community.

religious icons. Attached to that was what looked like an educational and recreational wing that had obviously been added at some point. And finally there was a relatively new looking sanctuary that gracefully preserved elements of the original building in a magnificent yet friendly looking style. Both the old and new stained glass windows were brilliant in the morning sun, and the steeple that rose high above the tree lined streets struck me as a beacon of hope in the community.

Inside, the place was already alive with activity. Greeters were in place at every door. People were already coming in and picking up their nametags and materials, and several were milling around the resource tables, coffee in hand.

"Good morning, Terry. Did you rest well?" It was the pastor.

"Yes, thank you. It's good to be here." He introduced me to the sound man who asked if I had any media I would be using. I gave him a flash drive and a couple of music CDs. "Can you load these up for me?"

"Not a problem. You let me know if there is anything else you need." He attached a wireless microphone to my jacket before heading up to the sound booth.

Next the pastor introduced me to the prayer coordinator, the one who had provided the basket in my room. I thanked her for the goodies and showed her the book of prayers in my briefcase. Her face flushed a little and I thought she might cry, "We're so glad you're here. I thought you might enjoy seeing just some of the prayers that have been offered for you over the past few weeks. Can I bring you anything—coffee, fruit, doughnuts? Did you get some breakfast?"

"Coffee would be great. Thanks." And she was off to the kitchen. I got the distinct feeling that these people would have pulled up the carpet if they had thought it would make me happy.

I walked into the sanctuary and headed down the wide aisle toward the lectern at the front. As the doors to the foyer swung closed behind me, the relative stillness of the sanctuary washed over me. It felt spacious and open; I drew in a deep breath. Drums and guitars stood silent between the organ and piano, and two women were weaving in and out of the pews, praying in hushed whispers. They didn't seem to notice I was there. The Presence of God was so real and tangible in the room that the fragrance was sweet. I stopped before I reached the front and just stood there, relishing the communion. I lifted my hands, looked up and spoke out loud, "God thank you for this church and this pastor who is so in love with you. Thank you for allowing me to do this. Come, Holy Spirit."

After finding a spot in the front row to spread out my teaching materials for the day, I wandered back behind the pulpit area to find a restroom. I heard the din of voices and followed it around the corner to a door marked, "Prayer Room." I stopped outside and listened. The sound of several people praying and worshiping individually but all at once gave me goose bumps. Yes, I knew God would show up in a powerful way.

At War

Make no mistake about it—we are in a spiritual war. Strongholds are real. Whether you want to think about it or not, every one of us as Christians, and every local church that professes the name of Jesus is a target of the enemy by association. As a result, every church—your church—falls somewhere along the spectrum between control-driven lock down and divine habitation. If you find yourself in a comfortable, nothing-ever-changes church environment; in other words, if you are not at times feeling the heat of this battle, that is probably not a good thing. There is a good chance that it means you are not enough of a threat to the enemy, or worse yet, that you are completely irrelevant. Too many churches today are just rocking along, blissfully unaware of their own inconsequence in spiritual affairs. Read what John Piper says:

> Life is war. That's not all it is. But it is always that.... But most people do not believe this in their hearts. Most people show by their priorities and their casual approach to spiritual things that they believe we are in peacetime, not wartime...Very few people think that we are in a war that is greater than World War II, or than any imaginable nuclear war. Few reckon that Satan is a much worse enemy than any earthly foe, or realize that the conflict is not restricted to any one global theater, but is in every town and city in the world. Who considers that the casualties of this war do not merely lose an arm or an eye or an earthly life, but lose everything, even their own souls, and enter a hell of everlasting torment? Until we feel the force of this, we will not pray as we ought. We will not even know what prayer is....[2]

Our oblivion to this battle raging around us in the spirit realm is what makes the American church an easy target for the enemy. We build nice buildings and then fill them with nice things and fun activities. We get together to learn and pray for each other and worship God for all he has done for us. But we don't perceive clearly either the battle or the battlefield. And when we do feel threatened, we lack the training to fight. We don't understand our weapons; we don't recognize the enemy; and we start shooting at anything that moves. We sometimes do more damage than good.

This book is a war plan. It is an attempt to help you discern the battle and employ a strategy for victory before you are completely surrounded. Don't wait! Not only is the health and vitality of your church at stake, but all the hearts and lives that God wills your church to touch.

Sistine Chapel

When Michelangelo was first asked by Pope Julius II to paint a dozen figures on the ceiling of the Sistine Chapel, history says that he contemplated turning the job down. Sculpting was his true passion, and painting the ceiling of a small part of the Vatican Palace apparently didn't excite him at first. Fortunately he reconsidered.

For four years, Michelangelo painted, sometimes lying flat on his back, high atop a scaffold. Although he was only in his 30's, he became so immersed in the project that his health suffered. He grew old and weary. The Pope's relatively simple request for a dozen figures was answered by the young artist with nine scenes containing close to 400 figures, all depicting the creation, fall and redemption of mankind. When Michelangelo took hold of the project, it took hold of him. With each stroke of his brush he must have felt more and more passion for the story his artistry was retelling.

One explanation for Michelangelo's inspiration: the answer he gave to one oberserver who asked why he focused so much attention on the details of the chapel corners, when it was obvious that no one would ever see them.

"God will," he replied.[3]

I believe that if you will begin to worship God personally, asking him to grant you the heart of a Levite, and begin to pray for God's Presence to become a stronghold in your church, you will find yourself so caught up in him that just like it did for Michelangelo, the everyday work will become an extraordinary adventure. It will become less and less about an end result and more about the sheer wonder and fascination of experiencing God. He is so worthy of our praise and attention, even in the times and places that no one sees.

It may not seem possible for you to bring about radical change in your church if you are the only one praying. But the adage is true: "God plus one makes a majority." When eighteenth-century German scholar Johann Wolfang von Goethe admired Michelangelo's masterpiece on a tour of Italy, he noted, "Without having seen the Sistine Chapel, one can form no appreciable idea of what one man is capable of achieving."[4] And until you give yourself to the sacrifice of worship, pouring yourself out to become an empty vessel for God's purposes, you will never taste the joy of a life touched by the divine.

Notes

Introduction
1. Francis Frangipane, *The Three Battlegrounds* (Cedar Rapids, IA: Arrow Publications, 1995) 7.

Chapter One—What is a Stronghold?
1. Beth Moore, *Praying God's Word* (Nashville, TN: Broadman & Holdman, 2000) 3.
2. Phillip Yancey, *Finding God in Unexpected Places* (New York, NY: Doubleday, 2005) 15.
3. Matthew George Easton, "Entry for 'Asherah'" *Easton's Bible Dictionary* (Thomas Nelson, 1897) <http://www.studylight.org/dic/ebd/view.cgi?number=T337>.
4. Graham Kendrick, quoted in Carol Owens, "Praise Factor: Perpetuating the Circle of Blessing," *Pray!* 49 (July/August 2005) 20.
5. William Easum, *Sacred Cows Make Gourmet Burgers* (Nashville, TN: Abingdon Press, 1995) 32.
6. Walter A. Elwell, "Entry for 'God, Names of'," *Baker's Evangelical Dictionary of Biblical Theology* <http://www.studylight.org/dic/bed/view.cgi?number=T298>. 1897.

Chapter Two—Religion vs Passion
1. The Internet Movie Database, *Talladega Nights* <http://www.imdb.com/title/tt0415306/quotes>.
2. William Shakespeare, *The Tragedy of Macbeth* (Act V, Scene V).
3. Donald Miller, *Blue Like Jazz* (Nashville, TN: Thomas Nelson, 2003) 13.
4. Brown, Driver, Briggs and Gesenius, "Hebrew Lexicon entry for Paniym," *The Old Testament Hebrew Lexicon* <http://www.studylight.org/lex/heb/view.cgi?number=6440>, "Hebrew Lexicon entry for Panah," <http://www.studylight.org/lex/heb/view.cgi?number=6437>.
5. Brown, Driver, Briggs and Gesenius, "Hebrew Lexicon entry for No`am," *The Old Testament Hebrew Lexicon* <http://www.studylight.org/lex/heb/view.cgi?number=5278>.
6. Mike Bickle, *After God's Own Heart* (Lake Mary, FL: Charisma House, 2004) 11.

Chapter Three—Pride vs Humility

1. Beth Moore, *Praying God's Word* (Nashville, TN: Broadman & Holdman, 2000) 18.
2. William Barclay, *The Gospel of Matthew*, Volume 2 (Philadelphia, PA: Westminster Press, 1958) 19.
3. Thayer and Smith, "Greek Lexicon entry for Anapauo" *The New Testament Greek Lexicon* <http://www.studylight.org/lex/grk/view.cgi?number=373>.
4. Watchman Nee, *Sit, Walk, Stand* (Carol Stream, IL: Tyndale House, 1977) 12, 14.
5. Samuel H. Moffett, "What Makes the Korean Church Grow?" *Christianity Today* online, January 2007 <http://www.christianitytoday.com/ct/2007/januaryweb-only/105-33.0.html>.

Chapter Four—Sedition vs Honor

1. William Easum, *Sacred Cows Make Gourmet Burgers* (Nashville, TN: Abingdon Press, 1995) 9.
2. Fawn Parish, *Honor* (Ventura, CA: Renew Books, 1999) 32.
3. Terry Teykl, *Prayed On or Prayed For* (Muncie, IN: Prayer Point Press, 2000).

Chapter Five—Parochialism vs Unity

1. Jack Deere, *Surprised by the Voice of God* (Grand Rapids, MI: Zondervan, 1998) 246.
2. Ibid, 274.
3. George Otis, Jr., *Transformations II* Video (Lynwood, WA: The Sentinel Group, 2001).
4. "Fiji Overview," Fusion Ministries, 2007 <www.fusionministry.com/fijivideo.php?page=1>.
5. Jackson Senyonga, "We Want it Quick, Big and Cheap," *Pray!* 37 (July/August 2003) 35.
6. The 700 Club, Guest Bio "Jackson Senyonga: Uganda Revival," CBN online, 2008 <www.cbn.com/700club/guests/bios/Jackson_Senyonga_032404.aspx>.

Chapter Six—Judgment vs Grace

1. William Temple (1881-1944), Archbishop of Canterbury, source unknown.
2. Eugene Peterson, *The Message* (Colorado Springs, CO: Navpress, 2002) 1846.

3. Mark Landsbaum, "Legendary Hollywood Presbyterian Church is in Turmoil," *Christian Examiner*, Keener Communications Group, July 2005 <http://www.christianexaminer.com/Articles/Articles%20 Jul05/Art_Jul05_13.html>.

4. Philip Yancey, *What's So Amazing About Grace?* (Grand Rapids, MI: Zondervan, 1997) 31.

5. Dream Center online newsletter, Aug 2007 <http://www.dreamcenter. org/media_archives.shtml>.

6. Tara Dooley, "Bridging Racial, Cultural Divides—Transforming Lives by Touching Hearts," *Houston Chronicle*, 2007 <http://www.pastor-rudy.net/Chron4607_article.html>.

7. Ed Silvoso, *That None Should Perish* (Ventura, CA: Regal Publishing, 1994) 81.

Chapter Seven—Fear vs Faith

1. Franklin Delano Roosevelt, First Inaugural Address, March 4, 1933, transcribed from audio in the Scripps Library and Multimedia Service <http://www.americanrhetoric.com/speeches/fdrfirstinaugural. html>.

2. *Student Bible* with notes by Philip Yancey and Tim Stafford (Grand Rapids, MI: Zondervan, 2002) 1315.

3. Anne Frank, *Diary of Anne Frank* (New York, NY: Bantam Books, 1997) Saturday, 15 July, 1944, p 237, online at BookRags Book Notes <http://www.bookrags.com/notes/daf/QUO.htm>.

4. Ibid, Tuesday, 7 March, 1944, p 152.

5. Freedom Writers Foundation website, Long Beach, CA: 2006 <http:// www.freedomwritersfoundation.org>

6. Vineyard Community Church website, Cincinnati, OH: 2006, <https:// www.vineyardcincinnati.com/>.

7. Matthew George Easton, "Entry for 'Dance'" *Easton's Bible Dictionary* (Thomas Nelson, 1897) <http://www.studylight.org/dic/ebd/view.cgi?number=T968>. 1897.

Chapter Eight—Get a (Worship) Life

1. William Temple (1881-1944), Archbishop of Canterbury, *Readings in St. John's Gospel*.

2. Eugene Peterson, *The Message* (Colorado Springs, CO: Navpress, 2002) 669.

3. "Hymns" <http://www.music-for-church-choirs.com/hymns.html>.

4. Ernest Gentile, *Worship God: Exploring the Dynamics of Pslamic Worship* (Portland, OR: City Bible Publishing, 1994).

5. "131 Christians Everyone Should Know: Fanny Crosby," *Christianity Today* archive, 2008 <http://www.christianitytoday.com/history/special/131christians/crosby.html>.

6. Cyber Hymnal biography: Frances Jane Crosby <http://www.cyberhymnal.org/bio/c/r/o/crosby_fj.htm>.

7. Oswald Chambers, *My Utmost For His Highest* (New York, NY: Dodd, Mead & Company, 1935) 54.

Chapter Nine—Crafted Prayer

1. Graham Cooke, *Crafted Prayer* (Grand Rapids, MI: Chosen Books, 2004).

2. David S. Kidder and Noah D. Oppenheim, *The Intellectual Devotional* (New York, NY: Rodale, 2006) 246.

Chapter Ten—A Tale of Two Cities

1. John Paul Jackson, *Needless Casualties of War* (Fort Worth, TX: Streams Publications, 1999) 140.

2. John Piper, *Let the Nations Be Glad* (Grand Rapids, MI: Baker Academic, 2003) 41-45.

3. Max Lucado, *Cure for the Common Life* (Nashville, TN: W Publishing Group, 2005) 93-94.

4. David S. Kidder and Noah D. Oppenheim, *The Intellectual Devotional* (New York, NY: Rodale, 2006) 115.

Encounter something new...

Inspiring.
Hilarious.
Motivational.
Informative.
Prophetic.

If you would like to invite Terry Teykl to conduct a
Prayer Encounter in your community,
or be a speaker at your conference,
contact Renewal Ministries:
www.renewalministries.com
(765) 759-5165

PRAYER ENCOUNTER SEMINAR TOPICS

Divine Strongholds
The Presence Based Church
Personal Prayer
Personal Prayer Ministry
Praying for Pastors and Leaders
Prayer Rooms
Mobilizing Your Church to Pray
Strategic City-Wide Prayer

THE VIRTUAL PRAYER ROOM

www.virtualprayerroom.net

The Virtual Prayer Room is the perfect vehicle to handle all the prayer needs of your congregation 24 hours a day, 7 days a week. As a launching point for local church prayer, a Virtual Prayer Room offers many unique benefits:

- real time prayer request and praise report station that scrolls as you watch
- easily accessible for every member of your church from any computer, night and day, year around
- select from several style choices for personalized appearance that suits your church
- a variety of prayer stations covering all aspects of church life
- build your stations from a wealth of prayer helps, or write your own
- bring your site to life by adding photos from our album or from your own digital camera
- customize two "wild card" stations to use as a church home page or for any other special emphasis
- manage your own site easily with a password protected administrative tool (no html knowledge needed)
- connect your church family in prayer instantly

WWW.VIRTUALPRAYERROOM.NET

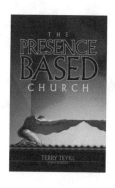

THE PRESENCE BASED CHURCH
by Terry Teykl

The Presence of God on the Ark of the Covenant was Israel's provision, authority, identity and joy.

Today, the same divine Presence is perfected and glorified in the Ark of the New Covenant—Jesus Christ. We are to put him at the very center of our camp and minister first to him, as a living offering of worship.

He is the source of our provision, authority, identity and joy, and he is the reason we exist as a church.

OTHER TITLES BY TERRY TEYKL

Acts 29
Encounter: Blueprint for the House of Prayer
How to Pray After You've Kicked the Dog
Making Room to Pray
Mosquito on an Elephant's Rump
Outside the Camp
Pray the Price
Praying Grace
Preyed On or Prayed For

PRAYER POINT PRESS

(888) 656-6067
www.prayerpointpress.com

For booking information, call (765) 759-5165 or visit www.renewalministries.com.

WORSHIP CDs AVAILABLE FROM PRAYER POINT PRESS

Terry MacAlmon	*Live at the World Prayer Center*
	I Came to Worship You
	Sounds of Heaven
	Visit Us
	You're My Glory
	The Glory of His Presence
The Zoe Group	*Ancient Future*
	When the Music Fades
	Desperate
	Closer
	In Christ Alone
David Teems	*No Language But a Cry*
Stanton Lanier	*Draw Near*
	Still Waters
	The Voice
	Walk in the Light
Nick and Anita Haigh	*Celtic Seasons of Worship*
	Volumes 1, 2, 3, 4
Various Artists	*Hymns 4 Worship - Just as I Am*
	Hymns 4 Worship - Amazing Grace
Dan Gariepy	*Secret Place*
Eoghan Heaslip	*Deeper Still*

PRAYER POINT PRESS

(888) 656-6067

www.prayerpointpress.com